LOEB CLASSICAL MONOGRAPHS
14

EAST & WEST

EAST & WEST

PAPERS IN ANCIENT HISTORY PRESENTED TO
GLEN W. BOWERSOCK

Edited by

T. COREY BRENNAN
and
HARRIET I. FLOWER

Department of the Classics, Harvard University
Distributed by Harvard University Press
Cambridge, Massachusetts, and London
2008

Image of Glen W. Bowersock courtesy of the Institute for Advanced Study, Princeton, NJ. Photograph by Randall Hagadorn.

Library of Congress Cataloging-in-Publication Data

East and west : papers in ancient history presented to
Glen W. Bowersock/ edited by T. C. Brennan and H. I. Flower.
    p. cm. -- (Loeb classical monographs ; 14)
Includes bibliographical references and index.
Summary: "Essays relating to the work of Glen W. Bowersock
and exploring classical antiquity from the second century BC to late
antiquity, from Hellenistic Greece and Republican Rome to Egypt and
Arabia"--Provided by publisher.
    ISBN 978-0-674-03348-1 (paperback : alk. paper)
1. Civilization, Classical. 2. Civilization, Greco-Roman. 3. Mediterranean Region--Civilization. I. Bowersock, G. W. (Glen Warren), 1936–
II. Brennan, T. Corey. III. Flower, Harriet I. IV. Title: East and west.
DE3.E2 2008
930--dc22

                                        2008044551

CONTENTS

PREFACE

THIS VOLUME, and the conference whose proceedings it publishes, is meant as a small but heartfelt tribute to Glen W. Bowersock, as a scholar, teacher, thinker, and friend. Above all, however, it celebrates the enormous positive influence he has exercised in the fields of Classics and Late Antiquity, through his fostering of the ideas, creativity, and careers of numerous ancient historians and Classicists, both in America and in Europe. His career at Harvard and at the Institute for Advanced Study in Princeton has been marked by the depth of his involvement in his scholarly community and his tireless energy in promoting the academic progress of pupils, colleagues, and friends.

No one volume of essays could encompass all of Glen's wide-ranging interests in the ancient world, as should be clear from Aldo Schiavone's introductory chapter. Just one theme was chosen here: East and West. The seven papers that follow Schiavone's contribution range across time from Classical and Hellenistic Greece (Walter Ameling) to the Roman Republic (Andrea Giardina, Miriam T. Griffin) to the Second Sophistic of the high empire (Christopher Jones), and on to later antiquity (Robert J. Penella, Peter Brown, Maurice Sartre). The papers are also set in very different locations throughout the Mediterranean world. They stress the meeting and interaction of cultures and ideas, of religions and empires. Each makes an original contribution to its own historical and geographical subject, while also looking beyond to the connections and clashes taking place between ancient cultures. The authors have designed their individual discussions to highlight Glen's impact on scholarly thinking and writing.

The conference that led to this volume was held at Princeton University on 7th April 2006 in the Andlinger Center for the Humanities. This celebration coincided with Glen Bowersock's retirement from the Institute for Advanced Study (Princeton, NJ), where he had been a faculty member in the School of Historical Studies for just over twenty-five years. The conference was made possible by the generous sponsorship of the following programs and departments at Princeton University: Classics, History, the Program in the Ancient World, Hellenic Studies, and the Council for the Humanities. The success of the conference also depended on the special help and support of Denis Feeney (Chairman of the Classics Department), Jill Arbeiter (Undergraduate Coordinator), and Donna Sanclemente (Technical Support Specialist).

It is most fitting that this volume should be published as a Loeb Classical Monograph, under the aegis of the Department of the Classics at Harvard University, and distributed by Harvard University Press. Educated at Harvard (AB summa cum laude 1957) and, after winning a Rhodes Scholarship, Oxford (BA 1959, MA, DPhil. 1962), Glen Bowersock then taught at Harvard in the Departments of History and the Classics from 1962 to 1980 before receiving an appointment to the Institute for Advanced Study faculty in 1980. At Harvard, Bowersock served as Chair of the Classics department from 1972–1977, and also as Associate Dean of the Faculty of Arts and Sciences (1977–1980), Acting Senior Fellow of the Society of Fellows (1979–1980), and Syndic of Harvard University Press (1977–1981). In addition, he has been a Senior Fellow of the Center of Hellenic Studies (1976–1989) as well as of Dumbarton Oaks (1984–1993, in the capacity of Chair for the last two of those years). Then there is his work with Harvard University Press, most visibly as general editor of its immensely successful Revealing Antiquity series. Indeed, Glen Bowersock also published some of his most notable titles with Harvard, including the co-edited *Edward Gibbon and the Decline and Fall of the Roman Empire* (1977) and *Late Antiquity: A guide to the Postclassical World* (1999), and his authored *Julian the Apostate* (1978) and *Roman Arabia* (1983). There is even a Loeb Classical Library title (*Pseudo-Xenophon, Constitution of the Athenians* [1968]), as well as seven articles over the years in *Harvard Studies in Classical Philology*.

The publication of this volume was made possible in part by the generosity of the Gladys Krieble Delmas Foundation, the Institute for Advanced Study, the Princeton University Program in Hellenic Studies, and the Princeton Department of Classics (whose Chair, Denis Feeney, energetically supported this phase of the project). David Danbeck (Rutgers '08) expeditiously produced the index to the volume; Christine Ferrara (Institute for Advanced Study) provided invaluable assistance with the cover and frontispiece images. In addition, the editors would like to extend a special thanks to the following individuals in Harvard's Department of the Classics for their help in the process of bringing this book to publication: John Duffy (Chair), Christopher Jones, Richard Thomas, Jan Ziolkowski, and (especially) Ivy Livingston, who expertly saw to all the aspects of physically producing the volume.

It has been both an honor and a pleasure to work with all the contributors to this endeavor, who were prompt, professional, and enthusiastic in making the conference and the volume a reality.

1 August 2008
T. Corey Brennan (Rutgers University)
Harriet I. Flower (Princeton University)

1

"ONLY CONNECT"*

Aldo Schiavone

I.

Glen Bowersock occupies a position of the utmost importance in the unprecedented development of American studies in ancient history over the last fifty years. Few other historians have contributed the same drive and breadth of vision or achieved as much as he has. We can safely say that he has been one of the great protagonists of the growth in this field, as, in other ways and more or less in the same period, have Ernst Badian, Peter Brown, and Erich Gruen.

It would be interesting to examine the whole of what is undoubtedly an important chapter in the story of American historiography and the university system that fostered it. This is a story, I believe, that has yet to be written, and one that could teach us a good deal about the origins of major trends and directions in contemporary classical studies, and also about some of the underlying features of American culture since the Second World War. I remember Arnaldo Momigliano holding forth on these matters over dinner during his stays in Chicago, with his customary flow of observations, anecdotes, and remarks. Of course, this is a far bigger topic than the much more limited task I have set myself here. But when focusing on such an exceptional single figure, what we seem to lose in range and scope is made up for by depth and detail as an entire world unfolds before us.

Glen Bowersock's life and career is the essence of what a long-standing European tradition—in particular English and German—has

---

* The title of this contribution is taken from the epigraph to Forster 1910.

consecrated as the biographic model of the great academic. He exemplifies it with a perfection, one might say purity, that is hard to find anywhere in the world nowadays: a solid bourgeois background, libraries and travel, discretion, wide-ranging knowledge, extensive contacts, good taste, understatement. The key places in his education and career were those of the English-language intellectual elite on both sides of the Atlantic: Harvard, Oxford, back to Harvard, and then on to his beloved Princeton and the Institute for Advanced Study, for which he rapidly became an irreplaceable *genius loci*.

Over the years Glen Bowerstock's unflaggingly rigorous scholarship and powers of concentration resulted in an impressive sequence of publications whose immediate success has made them familiar to us all: *Augustus and the Greek World* in 1965, *Greek Sophists in the Roman Empire* in 1969, *Julian the Apostate* in 1978, *Roman Arabia* in 1983, *Hellenism in Late Antiquity* in 1990, *Fiction as History* and *Studies on the Eastern Roman Empire*, which both appeared in 1994, *Martyrdom and Rome* in 1995, *Selected Papers on Late Antiquity* in 2000, *Mosaics as History* in 2006, and *Saggi sulla tradizione classica* in 2007. And that is not to mention the volumes he has edited, including *Edward Gibbon and the Decline and Fall of the Roman Empire* (with J. L. Clive and S. R. Graubard) in 1977, *A. D. Momigliano: Studies on Modern Scholarship* (with T. J. Cornell) in 1994, and *Late Antiquity. A Guide to the Postclassical World* (with P. Brown and O. Grabar) in 1999, plus some three hundred articles that have appeared since 1961 in European and American ancient history journals, as well as in *The New Republic*, *The New York Times Book Review*, *The Los Angeles Times Book Review*, and the *Times Literary Supplement*.

II.

This is not the place to attempt an in-depth analysis of such an imposing body of work. Instead I will simply concern myself with trying to shed some light on a number of core themes and elements, proceeding by way of successive approximations.

Two distinct traits are immediately and clearly discernible in Glen Bowersock's research activities. It is rare to find them with such intensity in current trends in North American historiography dealing with the ancient world, but they have always shaped his work, conferring on it a very distinctive and in a certain sense unique approach and style.

The first is what I would describe as an insatiable and multifarious intellectual curiosity, which prompted him to explore a wide variety of themes and issues, even though they all lie within an essentially unified field (more about this shortly). This is far removed from the precocious and demanding hyperspecialization—the tendency to know more and more about an increasingly narrow subject—which, especially in America, is becoming the hallmark of the up-and-coming generations of scholars who are gradually taking our places. In Glen Bowersock this curiosity does not just relate to his specific research interests; I would say it is inherent to his whole attitude to the world, making him, for example, an incomparably perceptive traveler with a gift for picking up on tiny details and the subtlest shades of meaning, whether he is in Helsinki or Istanbul, Palermo or Paris. This quality makes him an extraordinary, albeit extremely reserved, observer who misses almost nothing about the contexts and people surrounding him.

The second distinctive trait is his constant attention towards the European intellectual environment (especially France, Germany, and Italy), with which Glen Bowersock is very familiar, and not only insofar as it relates to his own studies. He has always been unsparing in his efforts to foster and maintain dialogue between the American and European academic worlds, serving as an authoritative and prestigious go-between—and one which we have all had endless occasion to turn to and appreciate—first at Harvard and then, above all, at the Institute in Princeton. Again, this attitude runs against the tide of what seems to me to have been the prevailing trend in American historiography in recent decades, dominated by what I might describe as a rather "isolationist" stance, the expression of an increasingly deep-rooted belief in the basic self-sufficiency of Anglophone research. (A cursory look at bibliographies of American academic studies in the last twenty years, with the possible exception of strictly philosophical research, will suffice to demonstrate what I mean here: the percentage of works not written in, or translated into, English is minimal, and is decreasing all the time.)

Around these two qualities, Glen Bowersock's research moves, as I said, in different thematic directions. At the same time, however, they betray the presence of a unifying motif that is identifiable with relative ease. It can perhaps be defined as the study of Greece—its culture, traditions, identity, and language—but always observed from within the reality of imperial Rome or its legacy, from Augustus to Byzantium and beyond. Greekness, but inside the container of the Empire. Athens, but within the spatiality of Rome.

This perspective orients Glen Bowersock's entire output, from his book about Augustus, a ground-breaking debut packed with scholarship and ideas, through to his recent work on Byzantine mosaics. Even *Roman Arabia*, which at first glance might seem the least related to such a theme, is entirely pervaded by it.

Rome has always been, in a certain sense, a "Greek" city; however, what attracts Glen Bowersock's attention is not the history of the origins of this relationship, because ultimately he is not particularly intrigued by Archaic and Classical Greece, the Greek "miracle" of Snell and Vernant. It is when Greece becomes part of the Roman construction of the Empire that things really start getting interesting for him, that is when Greek culture, with and after Hellenism, was projected into the foreground of a Mediterranean scenario that it had previously only glimpsed through Herodotus and Plato; and above all when Greek culture became compromised by Roman power, from Polybius onwards, eventually becoming its instrument; while, in turn, the Roman Empire, which was itself influenced by the meeting of cultures, became in some way or other a "Greek" empire (a theme also very dear to Paul Veyne). It is clearly not just a question of bilingualism (symbolized most powerfully by the diaries of Marcus Aurelius), upon which Arnaldo Momigliano was to place such emphasis. The root issue is the civic and political form taken by Roman dominion, after it incorporated an "other" which, however, had always nurtured, through its thought and culture, the history of Rome and its ruling classes. This was apparent to the Roman elites as well, at least from the time of Cicero onwards: the empire was a culturally and geopolitically asymmetric construct; governing Gaul and Britain was a very different proposition to integrating Greece and the East.

Of course it was not just Rome that changed: it was not solely a matter of Greece, having been defeated in arms, managing in turn to conquer Rome through the strength of its civilization. The empire was not a neutral container for Greek culture. The web of power relations established by the empire—spaces, contacts, hierarchies, the forming of city elites—retroactively modified the cultures that expressed them, transforming them in often radical ways. The categories of "contamination" and "assimilation" do not provide an adequate or full description of the complexity of the phenomena at work here. The Roman imperial reality was to prove a crucial influence on the education and writings of every Greek intellectual after Polybius. Imperial bilingualism—one of the great boasts of Hadrian's court—did not simply express the coexistence of two different cultures that had had dealings with each other since very remote times, but the coming together of two traditions which, although remaining distinguishable, had given rise to an unprecedented degree of fusion. Each component was transformed by the impact of the other, making possible a new synthesis in which the difference in language was no longer a sign of an authentic duality of worlds, but of a complex wealth of expressive codes; although these obviously derived from different origins and histories, they were by then firmly part of a single *koine*. Aelius Aristides, Lucian, or Plutarch, but also Apuleius, Gellius, or Favorinus would be utterly incomprehensible outside such a context and equilibrium.

Glen Bowersock is an acute interpreter of this tangle, of this Romanized Greekness, which preserved its integrity precisely because it was capable of change. The fruits of his historiographic labors, from the book about Greek sophists in the Roman Empire to the one about Hellenism in Late Antiquity are turning points in studies of this field and cannot be ignored by any scholar setting out to research them.

III.

But I believe that in addition to the thread outlined above, Glen Bowersock's work is also unified by something much more profound. It is a frame of reference that encapsulates the distinctiveness of his intellectual approach and reveals his personal historian's style, if I can put it like that. It is a constant presence in his work, irrespective of whether he is examining Roman Arabia or the relations between historic truth and literary construction, as he does in *Fiction as History*, in some ways his most mature and insightful book. It is what I would define as "the border paradigm," where, however, "border" is not a barrier, a limit or an obstacle, but a point of encounter, hybridization, a line of permeability, contiguity, and uncertainty, where everything is *sfumato* and one shade of color runs irresistibly into another. Glen Bowersock is the quintessential historian of connection, interweaving and displacement.

His attention is drawn to sites of crossing and intersection, both physical, geographically defined places and cultural and mental ones. He focuses on the slip planes between one culture and another, one tradition and another, one literary genre and another—the imperial Romanization of Arabia, but also the continual shifts in demarcation that mix up and bring closer (rather than separating) literature and historiography, the elaboration of the fantastic and the recording of facts and events under the common sign of narrative.

It seems to me that this accounts for Glen Bowersock's powerful interest in the more mature Roman imperial period from the Principate to Late Antiquity, because more than any other this represents for him the world of plurality and of the multifarious, of the ethnic and cultural melting pot, the world of Romanized Greekness and Hellenized Romanness, of open, shifting identities, of travels, curiosities and exchanges, of East permeating West and the West understanding the East, of seas that unite much more than they divide, of malleability, pliability, and constant integration. Perennial fluidity interests Glen Bowersock much more than close observation of the political and institutional forms of Roman supremacy and control. He is much more struck by the cultural flexibility of the empire, where dominion melts into consensus, than by institutional rigidity and repressive violence, though he never seeks to hide the latter. What emerges is the outline, albeit in pieces, of a kind of protohistory or archaeological grammar of an instance of imperial globalization capable of reducing the world to a "small world."

This explains equally well his interest—which, I believe, has grown in recent years, from *Studies on the Eastern Roman Empire* (1994) through to *Mosaics as History* (2006)—in Late Antiquity. I am not sure to what extent this interest was originally inspired by the reflections of his greatly loved and much-studied Edward Gibbon; at any rate this age appears to Glen Bowersock, as it does to Peter Brown, to be a huge and feverishly active laboratory of new structures and behaviors just waiting to be explored. But it was also one of continuity and enduring traits; especially in the East (the focus of his attention), the uninter-rupted blending together of often very heterogeneous elements—and this brings us back to a theme that is very close to his heart—yielded cultural and social forms that went way beyond the boundaries of the "classic" and towards a future rich in prospects and developments.

Glen Bowersock has therefore played an active and prominent part in what Andrea Giardina recently and very aptly described as the "esplosione di tardo antico."[1] Underlying this trend, which has undoubt-edly brought important historiographic benefits—many of which can be traced back to the work of Glen Bowersock and of Peter Brown, in addition to the researches of French and Italian scholars—there is often a more or less explicitly expressed tendency to opt for a continuist and gradualist reading of historical processes that basically denies the notion of any genuine break between Antiquity and the Middle Ages, replacing it with one of a slow, almost imperceptible and painless transi-tion describable only in fragments. It is a reconstruction with which I have long been in disagreement; the risk, in my view, is that of losing the most powerful specificity in Western history, whose distinctive char-acteristic is precisely that of discontinuity and rupture, marked by the "end" of Antiquity. The critical observations advanced by Giardina in the work cited above seem to me particularly pertinent in this respect.

Although Glen Bowersock's pondered view diverges from my own, he was nonetheless keen that *La storia spezzata: Roma antica e Occidente moderno*, the book in which I first expressed my dissent about this approach, should be translated and published in America in a pres-

---

[1] Giardina 1999.

tigious series of which he is the general editor.[2] It was an example of balance, generosity, and respect one rarely comes across in life.

More recently, Glen Bowersock and I have had two further opportunities to discuss this issue.[3] And the measure and composure of his argumentation, and of all the essays in his *Selected Papers on Late Antiquity*, make me increasingly convinced that the time is ripe to make an attempt to bring together the interpretation based on notions of "crisis" and of the "end" (of the ancient world) and the one founded on the idea of "transformation" and "transition," and to integrate the two schemata into a unified vision that takes both perspectives into account. If this ever proves possible, it will also be thanks to Glen Bowersock.

IV.

With his long-time friend Arnaldo Momigliano, Glen Bowersock shared an interest in the study of the history of historiography and of the classical tradition in the modern age, in particular from the eighteenth century onwards. His essays, published in a recent Italian volume,[4] offer a broad-ranging and significant collection. Glen Bowersock is exceedingly well informed about European culture, capable of grasping and giving importance to aspects and figures in an original, unfailingly meticulous and reliable fashion, in keeping with a model that I fear American academia is losing. The French and English Enlightenment, which remains his favorite subject in this area, is always treated with great interpretative vigor. And more than a trace of the Enlightenment frame of thinking and perspective on reality can be found in his own personality, a kind of rationalizing impulse that is ever-present but that never chills his heart (although Glen Bowersock himself simply attributes it to his New England roots)—not to mention his extraordinary and truly eighteenth-century gift as a sparkling conversationalist. However, his intelligence roams with equal competence from England

[2] For the English edition, see Schiavone 2002, published in the *Revealing Antiquity* series.

[3] In Bowersock et al. 2002 and in Bowersock 2004.

[4] Bowersock 2007, published by Einaudi.

and France to Mommsen's Germany and the Italy of the "grand tours." His narrative style is always clear and elegant, with a very English taste for biographic detail that borders on the anecdotal and at times is tinged by barely perceptible flickers of irony.

Glen Bowersock is also capable of tracing the echoes of antiquity when this is a source of inspiration and culture for poets. His beloved Kavafis is a case in point; he brings to light sources and intellectual genealogies with acute perspicacity and reads him with a sensitivity and degree of attention that is as philological as it is literary. What comes to the fore once again is Roman and Byzantine Greekness, explored now in its most recent and sophisticated twentieth-century echoes, in Athens, Cairo, and Constantinople. Another example is Auden (who also admired Kavafis), whose relationship with classicism and Late Antiquity and the influence he had on Dodds is read by Glen Bowersock with care and subtlety.

Besides poetry, his aesthetic sense and powers of understanding have also been nurtured by music, a crucial passion in his education and a real initiation into modernity and beauty. I do not know if Glen Bowersock has ever written about music (he touches on it in his essay on Berlioz and Vergil, though he explicitly states that he is writing as a classicist and not as a musicologist),[5] but certainly the Metropolitan Opera House Theater in New York is one of the key places in his life, no less so than the Institute.

Finally, there are his ties with Italy. Our friendship (if I might be allowed such a personal reference) arose out of and flourished in the context of Glen Bowersock's fondness for and long-standing bond with my country. He has visited Italy ever since he was a young man, returns regularly, and rightly feels very much at home there, in Tuscany as in Sicily, in Florence as in Rome or Pavia (a place familiar to him thanks to his friendship with Emilio Gabba).

In the last decade (we first met one evening in Princeton, in the summer of 1993, and Christopher Jones, who was with us, was helpful in breaking the ice) he has followed the foundation and organization

---

[5] In an essay in Bowersock 2007:91n1.

first of the Istituto di Studi Umanistici (he currently presides over the Scientific Committee of the doctoral program Antiquity, Middle Ages, and Renaissance section) and then of the Istituto Italiano di Scienze Umane. His support made an important contribution to the initial success of a difficult and by no means certain undertaking.

In these last few years he has been an invaluable guide in the growth and development of our new institution, with his suggestions, intellectual openness and receptiveness, and with his network of contacts. But this is all part of a story that we are both still writing.

Istituto Italiano di Scienze Umane (Florence, Naples)

Bibliography

Bowersock, G. W. 1965. *Augustus and the Greek World*. Oxford.

———. 1969. *Greek Sophists in the Roman Empire*. Oxford.

———. 1978. *Julian the Apostate*. London and Cambridge, MA.

———. 1983. *Roman Arabia.* Cambridge, MA.

———. 1990. *Hellenism in Late Antiquity*. Ann Arbor, MI and Cambridge.

———. 1994a. *Fiction as History, from Nero to Julian*. Berkeley, CA.

———. 1994b. *Studies on the Eastern Roman Empire*. Goldbach.

———. 1995. *Martyrdom and Rome*. Cambridge.

———. 2000. *Selected Papers on Late Antiquity*. Bari.

———. 2004. "Riflessioni sulla periodizzazione dopo 'esplosione di tardoantico' di Andrea Giardina." *StudStor* 45:7–13.

———. 2006. *Mosaics as History: The Near East from Late Antiquity to Islam*. Cambridge, MA.

———. 2007. *Saggi sulla tradizione classica dal Settecento al Novecento*. Turin.

Bowersock, G. W., P. Brown, and O. Grabar, eds. 1999. *Late Antiquity: A Guide to the Postclassical World*. Cambridge, MA.

Bowersock, G. W., J. L. Clive, and S. R. Graubard, eds. 1977. *Edward Gibbon and the Decline and Fall of the Roman Empire*. Cambridge, MA.

Bowersock, G. W., and T. J. Cornell, eds. 1994. *A. D. Momigliano: Studies on Modern Scholarship*. Berkeley, CA.

Bowersock, G. W., L. Ruggini, A. Schiavone, and D. Vera. 2002. "Antico e Tardoantico Oggi." *RSI*114:349–379.

Forster, E. M. 1910. *Howard's End*. London.
Giardina, A. 1999. "Esplosione di Tardoantico." *StudStor* 40:157–180.
Schiavone, A. 2002. *The End of the Past: Ancient Rome and the Modern West*. 2nd ed. Transl. M. J. Schneider. Cambridge, MA.

2

ETHNOGRAPHY AND UNIVERSAL HISTORY IN AGATHARCHIDES

Walter Ameling

I.

Historians of both classical and late antiquity have a natural tendency to view the world they study as fundamentally divided into East and West,"[1] which is at best an arbitrary division, depending on your point of view, and usually confines the historians to the traditional hunting-grounds of Greek or Roman history. Whenever a historian wishes to move to the periphery and to transcend these boundaries, there is "a concomitant effort ... to move downward in the societies they study in order to delineate the life of the lower, rather than the upper classes."[2]

The relations of east and west, the move to the eastern periphery, and the view beyond the limits of empire give an idea of Glen Bowersock's work and achievements. These are subjects central to different epochs in history, and I want to concentrate on an epoch that may be seen as a *praeparatio historica* of the times and phenomena the addressee of this tribute has worked on. Hellenism, like late antiquity, "is conspicuously not confined to the Mediterranean,"[3] and strong centrifugal forces were at work to move the Greek world away from its Aegean center—and not only the political world, but also the geographical and intellectual world. With Alexander, the Greek world

---

[1] Bowersock 2005:167.
[2] Bowersock 2004:20.
[3] Bowersock 2004:23.

had experienced a push to the margins, not only to the margins in the east, but also in the south.[4] East and West became ambiguous terms, and some intellectuals reacted to the new challenges. One of these was Agatharchides of Cnidus, who is best known as the author of a work *On the Red Sea* and as somebody who described the life of the lower classes with much sympathy, giving a voice to people who seldom came to the attention of writers of history.

This brought him to the attention of Strasburger, who wrote influential pages on Agatharchides' "Hinwendung zum pathos" and on the way he wrote the history of a people usually not thought to be worthy of the historian's interest. Strasburger, himself a "Historiker der Opfer, der Leidenden (ganz im Sinne Jacob Burckhardts),"[5] thought him a congenial spirit, and while Peter Fraser stated that "the absence of creative historical writing ... is one of the most striking lacunae in Alexandria at this time,"[6] Strasburger saw in Agatharchides an historian of exceptional creative power.[7]

Hellenistic intellectuals moved in a completely new world: the horizons for enquiries of all sorts had broadened dramatically, and there were many areas to be covered—zoology, botany, geography, ethnography, history. Some of these subjects were closing ranks fast, thereby returning to a proximity they had lost already in the late fifth century. Agatharchides provides the most outstanding—but not the only—example of geography, ethnography, and history coming together.[8]

Geographically, the world of Agatharchides had dramatically shrunk, and he demonstrates his awareness of this fact by describing it

---

[4] Cf. Bowersock 2004:22: "push to margins can be seen along the north-south axis of the late antique world."

[5] Meier 1986:180–181. Strasburger's pages, in 1982:1006–1010, are still the most influential discussion of Agatharchides. A synopsis of the current thinking on Agatharchides is given by Engels 2004:179–192.

[6] Fraser 1972:514.

[7] Strasburger 1982:1006: "sein Versuch, als geschichtsunwürdig geltende Menschenklassen und Völker in die Geschichte einzuführen, hat im 20. Jahrhundert eigentlich eine Aktualität, die von der des Thukydides nicht weit absteht."

[8] Engels 2004:180–181 on the difficulty of defining "history" as a literary genre in this period; Clarke 1999 on the interaction of the two subjects.

in a straight north-south direction (Phot. 66.454b–455a):[9] ὅτι τοὺς τῶν ἀνθρώπων διαφορωτάτους βίους οὐ πολὺς διαμετρεῖ καὶ διορίζει τόπος. ἐκ γὰρ τῆς Μαιώτιδος λίμνης πολλοὶ τῶν φορτιζομένων ἐν φορτηγοῖς ἀκάτοις δεκαταῖοι κατῆραν εἰς τὸν Ῥοδίων λιμένα, ἀφ' ὧν ὑπὸ τὸν αὐτὸν καιρὸν τεταρταῖοι μὲν ἀφίκοντο εἰς τὴν Ἀλεξανδρείαν, ἐκ δὲ ταύτης ἐναντίῳ τῷ ῥεύματι πλέοντες ἀνὰ τὸν πόταμον ἐν ἄλλαις δέκα παραγένοιντ' ἂν οὐ χαλεπῶς εἰς Αἰθιοπίαν· ὥστε ἀπὸ τῆς ὑπερβολῆς τοῦ ψύχους εἰς ἄκραν τοῦ καύματος τὴν ἀκμὴν μὴ πλείους εἴκοσι γίνεσθαι καὶ πέντε τοῖς κομιζομένοις ἐνδελεχῶς ἡμέραις.[10] Agatharchides was not only interested in the east, that is, he was not only interested in the reaction of a western, i.e., Greek, mind to eastern, i.e., Arabian, realities. He was interested in the south, too, and he believed that he was the first to introduce his readers to this part of the world (Phot. 65.454b).

As we shall see, Agatharchides tried to use his knowledge of the "Eastern" world and its inhabitants to come to grips with one of the main problems with which a historian living in the third or second century BC had to deal, universal history. To do this, I have to touch upon some other points, first, on Agatharchides' biography (II), his literary output (III), and his attitudes towards historical method and universal history (IV, V). Only then shall we occupy ourselves with the way Agatharchides used his ethnographical knowledge to further his aims as a historian (VI), and shall be able to compare him with one of his intellectual predecessors, Dicaearchus of Messana (VII).

---

[9] The numbering of the chapters follows that used since Müller's edition in *GGM*, used also by Henry's edition of Photius. Preference is given to the text of Photius, if possible, in accordance with Palm 1955:25–26; if another tradition (e.g. Diodorus) is cited, it usually concerns a passage not in Photius. Woelk 1966 and Burstein 1989 provide modern translations; Burstein's translation is sometimes used without further acknowledgment. I cite the fragments of Dicaearchus according to the edition by Mirhady, providing Wehrli's numbers as a convenience.

[10] Cf. Bowersock 2005:170: "It seems to have been rare for an ancient author to describe the civilized world by longitude, in a straight north-south direction. Aristotle did it in the *Meteorologica* to make his point that the distance between Ethiopia and Lake Maeotis (the Sea of Azov) was less than the distance between the west coast of Spain and India by a ratio of three to five. North-south communications were clearly not determined by sea travel in the same way as east-west communication." Bowersock 2005:174: "What is consistently striking about the north-south axis is that there is never any suggestion that the inhabitants of the ancient world would travel along it from one extremity to the other."

II. Agatharchides' Life

Agatharchides was a native of Carian Cnidus,[11] a city under Ptolemaic rule during most of the third century. Like many intellectuals, he gravitated to Alexandria, the city that had supplanted Athens as the new intellectual center of the Greek world. He started as the θρεπτός of a certain Cineas, who occupied a high position in court circles and is best known as one of the counselors of Ptolemy VI in his negotiations with Antiochus IV, but had held high offices long before that.[12] Agatharchides' second patron and employer was Heraclides Lembus,[13] who was not only an influential member of the court in the days of Ptolemy VI,[14] but also one of the most important intellectuals of the day—who wrote, *inter alia*, a history in 37 books, made extracts from Aristotle's Πολιτεῖαι and Νόμιμα βαρβαρικά,[15] both of which must have influenced Agatharchides.[16] Thus Agatharchides is put in the first half of the second century, not necessarily in the middle of the century.

It is usually assumed that Agatharchides wrote his work at the end of his life and did not finish it, because certain disturbances, or revolts, ἀποστάσεις, made him flee from Alexandria.[17] Different

---

[11] Strabo 14.2.15 p656 (*FGrH* 86 T 1): ἄνδρες ἀξιόλογοι Κνίδιοι ... Ἀγαθαρχίδης ὁ ἐκ τῶν περιπάτων, ἀνὴρ συγγραφεύς; Photius, *Bibl.* 213 p171a (86 T 2): τούτῳ πατρὶς μὲν ἡ Κνίδος ἦν, ἡ δὲ τέχνη γραμματικὸν ἐπεδείκνυτο· ὑπογραφέα δὲ καὶ ἀναγνώστην ὁ τοῦ Λέμβου Ἡρακλείδης, δι' ὧν αὐτῷ ἐξυπηρετεῖτο, παρέσχε γνωρίζεσθαι. ἦν δὲ καὶ θρεπτὸς Κινέου; Joseph. *AJ* 12.5 (*FGrH* 86 T 4). Cf. *Prosopographia Ptolemaica* (= *PP*) VI 16892.

[12] *PP* II/VIII 1926, III/IX 5169, VI 14610; Walbank 1979:353–354.

[13] *PP* VI 16922; Runia 1998:375–376 (bibliography).

[14] Agatharchides may have known him even earlier, if Fraser 1972:741n172 is right and the relative clause in Diog. Laert. 5.94 refers to Ptolemy VI, king since 181: Ἡρακλείδης ... γεγονὼς ἐπὶ Πτολεμαίου τοῦ ἕκτου, ὃς τὰς πρὸς Ἀντίοχον ἔθετο συνθήκας (*Suda* H 462 Adler is taken from Diogenes).

[15] On this work, Fraser 1972:515; Schepens and Bollansée 2004:61: "A limited number of authors produced works on *Barbarian Customs* ... but this type of writing never seems to have risen from the level of ethnography to that of historiography, and over the years it even acquired a markedly paradoxographical slant."

[16] Bloch 1940:38 believes that Heraclides got the idea of epitomizing larger works from Agatharchides; usually the opposite is assumed.

[17] Immisch 1919:9n3; Jacoby 1926:151 assumed that Agatharchides fled to a place like Athens, where there were good libraries, but no eyewitnesses. Woelk 1966:253 is sceptical.

dates are suggested for these disturbances,[18] but the whole approach seems to be flawed, since the crucial sentence says (Phot. 110.460b): οὔτε τῶν ὑπομνημάτων διὰ τὰς κατ' Αἴγυπτον ἀποστάσεις ἀκριβῆ παραδιδόντων σκέψιν, translated by Desanges: "Et les archives royales ne nous donnant pas une vue précise des faits en raison des mouve-ments de sécession ... qui ont eu lieu en Égypte."[19] Agatharchides could not consult records, because—due to the ἀποστάσεις—there were no records for a certain place and time. The ἀπόστασις of the Thebaid under Ptolemy IV and Ptolemy V could be meant,[20] but this is mere guesswork. Nevertheless, we have to cease using this sentence to deter-mine the date of Agatharchides' death, and have to assume in accor-dance with the few indications on his life that he wrote in the first half of the second century.[21] Such a date is supported by the complete lack of any Atticist bias (even if Photius thinks differently[22]), and we have no reason to assume that Agatharchides lived to see the destruction of Corinth or Carthage.[23]

Agatharchides was a Peripatetic, and his close relations with Heraclides may be thought to confirm this designation. His τέχνη was that of a γραμματικός,[24] and his activities as ὑπογραφεὺς καὶ

[18] Notably the years 145, 132, and 107 (the last date is favoured by Jacoby, *Comm.* on 86 T 3; Susemihl 1891:1.687–688 and Brown 1973:198n68 are in favor of 132, whereas Müller 1882:LIV–LVIII opted for 107).

[19] Desanges 1999:72.

[20] On this revolt, lasting from 207/6 until 187/6, see Véïsse 2004:11ff.

[21] Already Schneider 1880:234–241 argued for an early date. This has certain conse-quences for the interpretation of his writings, since some of them depend very much on an Agatharchides working only from the 160s on: Alonso-Núñez 1997:66 (e.g.) believes that Agatharchides set all his political hopes after the fall of Macedon on a vigorous Ptolemaic monarchy, was disappointed, and was therefore critical of the Ptolemies. For the presumed end of Agatharchides' history, see text below with n59.

[22] Phot. 62.454a: ὅτι κέχρηται ὁ συγγραφεύς, ἀττικιστὴς καίτοι ὤν, τῇ τῆς καμάρας λέξει. Contra: Leopoldi 1892:77–81; Immisch 1919:7; Marcotte 2001:426–427.

[23] Diod. Sic. 3.44.8 mentions the Carthaginian harbour, κώθων, but this is an addition by Diodorus, since he promises (falsely) to return to the matter ἐν τοῖς οἰκείοις χρόνοις.

[24] Marrou 1977:308–309: "Der eigentliche Gegenstand seines Unterrichts, sein Hauptstoff ... ist das vertiefte Studium der Dichter und der anderen klassischen Schriftsteller. Dies ist sein besonderer Gegenstand, der die Grammatik im Sinne des höheren Unterrichts von dem Unterricht des Elementarschul-Grammatisten unter-scheidet."

ἀναγνώστης—in which he was supported by Heraclides[25]—are specifically noted (Phot. *Bibl.* 213.171a = *FGrH* 86 T 2). A γραμματικός in the third century BC was a philologist, an author of interpretations and monographs,[26] somebody who had an intimate empirical knowledge of the usual contents of books in prose and poetry, as is shown by Dionysius Thrax:[27] γραμματική ἐστιν ἐμπειρία τῶν παρὰ ποιηταῖς τε καὶ συγγραφεῦσιν ὡς ἐπὶ τὸ πολὺ λεγόμενων.[28] Not many years later Asclepiades of Myrlea, a pupil of the Pergamene scholar Crates, introduced the ἱστορικὸν μέρος into the γραμματικὴ τέχνη.[29] Photius praises Agatharchides' excellence as a grammarian (*Bibl.* cod. 213): ἀλλὰ γὰρ ἔμοιγε δοκεῖ οὐδὲν ἔλαττον τῶν γραμματικῶν οὐ δεύτερος ἢ τῶν ῥητόρων, δι' ὧν καὶ γράφει καὶ διδάσκει, καταφαίνεσθαι.

Intellectually, therefore, Agatharchides' origins can be roughly described, but his social status is defined almost completely by negations. He did not belong to the court of the kings, he had no officially recognized relation to the Alexandrian library, and he was not a member of the Ptolemaic bureaucracy.[30] Instead, he depended completely on Alexandria's social elite. His starting point in history was the newly established philology—perhaps the intellectual career

[25] See the translation by Schamp 1987:370: "grâce aux services qu' [Agatharchide] lui rendit, Héraclide Lembos lui procura l'occasion de gagner de la notoriété en tant que sécretaire et lecteur."

[26] Schol. Dion. Thrax (*Grammatici Graeci* 3 p160.10): Ἐρατοσθένης ἔφη ὅτι γραμματική ἐστιν ἕξις παντελὴς ἐν γράμμασι, γράμματα καλῶν τὰ συγγράμματα.

[27] Dion. Thrax *Gram.* 1. Cf. Pfeiffer 1978:324–325, who cites Cic. *De or.* 1.187 (*pertractatio poetarum*): "Die Prosaschriftsteller sind in Dionysios' Eingangssatz nicht ausgeschlossen; aber er setzte sie an die zweite Stelle, weil vor Aristarch kein Philologe sie behandelt hatte" (325).

[28] One of the subdivisions of the τέχνη γραμματική is reading, ἀνάγνωσις: Dion. Thrax *Gram.* 2; Pfeiffer 1978:325.

[29] Cic. *De or.* 1.187; Quint. *Inst.* 1.9.1 (even if Asclepiades did not belong to the Alexandrian circles, he lived roughly in the same time as Agatharchides); ἱστορικὸν μέρος is translated as "philologische Realienkunde" by Ax 1991:277. Especially important in this context is the chapter on "grammatica e storiografia" in Nicolai 1992:178–247. Augustine's *grammaticus* is a *custos historiae* (*De musica* 2.1.1).

[30] For a different view, see Jacob 1991:134; also Gozzoli 1978:59–60 and Zecchini 1990:221–222, who postulate some kind of relation to the court for a whole group of historians: Demetrius of Kallatis, Ptolemaeus of Megalopolis, Heraclides Lembus, and Agatharchides. Unfortunately, his arguments are not always strong.

typical for an Alexandrian.[31] He was no politician and had no political experience,[32] but he had seen or heard enough to be sensitive about the problems a historian faced at the court of a king, as his treatment of Hieronymus of Cardia shows.[33] There is no indication that Agatharchides believed in history as a school for future politicians. It is therefore not too surprising that he seems not to have bothered with the politics of his day, nor tries to convey a specific point of view on the politics and politicians of his day.[34] Even though he was a close contemporary of Polybius, he had not only a different background, but also very different aims.

III. Agatharchides' Writings

Agatharchides wrote several books, most of which are known only through a short notice by the Byzantine patriarch Photius—a notice not without problems.[35] It is evident that some of these books accrued

[31] Istrus the Callimachean might provide a good comparison, *FGrH* 334 T 1: Καλλιμάχου δοῦλος καὶ γνώριμος. Cf. *ad personam* Fraser 1972:511, 737n140. Jacoby 1926:223 seems to think that Menecles of Barca (*FGrH* 270) belonged to the same social group.

[32] For historians who had been politicians or soldiers, see Meißner 1992:215–315 (politicians), 316–361 (soldiers).

[33] *FGrH* 86 F 4b (= Lucian, *Macr.* 22); Phot. 13.445a: τὰς τῶν δυναστῶν φιλίας ὁ καιρὸς σφραγίζεται καὶ λύει. Cf. Meißner 1992:505.

[34] Gozzoli 1978 sees an allusion to the reign of Ptolemy VIII in the τύραννις of the gold mines (Phot. 24.447b), but this is difficult on many levels, not the least because the book can easily have been finished before the reign of Ptolemy VIII, and because, *pace* Gozzoli 71, Diod. Sic. 3.12.1 convinces the reader that the working of the gold mines, however abominable, was no "altro momento dell'azione di violenza dei Tolomei contro gli indigeni del sud." (Against Gozzoli, see Urías Martínez 1993:57–67.) The same set of problems applies, if one tries to interpret 49.451b as an ideal Ptolemy VI and Ptolemy VIII should apply to their behavior (Engels 2004:188–189). Verdin 1983:418 calls our attention to the fact that—while Photius used τύραννις—Diod. Sic. 3.12.2 mentions only the βασιλεῖς, and Verdin believes this to be closer to Agatharchides' own use (but see Fraser 1972:513, 779).

[35] Phot. *Bibl.* 213 (*FGrH* 86 T 2.3): πλήν γε εἰσὶν οἵ φασιν αὐτὸν καὶ ἑτέρας συγγεγραφέναι πραγματείας, ὧν ἡμεῖς οὐδένα (οὐδὲν?) οὐδέπω ἴσμεν. ἐπιτομὴν δὲ αὐτόν φασι τῶν περὶ τῆς Ἐρυθρᾶς θαλάσσης ἀναγεγραμμένων ἑνὶ συντάξαι βιβλίῳ, καὶ μὴν καὶ περὶ τρωγλοδυτῶν βιβλία ε΄, ἀλλὰ καὶ ἐπιτομὴν τῆς Ἀντιμάχου Λύδης, καὶ πάλιν ἄλλην ἐπιτομὴν τῶν συγγεγραφότων περὶ συναγωγῆς θαυμασίων ἀνέμων, ἐκλογάς τε ἱστορίων αὐτὸν συντάξαι, καὶ περὶ τῆς πρὸς φίλους ὁμιλίας. On the difficulties of the text, cf. Susemihl 1891:1.686n248. The epitome περὶ τῆς Ἐρυθρᾶς θαλάσσης should be the work of a later author; the work on the Troglodytes is perhaps to be identified with a passage

from his work as a γραμματικός[36] and thus are further testimonies to his philological, perhaps Peripatetic background.[37] The list of books points to another fact, too: Agatharchides' call to history came only late, and he started his work as a historian after having worked as a philologist.[38]

Jacoby divided the fragments of the historian Agatharchides into a history of Asia in ten books (τὰ κατὰ τὴν Ἀσίαν ἐγνωσμένα, τὰ περὶ τὴν Ἀσίαν, Ἀσιατικά, περὶ Ἀσίας, αἱ περὶ τῆς Ἀσίας ἱστορίαι) and a much longer history of Europe in 49 books (τὰ κατὰ τὴν Εὐρώπην, Εὐρωπιακά, Ἱστορίαι)—promising us to present *On the Red Sea* (περὶ τῆς ἐρυθρᾶς θαλάσσης, ἱστορία ἡ περὶ τὴν ἐρυθρὰν θάλασσαν) in a later part of his collection.

Agatharchides was read in antiquity by Artemidorus and Posidonius—who shared his fate and survive only in fragments. He was used by Strabo, if the Augustan geographer did not use him exclusively via Artemidorus,[39] and Diodorus. He is still acknowledged as a source by Aelian and Athenaeus in the second or early third century AD.[40] And

---

of περὶ τῆς Ἐρυθρᾶς θαλάσσης (Susemihl refers to Frieten 1847:24, and see now Mazza 2002:63, but Desanges 1998:69, is sceptical and believes only in a partial overlap of two different works). The end of the notice, περὶ συναγωγῆς θαυμασίων ἀνέμων, has been emended in different ways: see Jacoby's apparatus criticus (Schwartz 1893:740 talks about only a συναγωγὴ θαυμασίων). The last title may relate to a work of Heraclides Lembus.

[36] According to Schwartz 1893:740 the *Epitome of the Lyde* and the ἐκλογαὶ ἱστορίων, which he holds had stylistic purposes, are to be counted as grammatical works.

[37] Schwartz 1893:740 refers to Arist. *NE* 1242a19 to explain the περὶ πρὸς φίλους ὁμιλίας and reminds us that the Peripatos of the third and second century produced a mass of works on popular morality. Not everybody took Agatharchides' designation as a Peripatetic seriously. See Schwartz 740: "d. h. ein Peripatetiker des 2. Jhdts., der sich um Metaphysik nicht kümmerte und in philosophischen Gedanken das beste Mittel sah, ein reiches empirisches Material zu ordnen und zu beleben;" Dihle 1994:86: "was nach dem Sprachgebrauch der Zeit wohl nur ... zu sagen hat, daß er sich als gelehrter Literat hervortat." A bit different is Palm 1955:45–46: "Auch im Wortvorrat kann die Abhängigkeit des Ag. von den grossen Vertretern der peripatetischen Schule beobachtet werden." But this does not necessarily make him a Peripatetic: it attests only that his interests and those of the Peripatetics coincide in many points.

[38] He was not the only one to do so; Meißner 1992:186–190 supplies further examples.

[39] Capelle 1953:170 insisted on this.

[40] Jacoby prints fragments originating from the following authors: Pliny, Josephus, Athenaeus, Aelian (on Agatharchides as his source, cf. Palm 1955:52–53). I do not believe that Agatharchides was used directly by the authors of the μακρόβιοι tradition (F 4). Capelle 1953:168–169, 172–175 noticed some passages in which Heliodorus and Strabo

then he is cited again only in the second half of the ninth century AD: the patriarch Photius read a codex, from which he took a short sample with a very flattering stylistic evaluation. More important, he made also long extracts from—as he says—the first and fifth book περὶ τῆς ἐρυθρᾶς θαλάσσης καὶ ἑτέρων παραδόξων (more than 50 printed pages in Henry's edition).[41] Nobody is known to have read Agatharchides after Photius.

A close reading of Photius shows that he described not three different historical works, but only one.[42] He says (*Bibl.* cod. 213 p171a): ἀνεγνώσθη Ἀγαθαρχίδου ἱστορικόν[43] ... γράψαι δὲ τὸν ἄνδρα τοῦτον τὰ κατὰ τὴν Ἀσίαν ἔγνωμεν ἐν βιβλίοις ι᾽· καὶ τῶν κατὰ τὴν Εὐρώπην δὲ εἰς θ᾽ καὶ μ᾽ παρατείνεται[44] αὐτῷ ἡ ἱστορία. This is to be translated: "Lu d'Agatharchide un traité de genre historique ... il est établi que notre auteur a écrit des *Affaires d'Asie* en dix livres. Avec ses *Affaires d'Europe* son enquête en couvre jusqu'à quarante-neuf."[45] Photius continues: ἀλλὰ καὶ ε᾽ βίβλια τὴν Ἐρυθρὰν αὐτῷ πᾶσαν καὶ τὰ περὶ ταύτην ἐξιστοροῦσι. "Mais à noter aussi que cinq livres à lui explorent la mer Érythrée dans son ensemble et les régions alentour."

Clearly, therefore, the five books *On the Red Sea* are (at least in the eyes of Photius) part of the grand total of the 49 books. It gets clearer still. According to Photius, Agatharchides gave his reasons why he did

---

seem to have used a common source: Heliod. *Aeth.* 9.22 and Strabo 17.1.48 p817; Heliod. *Aeth.* 10.5 and Strabo 17.2.2 p821; Diod. Sic. 1.33.2. Capelle 1953:174 believes, too, that Heliod. *Aeth.* 8.16, 9.16–18 depends finally on Agatharchides–but assumes that Heliodorus knew Agatharchides only via Artemidorus.

[41] Schamp 1987:274 argues that even Photius knew only extracts, but this does not seem to be evident from his wording, and the closeness of the accounts of Diodorus and Photius is a problem for this thesis, too: certainly nobody wants to argue that Diodorus read only extracts.

[42] The argument of Marcotte 2001:385–435, esp. 385–416. Engels 2004:182 does not agree.

[43] The introduction of *Bibl.* cod. 250 is very similar: ἀνεγνώσθη Ἀγαθαρχίδου λόγοι δύο, ὁ πρῶτος καὶ ὁ πέμπτος κτλ. The reading of M and A *pinax* however is: ἀνεγνώσθη ἐκ τοῦ πρώτου λόγου Ἀγαθαρχίδου τῶν περὶ τῆς ἐρυθρᾶς θαλάσσης A. This difference has been exploited to prove that Photius himself had only excerpts of the work, but see on the significance of ἀνεγνώσθη ἐκ Hägg 1975:136–137.

[44] Lampe 1961 s.v. παρατείνω 3: "continue, go on doing."

[45] Marcotte 2001:391, 394.

not treat some topics his readers could expect him to treat in the fifth book of ἡ πᾶσα συγγραφή–and exactly this passage is known from the extracts of the so-called *On the Red Sea*.[46]

Who was the author of this συγγραφή? Was it the work of Agatharchides—or was it just a bookbinder gluing together three different works of the same author and fooling the Byzantine patriarch? It seems to me that Agatharchides was responsible for ἡ πᾶσα συγγραφή—perhaps himself forming a single whole out of earlier writings.[47] This is the best explanation for the fact that the historical content of the *Asian Affairs* and the *European Affairs* does not overlap (at least according to the surviving fragments).[48] Moreover, the identity of Book 5 of the συγγραφή, which started with the ten books *On the Affairs of Asia* with Book 5 *On the Red Sea*, would be difficult to explain by any other hypothesis.[49] In this way, the work of Agatharchides is an important parallel to the 20 books περὶ Ἀσίας καὶ Εὐρώπης written by Demetrius of Kallatis—in Alexandria.[50]

What have we got, then?[51] Photius transmits excerpts of the first book, very uneven and without any discernible train of thought (*Bibl.*

---

[46] *Bibl.* cod. 213 p171a: τὴν οὖν εἰρημένην ἅπασαν συγγραφὴν καὶ αὐτὸς ἐπὶ τέλει τοῦ έ λόγου εἰς μνήμην ἀνάγει, ἐν ᾧ καὶ πεπαῦσθαι τοῦ γράφειν διά τινάς τε αἰτίας ἄλλας, καὶ ὅτι τὰ τῆς ἡλικίας ἀποκλίνοι πρὸς τὸ ἔξωρον. This refers to cod. 250 (110.460b).

[47] This could explain why Athenaeus still cited the different parts (he is, by the way, the only author who cites from the *Europiaka* [Alonso-Núñez 1997:59]), and it could explain Phot. *Bibl.* cod. 213 p171: πλήν γε εἰσὶν οἵ φασιν αὐτὸν καὶ ἑτέρας συγγεγραφέναι πραγματείας ὧν ἡμεῖς οὐδένα οὐδέπω ἴσμεν. Wachsmuth 1891:329–331 emphasized the importance of editions organized in pentads for the transmission of ancient books in general; we may presume that Photius read only the last remnants of such an edition in pentads.

[48] Cf. Alonso-Núñez 1997:59–60, who interpreted the *Europiaka* as a continuation of the *Asiatika*.

[49] Marginally relevant may be other forms of overlap. To cite just one instance: Diod. Sic. 3.8.6 is usually thought to belong to the *Asiatika* Book 2, but corresponds to Phot. 30.448b.

[50] *FGrH* 85; "una storia universale disposta secondo criteri geografici di impronta ionica e quidi arcaizzante" (Zecchini 1990:218). Agatharchides knew this book: *FGrH* 85 T 3.

[51] Many attributions did not stand the test. Immisch claimed the Pythagorean cod. 249 as Agatharchidean (Wilson 1994:219–225 offers a translation); however, Immisch has had few followers (most importantly, Thesleff 1961:30, 109; id. 1965:237n4). Eudoros was suggested by Theiler 1970:494–497, the ubiquitous Posidonius by Reinhardt 1953:764–768

cod. 250.1–20). Diodorus cites the second book for his remarks on the
Ethiopians at the Nile (3.5–10),[52] and this has to be connected with
his discussion of the sources of the Nile (1.32–41 [= *FGrH* 86 F 19]).[53] A
description of Arabia might be taken from Agatharchides, too (Diod. Sic.
2.49–54),[54] and the fifth book consists of the famous excerpts on the Red
Sea (Diod. Sic. 3.12–48,[55] Phot. *Bibl.* cod. 250.21–111); a description of the
Libyan tribes may have followed (Diod. Sic. 3.49–51).[56] After quite a gap,
Book 8 records events of 324 BC, Book 9 advances to ca. 300, and Book
10 will have ended with the battle of Corupedium.[57] Jacoby believed
that the European history ended around the time of Pydna, thereby
providing a sequel to the Asian history[58]—but the latest datable frag-

---

and Fraser 1972:540, 774n166. Dihle 1984:59n21 (cf. Woelk 1966:89) denied Agatharchidean
and Posidonian authorship. Kunz 1935 (esp. 104–107) assigned several Diodorean prefaces to Agatharchides, e.g. the prefaces of Book 1 and "Buch 21ff.", perhaps even of Book
33. But Diod. Sic. 21.1.4a is sometimes claimed for Hieronymus of Cardia (Hornblower
1981:50n104), whereas Sacks 1990:19 n32 and 21 sees Diodorus as the writer of all prefaces—rightly, in my opinion.

[52] Leopoldi 1892:32–36; Bommelaer 1989:XI–XII.

[53] The Nile is the border between Asia and Africa, therefore the Ethiopians could form
a part of the *Asiatika*, Desanges 1998:70; on the general concept see Zimmermann 1999:84,
109.

[54] Leopoldi 1892:38–50; Schwartz 1893:739. Jacoby, *FGrH* 87 F 114 prints this as
Posidonius (as does Theiler F 78), but acknowledges the possibility of an Agatharchidean
origin, as did Rudberg 1918:18n4. Diod. Sic. 2.51.3–4 is certainly Agatharchidean (*FGrH* 673
F 104a). Leopoldi and also Mazza 2002:62 argue for Agatharchides as the source of the
whole passage. Alonso-Núñez 1997:60 believes that Books 2–4 concerned the Ethiopians
and the Indian Ocean.

[55] Diod. Sic. 3.22 is sometimes attributed to another source, Müller 1882:140;
Bommelaer 1989:XXVI –XXVII, but cf. Woelk 1966:138–139.

[56] Leopoldi 1892:37–38. The parts of Artemidorus found in Strabo open no further
vistas on the contents of Agatharchides.

[57] Flavius Josephus described Agatharchides as historian of the *diadochi* (*AJ* 12.5 = *FGrH*
86 F 20b).

[58] Jacoby 1926:151 on the *Europiaka*: "wann diese einsetzten, ist nicht zu sagen, da F 5–6
undatierbar sind; aber spätestens von der zweiten dekade an enthielten sie die geschicke
Makedoniens und der staaten des hellenischen Mutterlandes im s. III in großer ausführ-
lichkeit. die FF gehen nicht über die regierung des Philippos V; und daß der Perseuskrieg
und der untergang des makedonischen reiches den schluß bildete (C. Mueller), ist zwar
nicht zu beweisen, aber recht glaublich." One of the reasons for Pydna as the end-date
of Agatharchides' history is the belief that Agatharchides wrote in the second half of the
second century.

ment (F 16) refers to an event in the year 197, and the peace of Apamea or some other event may have provided an appropriate end.[59] There is no real proof that Rome played any role in Agatharchides' thinking.[60]

The structure of the 49 books seems odd, but we have to keep in mind that we know quite a lot about Books 1 and 5, but much less about the other books. We would surely like to understand the composition of the opening books, about the transition from a setting somewhere in the third or second century to the earlier history, and we may remember Polybius Books 6 and 12 as not really being part of a coherent narrative.[61] The solution to these problems is lost with the rest of Agatharchides' histories:[62] later generations were not much

[59] Fraser 1972:516: "the *Events in Europe* ... certainly went down to the end of the third century, if not further;" cf. Zecchini 1990:220. Desanges 1998:73, 81 furnishes some indications for an early date: the coast is described only till Ptolemais Theron, established by Ptolemy II (Phot. 84.457a; Diod. Sic. 3.18.4); Syria is said to be under Ptolemaic rule (Phot. 102.459a: οὗτοι πολύχρυσον τὴν Πτολεμαίου Συρίαν πεποιήκασιν), which cannot be squared easily with a date in the late second century. Important, though not always heeded, is the remark by Immisch 1919:10n, who observed that 102.459b (see n60 below) could have been written any time after the Roman victory over Antiochus III. Engels 2004:183 believes that the end point of the work should have had some significance in terms of Ptolemaic history, suggesting 180/79 or the day of Eleusis, or 145—but this causes problems with the title of *Europiaka*, the idea of universal history, and the inferred date of writing in the first half of the second century.

[60] According to Engels 2004:189 there is an allusion not only to the end of Alexander's rule, but also to Pydna in Phot. 17.445b: καὶ τὰς μεγίστας βασιλείας ἄρδην ἀνῃρημένας, τὴν Κασσάνδρου, τὴν Λυσιμάχου, τὴν Ἀλεξάνδρου τηλικαύτην οὖσαν, τὴν Μήδων, τὴν Σύρων, τὴν Περσῶν, ὥστε μηδὲ σπέρμα καταλελεῖφθαι τοῦ γένους. More important is 102.459b, which is usually taken as a reference to Rome (Woelk 1966:249–250; Fraser 1972:545; further literature in Ferrary 1988:234n35): εἰ δὲ μὴ πόρρω διεστηκυῖαν τὴν οἴκησιν κατεῖχον τῶν ἐπὶ πάντα τόπον τὰς δυνάμεις στρεφόντων, οἰκονόμοι τῶν ἀλλοτρίαν ἂν ὑπῆρχον οἱ κύριοι τῶν ἰδίων ἄθλων. The parallel passage in Diod. Sic. 3.47.8 need not refer to Rome: ἀλλὰ γὰρ οὗτοι μὲν ἐκ πολλῶν χρόνων τὴν εὐδαιμονίαν ἀσάλευτον ἔσχον διὰ τὸ παντελῶς ἀπεξενῶσθαι τῶν διὰ τὴν ἰδίαν πλεονεξίαν ἕρμαιον ἡγουμένων τὸν ἀλλότριον πλοῦτον. Fraser 1972:786n212 concluded: "Diod. Sic. ... has emasculated the passage," but Ferrary 1988:233 sees in Diodorus "le texte le plus violent," even though he, too, believes Rome to be meant. Can it be criticism of the Ptolemies?

[61] See Immisch 1919:3 on the looser connection of prooemia and main text developing since the fourth century.

[62] Diod. Sic. 4.1 offers a certain possibility for such a transition, but since he used all kinds of μυθολογούμενα, we are unable to form any exact idea of the first part of Agatharchides' history from Diodorus. Agatharchides himself was fond of digressions, or perhaps better: he liked to move from a point coming up in his narrative to the broader

interested in Hellenistic history, or they were able to read more interesting narratives of this period.[63] Therefore only the geographical and ethnographical parts of Agatharchides' work survived for a longer time: their contents were almost unique.[64] The concentration on geographical and ethnographical matters will have been enhanced by Photius' excerpts. As can be seen in comparing the (extant) *vita Apollonii* with the patriarch's excerpts, Photius was especially interested in all kinds of descriptions of foreign lands.[65]

Embarrassing as it may seem to some, *On the Red Sea* can be read as historiography, even if the notion of fish-eaters and other outlandish people as part of history may seem strange at first sight. Nevertheless, it is supported by the famous remark of Agatharchides about the authors who had written on the four corners of the world (Phot. 65.454b): ὅτι, φησί, τῆς ὅλης οἰκουμένης ἐν τέτταρσι κυκλιζομένης μέρεσιν, ἀνατολῆς λέγω, δύσεως, ἄρκτου καὶ μεσημβρίας, τὰ μὲν πρὸς ἑσπέραν ἐξείργασται Λύκος τε καὶ Τιμαῖος, τὰ δὲ πρὸς ἀνατολὰς Ἑκαταῖος τε καὶ Βασιλίς, τὰ δὲ πρὸς ἄρκτους Διόφαντος καὶ Δημήτριος, τὰ δὲ πρὸς μεσημβρίαν, φορτικόν, φησί, τὸ ἀληθές, ἡμεῖς. Some of these authors are more than empty names to us. There is Timaeus, of course (*FGrH* 566), but also Hecataeus of Abdera (*FGrH* 264),[66] who is, incidentally,

---

aspects of the matter, as Phot. 7.442b–8.444b exemplify. These chapters begin with an exploration into the origin of the Red Sea's name, continue with a criticism of mythological traditions, and end with general remarks on the relation of poetry and history.

[63] Diodorus, who used Agatharchides in his first books, did not use his account of Hellenistic history. Quint. *Inst.* 10.1.75 (Timagenes, *FGrH* 88 T 6, and believed by Laqueur 1936:1065 to reflect directly the claims of Timagenes) shows clearly how Hellenistic historiography was discounted during the empire: *longo post intervallo temporis natus* (i.e., after Clitarchus) *Timagenes vel hoc est ipso probabilis quod intermissam historias scribendi industriam nova laude reparavit.* Cf., generally, Ameling 1996:126–130 for the real and perceived break in the middle of the second century.

[64] Burstein 1989:35 believes that Uranius' *Arabica* supplanted Agatharchides as the standard account of the area in late antiquity—which seems a little doubtful in the face of the characteristic Bowersock 2000:128–133 gives of this author.

[65] Palm 1955:16 and 20–25 noticed the same interests, not quite as distinct, in Photius' excerpts of Plutarch's *Lives.*

[66] But Jacoby prints this notice as 1 T 14—and has doubts about this assignation in the commentary to 264 T 9; Fraser 1972:788n241 is uncertain ("Hecataeus is presumably the Milesian and not the Abderite"), while Engels 2004:183n26 prefers the Abderite.

called a φιλόσοφος ... καὶ κριτικὸς γραμματικός in the *Suda* (T 1). And
we know at least the titles and a little bit more about Lycus (*FGrH* 570),
Diophantus (805), Basilis (718),[67] and Demetrius (85), whose 20 books
περὶ Ἀσίας καὶ Εὐρώπης were mentioned as an interesting parallel to
Agatharchides' work. All of them are historians, telling the story of
their very own part of the world—and Agatharchides, who is the historian of the south in his early books, claims precisely for these books
that they belong to history. Therefore, the standards of history are
valid for his work, too, and we may use Photius' résumé as a witness for
Agatharchides' attitudes to historiography and to the tasks of an historian during the early second century.

IV. Method

Time and again, Agatharchides insists on the importance of truth—
and although this topos is popular in historiography, he succeeded
in earning himself a solid reputation with modern classicists. His use
of sources is often approved and praised–especially in the light of
the following remark (Diod. Sic. 3.38.1): περὶ δὲ τοῦ καταλελειμμένου
μέρους, λέγω δὲ τοῦ Ἀραβίου κόλπου, ποιησόμεθα τὴν ἀναγραφήν, τὰ
μὲν ἐκ τῶν ἐν Ἀλεξανδρείᾳ βασιλικῶν ὑπομνημάτων ἐξειληφότες, τὰ
δὲ παρὰ τῶν αὐτοπτῶν πεπυσμένοι. A closer inspection, carried out by
Willy Peremans,[68] was sobering: the royal *hypomnemata* are the official
court-bulletins, originating from Alexandria, and when these bulle-
tins had been written (and published), nobody could scrutinize them,
because their sources were gone. Agatharchides' eyewitnesses were no
living persons, no voyagers sought out by the historian in an almost
Herodotean manner, but are the authors of monographs who had been

---

[67] Susemihl 1891:1.663–664.

[68] Peremans 1967:432–455; on the ὑπομνήματα see Peremans 438–445; Burstein
1989:30–31. This passage of Diodorus is usually seen as a direct copy of Agatharchides
(Müller 1882, *ad* ch. 79; Woelk 1966:257–258; Peremans 455; Burstein 30); Pirenne 1961:80–
81, 87, and 89 proposed cautiously that the remark was written by Diodorus himself,
who had sought out the eye-witnesses; Sacks 1990:85–86 is of the same opinion, but
see Altheim and Stiehl 1964:65–69. Bommelaer 1989:XVI–XVII suggests that Diod. Sic.
3.40.8 might be an example of Diodorus consulting the archives, but πρόσταγμα γάρ ἐστι
βασιλέως on ships in the Red Sea sounds more like Agatharchides—and Diodorus reports
in this chapter many items left out by Photius 83.456b–457a.

there and had come back again to write about their journeys and adventures.[69] It was emphasized several times in the last years that Agatharchides' geographical information had not been really up-to-date:[70] the knowledge he relied on was—at least in parts—almost fifty or sixty years old, going back to the times of Ptolemy II.[71] And, of course, Agatharchides never went himself.[72]

This has some implications for our interpretation of his work[73] and for his claim to truthfulness: truth is not the result of newly acquired knowledge, surpassing the information of earlier generations. Instead, the claim to truth is supported by the use made of—known—sources. This may be a consequence of Agatharchides' beginnings as a γραμματικός, but he shares this interest in written sources with many of his contemporaries, and there are many places where he enters into discussions with earlier authors.

The historian has to discriminate among his sources, if they offer more than one account of the same phenomenon. The Argive explanation of the Red Sea's name, to be found in the work of a certain Deinias, was τῇ μὲν τόλμῃ μέγας, τῇ δὲ δόξῃ κενός (Phot. 4.442a).[74] Without any

---

[69] Even Eratosthenes' knowledge derived from books written by τοῖς ἐν τοῖς τόποις γενομένοις (Strabo 2.1.5 p69).

[70] Fraser 1972:261n134 used F 22 to prove this. See also Woelk 1966:259–264; Desanges 1998:80. On the Arabian side, not even the Kattabaneis (known from Eratosthenes) are mentioned; the capital of Saba is not Mariaba, as in Eratosthenes, but Sabei—so that Anaxicrates may have been the latest author used, as Tarn 1929:14 suggested. Even the description of the Red Sea's fauna (Diod. Sic. 3.35–7; Phot. 66.455a –80.456a) contains elements older than Ptolemy II, perhaps going back to Ctesias: Desanges 1998:82.

[71] Simmias, Eumedes, and Ariston (F 84) belong to this time.

[72] This is clear from the evidence presented by Desanges 1998, but it is well worth noticing that Woelk 1966:110–111 finds no evidence for Agatharchides having visited the gold mines, the account of which had triggered Strasburger's interest in him. Burstein 1989:17 rightly notes that the requirements of a successor delineated in Phot. 110.460b do not require journeys or eye-witness experience of events.

[73] Jacob 1991:134: "Cet ouvrage ne s'adresse pas explicitement à des voyageurs, des marins ou des négociants. Il s'agit moins d'un texte à finalité pratique que d'un traité littéraire adressé à un public de lecteurs sans doute plus étendu que celui des destinataires habituels des textes géographiques." Since Agatharchides wanted to write history, we should accentuate a bit differently.

[74] Deinias was conjectured by Reinesius (306F7), defended by Woelk 1966:97; Κλεινίαν codd. The expression οἱ περὶ Δεινίαν means just Deinias himself.

facts capable of shedding knowledge on the subject under discussion,
silence is to be preferred to empty verbiage, as his remarks on the tides
make clear (Phot. 107.460a): ὅτι εἰπὼν περὶ ἀμπωτέων ὁ συγγραφεὺς
διαφόρους αἰτίας, καὶ πάσας ὡς οὐδὲν ἐχούσας ἀληθὲς ἀποδοκιμάσας,
ἐπάγει· ὅτι δὲ ταῦτα πάντα λαλιὰν μὲν ἔχει σιγᾶν αἰσχυνομένην,
πράγματος δὲ οὐδενὸς ἀντείληπται βοήθειαν δυναμένου τοῖς εἰρημένοις
παρασχεῖν, εὐχερές ἐστι μαθεῖν. In both, completely different cases,
Agatharchides tries to reach a decision with the aid of *ratio*—and
he asks for secure facts as basis for any explanation (otherwise your
explanation might come in for a sharp rebuke).[75] One of his predecessors is criticized harshly: ἀλλὰ γὰρ περὶ μὲν τοιούτων ἀνεφίκτου τῆς
ἐπινοίας ἡμῖν οὔσης οὐδὲν κωλύει τοὺς τὰ πλεῖστα ἀποφηναμένους
ἐλάχιστα γινώσκειν, ὡς ἂν τῆς ἐν τοῖς λόγοις πιθανότητος τὴν μὲν
ἀκοὴν πειθούσης, τὴν δ' ἀλήθειαν οὐδαμῶς εὑρισκούσης (Diod. Sic.
3.20.3).

In a comparable case, writing on the sources of the Nile,
Agatharchides gives a short summary of his most important predecessors and the reasons for their failure (Diod. Sic. 1.37.3–4 [= *FGrH* 86 F
19]): Cadmus, Hellanicus, Hecataeus and others, παλαιοὶ παντάπασιν
ὄντες, put trust in the answers offered by the myths (εἰς τὰς μυθώδεις
ἀποφάσεις ἀπέκλιναν); Herodotus followed contradictory guesses
(ἀντιλεγομέναις ὑπονοίαις)—two mistakes in one (cf. 1.38.12:
σχεδιάζων). Xenophon and Thucydides are praised for the truthfulness (ἀλήθεια) of their works—but did not treat Egypt at all. Ephorus
and Theopompus were almost completely wrong (ἥκιστα τῆς ἀληθείας
ἐπέτυχον), because they had no pertinent information: no Greek had
reached the confines of Egypt or traveled into Ethiopia.[76] Since nobody
had seen the sources of the Nile, everybody had to use ὑπόνοια and

---

[75] Nicely expressed in Diod. Sic. 1.40.1 (*FGrH* 86 F 19), for instance: ἀνεξέλεγκτος
μᾶλλον ἢ πιθανός.

[76] Even here Agatharchides thinks of his own work only in the categories of historiography: he mentions even historians that did not treat the subject, because he wanted to
be seen as standing in their succession; and he mentions only the different explanations
provided by historians, omitting all the other ones, even if he must have known them (cf.,
for instance, Keyser 2001:368–370, on the ideas Dicaearchus developed about the sources
of the Nile).

πιθανόν[77]—but, as Agatharchides put it, plausibility (πιθανότης) may persuade the hearing, but it does not discover the truth.[78]

For some facts and stories, as Agatharchides knew, there is no possible kind of evidence—notably for those to be found in the myths (Phot. 8.444a): ἐπεὶ διὰ τίνα αἰτίαν Ὅμηρον οὐκ εὐθύνω, Διὸς καὶ Ποσειδῶνος φράζοντα διαφοράν, ἀδύνατον ἀνθρώπῳ πίστιν παραδοῦναι?[79] This is supported by further examples, and the consequence is: ὅτι αὐτός, φησίν, ἑαυτῷ αἴτιος καθίσταται ἐλέγχων ὁ τὴν τῶν μυθοποιῶν ἐξουσίαν εἰς πραγματικὴν μετάγων ἐνάργειαν.[80] Agatharchides does not denigrate the myths, because they bring injury to the gods—but because it is impossible to know the truth about myth, and because no one had (or could have) undertaken a serious enquiry about these matters.[81]

The claim of poetry is not invalidated, but—according to Agatharchides—it is a different claim, which enables the poets to use myths: ὅτι πᾶς ποιητὴς ψυχαγωγίας μᾶλλον ἢ ἀληθείας ἐστὶ στοχαστής (Phot. 8.444b). Thucydides would have agreed,[82] but Eratosthenes is

---

[77] Diod. Sic. 1.37.6–7: τὰς δὲ πήγας τοῦ Νείλου, καὶ τὸν τόπον ἐξ οὗ λαμβάνει τὴν ἀρχὴν τοῦ ῥεύματος, ἑωρακέναι μὲν μέχρι τῶνδε τῶν ἱστοριῶν γραφομένων οὐδεὶς εἴρηκεν οὐδ' ἀκοὴν ἀπεφήνατο παρὰ τῶν ἑωρακέναι διαβεβαιουμένων. διὸ καὶ τοῦ πράγματος εἰς ὑπόνοιαν καὶ καταστοχασμὸν πιθανὸν καταντῶντος, κτλ.

[78] Cf. Diod. Sic. 1.38.5–6: ὅταν οὖν ἡ τῆς πείρας ἀκρίβεια κατισχύῃ τὴν τῶν λόγων πιθανότητι ... οὐ μόνον ἀναπόδεικτόν ἐστιν, ἀλλ' οὐδὲ τὴν πίστιν ἔχει διὰ τῆς ἐναργείας συγχωρουμένην. 3.20.3: ὡς ἂν τῆς ἐν τοῖς λόγοις πιθανότητος τὴν μὲν ἀκοὴν πειθούσης, τὴν δ' ἀλήθειαν οὐδαμῶς εὑρισκούσης.

[79] Cf. Phot. 7.444a: ἐν ταῖς μακάρων νήσοις, ἃς οὐδεὶς κυρίως ἱστόρηκε; 444b: οἱ οὖν ταῦτα τερατευόμενοι, πόρρω τῆς ἀληθείας ἱστάμενοι, οὐκ ἂν ἑτέροις ταύτην εἰσηγεῖσθαι κριθεῖεν ἂν ἀξιόλογοι. On the use of Homer and other poets in this chapter, see Battazzato 2003:282–302, esp. 282–287.

[80] It was, of course, evident to Agatharchides that a myth can have a profound effect on history, as kinship diplomacy attests so vividly—but the subject of the myth itself is still no subject of history. Cf. Phot. 95.458a: φιλόξενοι δὲ εἰς ὑπερβολήν, οὐ πᾶσιν ἀνθρώποις, ἀλλὰ τοῖς ἀπὸ Πελοποννήσου διεκβάλλουσι καὶ Βοιωτίας διά τινα μυθικὴν ἀφ' Ἡρακλέους ἱστορίαν. I believe Diod. Sic. 3.30.4 to be an addition by that author.

[81] Phot. 7.444a: ἃς οὐδεὶς κυρίως ἱστόρηκε. See in general Verdin 1990:6–11.

[82] The opposition between μυθώδης and ἀληθινὸς λόγος goes back at least to Thucydides (1.22.4), but cf. also Pl. *Plt.* 522a8. It may be added that Agatharchides was one of the few followers Thucydides had in Hellenistic times, as Photius tells us (*Bibl.* 213 = *FGrH* 86 T 2.6): καὶ ζηλωτὴς μέν ἐστι Θουκυδίδου ἔν τε τῇ τῶν δημηγοριῶν δαψιλείᾳ τε καὶ

even nearer to our author,[83] and his treatment of Homeric geography had culminated in the dictum that ψυχαγωγία, not διδασκαλία, was the poet's intention.[84] Neoptolemus of Parium, a near contemporary, dissented,[85] but Agatharchides went even further: the aim of the historian is not διδασκαλία, but ἀλήθεια. The historian has to face the constraints his researches and his sources put on him, whereas the poet may take every liberty his material requires.

We may wonder, whether Agatharchides expected history to supply dramatic μίμησις, hence ἡδονή. At least he knew—as did Polybius (20.12.8)—the value of ἐνάργεια conveying πίστις to a narrative, but at the same moment he distanced himself from somebody like Hegesias (Phot. 21.445b [= FGrH 142 T 3]),[86] who is characterized as εὐτελής, and whose manner of writing is seen without any sympathy: ἀλληγορικῶς τῷ τρόπῳ καὶ ταῖς διαλέκτοις, ὡς δοκοῦσι, περιττῶς. Of course, αὐτοπάθεια was a necessary requirement of the historian as a man of letters,[87] even if own political experiences or journeys were not.

διασκευῇ, τῷ μεγαλείῳ δὲ μὴ δευτερεύων τοῦ λόγου τῷ σαφεῖ παρελαύνει τὸν ἄνδρα. Το be a ζηλωτής of Thucydides is rare among Hellenistic historians (this is, I believe, the reason for the disclaimer of Hornblower 1994:61: "but this might just be a vivid way of saying that Photius himself saw resemblances"), but Walbank 1985:251 draws attention to Polybius. Cf. Pédech 1964:300–301 for a translation of Photius' phrase.

[83] Knaack 1907:376–377. On the concept of ψυχαγωγία, starting with Gorgias, see Pohlenz 1965:2.436–472. It may be noted in passing that Diod. Sic. 3.11.1–2 calls for diligent discrimination in the use of sources on Ethiopia and Egypt: ὧν οἱ μὲν ψευδεῖ φήμῃ πεπιστευκότες, οἱ δὲ παρ' ἑαυτῶν πολλὰ τῆς ψυχαγωγίας ἕνεκα πεπλακότες, δικαίως ἂν ἀπιστοῖντο. Ἀγαθαρχίδης μὲν γὰρ ὁ Κνίδιος ... καὶ ὁ τὰς γεωγραφίας συνταξάμενος Ἀρτεμίδωρος ὁ Ἐφέσιος κτλ.

[84] Strabo 1.2.3 p15: ποιητὴν γὰρ ἔφη πάντα στοχάζεσθαι ψυχαγωγίας, οὐ διδασκαλίας; Cf. 7 p18, also referring to Eratosthenes: τοὺς τ' ἐξηγητὰς φλυάρους ἀποφαίνων καὶ αὐτὸν τὸν ποιητὴν κτλ. (Berger 1880:36–37 with his remarks; Pfeiffer 1978:207). Geus 2002:267n35 specifies other connections between Eratosthenes and Agatharchides.

[85] Pfeiffer 1978:208, citing Philodemus, περὶ ποιημάτων 5 col. 16 pp143–144 Mangoni: [... τ]ῷ τελείῳ ποι[ητῇ μετ]ὰ τῆς ψυχαγω[γί]α[ς τὴν τῶν] ἀκουόντω[ν] ὠ[φέλησι]ν καὶ χρησι[μο]λ[ογία]ν καὶ τὸν Ὅμηρ[ον ....].

[86] On Hegesias, see now Staab 2004.

[87] Schepens 2005:162n60 cites in this context Phot. 21.445a: ὅτι πολλοί, φησί, καὶ τῶν πολιτικῶν ἀνδρῶν καὶ τῶν ποίημα γεγραφότων διηπόρηκασι πῶς τὰς ὑπερβαλλούσας ἐνίοις ἀκληρίας τὸν ἐκτὸς τῶν κινδύνων κείμενον πρεπόντως ἐξαγγελτέον. Agatharchides combines this with a long, essentially stylistic discussion, even if later on he contends that there has to be a reason (αἰτία) to depict misfortune (Phot. 21.446a). Marincola 1997:233

The danger to the historian, according to Agatharchides, lay in the use of ποιητικὴ ἐξουσία,[88] in the disregard of τὸ ἀκριβές, and the disdain of truth: Ephorus especially is singled out and criticized in this regard.[89] But the general claim of Agatharchides is that history is useless without truth.[90] To reach this aim, there is no other way but to concentrate on a narrative made out of facts that can be known: the task of the historian is to decide on these facts in a methodically responsible way and to base his true narrative on them.

This does not preclude ψυχαγωγία on the historian's part[91]—as Strasburger's insistence on the πάθος in Agatharchides shows. This πάθος is real, and Photius says about the portrayal of human existence (and misery) in the Ptolemaic gold mines, ὑπερβολὴν οὖν οὐδενὶ τὸ πάθος δυστυχήματι καταλιπεῖν ἐκτραγῳδήσας κτλ. (Phot. 24.447b). Style is no forbidden matter for Agatharchides, even if he is no poet,

---

sees an extension of Polybius' polemic against Phylarchus, but since Agatharchides was a contemporary of Polybius, both just seem to react to a contemporary tendency.

[88] Phot. 4.442a: ἀπὸ τῆς ποιητικῆς ἐξουσίας καὶ αὐτοὶ ἄδειαν λαβόντες κτλ. The theme was very much used by Christian authors in their criticism of pagan historical conceptions: see Tert. *Ad nat.* 2.7.9: *nam quotiens misera vel turpia vel atrocia deorum exprobramus, allegatione poeticae licentiae ut fabulosa defenditis*; Justin, *Apol.* 1.54.1, who notes the missing proof: οἱ δὲ παραδιδόντες τὰ μυθοποιηθέντα ὑπὸ τῶν ποιητῶν οὐδεμίαν ἀπόδειξιν φέρουσι τοῖς ἐκμανθάνουσι νέοις.

[89] Diod. Sic. 1.39.13 (*FGrH* 86 F 19; Ephorus, *FGrH* 70 T 16): ἀλλὰ γὰρ οὐκ ἄν τις παρ' Ἐφόρου ζητήσειεν ἐκ παντὸς τρόπου τἀκριβές, ὁρῶν αὐτὸν ἐν πολλοῖς ὠλιγωρηκότα τῆς ἀληθείας. Cf. Meister 1973/4:454–455.

[90] Marcotte 2001:418–419 recognized a reflection on the task of the historian in Phot. 11.445a, even though this chapter is usually taken to be a fragment of a speech (αὐστηρὸς ὁ λόγος, ἀλλὰ σωτήριος. δηλοῦται γὰρ οὐ λύπης, ἀλλὰ φυλακῆς ἕνεκεν, καὶ τὴν ἡδονὴν ἐκ τῶν λόγων ἦρκεν, ὅπως τῆς ἐκ τῶν πραγμάτων χάριτος ἀπολαύοντες μηδέποτε ἀντὶ τοῦ βελτίονος τὸ χεῖρον αἱρώμεθα, ἢ πρὸς Διὸς καὶ θεῶν, ἵνα μηδὲ τῶν ἐν μέσῳ κειμένων ἔνια παρίωμεν). Tempting as Marcotte's suggestion may be, I have found not a single instance of λόγος αὐστηρός employed to refer to a written book, but found many instances referring to (unwelcome) speeches. Nevertheless, we may perhaps think that Agatharchides' ideas of a historian's task were not very different from this. Cf., besides Thucydides, Polyb. 9.1.2–6 emphasizing the severity of his work, setting pleasure against profit; Joseph. *BJ* 1.30.

[91] Nevertheless, the rejection of ψυχαγωγία in Diod. Sic. 3.11.1 (cf. *FGrH* 86 F 1, on the sources for the history of Egypt and Ethiopia) is strongly influenced by Agatharchides: ὧν οἱ μὲν ψευδεῖ φήμῃ πεπιστευκότες, οἱ δὲ παρ' ἑαυτῶν πολλὰ τῆς ψυχαγωγίας ἕνεκα πεπλακότες κτλ.

and he will have argued that a pathetic style was allowed if it corresponded to its subject—thus keeping the discussion well within the limits of literary criticism. It is certainly his aim to arouse our pity (ἔλεος[92])—and the Aristotelian theory of tragedy is not far, even if tragic history is a "disgraced concept."[93] But what was the aim of his pathetic descriptions? Was it only ἐνάργεια,[94] or were they born out of a deep humanity? Is the experience and memory of πάθη a means to learn, should the reader come to respect the divine through his knowledge of suffering?[95]

Or is the answer to be sought in the realm of literary criticism, as might be argued from a (later) inscription in Priene? Instruction in literature had the duty to use the contemplation of mythological and historical examples to lead the students to τὰ κάλλιστα, portraying human greatness and human sorrow—τ[ὰς ψυχ]ὰς πρὸς ἀρετὴν καὶ πάθος ἀνθρώπινον προάγεσθαι. Perhaps this was the sole aim of Agatharchides—and perhaps it had its origin in his former life as a γραμματικός.[96]

---

[92] To cite the most significant occurrences: οὐκ ἔστιν ὃς ἰδὼν οὐκ ἂν ἐλεήσειε τοὺς ἀκληροῦντας διὰ τὴν ὑπερβολὴν τῆς ταλαιπωρίας (Diod. Sic. 3.13.2); τὸ δὲ περὶ τὰς ἐλεφαντηγοὺς κακὸν πολὺν ἔλεον τοῖς πάσχουσι ἀπὸ τῶν ὁρώντων ἐκκαλεῖται (Phot. 83.456b); cf. τοὺς ὁρῶντας εἰς οἶκτον καὶ συμπάθειαν ἄγει τῶν ἀπολωλότων (Diod. Sic. 3.40.8). His criticism of Hegesias has the emotions of the observer in mind, because Hegesias does not regard πῶς τὸ πάθος ὑπὸ τὴν ὄψιν ἀγάγοι διὰ τῆς ἐναργείας (Phot. 21.446b). Phylarchus, FGrH 81 T 2 (= Polyb. 2.56.6) speculates about ἔλεος, φόβος, and συμπάθεια as emotions of his readers. Mortley 1996:15 is certainly wrong in implying that terms like ἔλεος and φόβος are not to be found in historiography.

[93] Hornblower 1994:44.

[94] Reinhardt 1921:22–25 thought so: "Er appelliert an die Effekte, deren Emotion dem Dichter und Redner ihre Wirkungen sichern ... Was er jedoch in Wirklichkeit beschreibt, ist, was an Land und Leuten ihm geeignet erscheint, jenen Effekt zu machen, den er wünscht." Strasburger's own pupil, Woelk, was of the same opinion.

[95] At least comparable to this idea is Phot. 98.458b: οἱονεὶ φθονούσης τοῖς ἁδροῖς ἐπιτεύγμασι τῆς τύχης καὶ παραπλεκούσης τἀγαθῷ τὸ βλαβερόν, ὅπως μηδεὶς εἰς τέλος ἐξυβρίζων τιτανῶδες καὶ κατεγνωκὸς τοῦ θείου τὸ φρόνημα λαμβάνῃ τῶν ἀγαθῶν εὐτυχούντων, παιδεύηται δὲ τῇ παραθέσει καὶ μνήμῃ τῶν ἐναντίων.

[96] IPriene 112.73–76 (decree in honor of Zosimus, after 84 BC): ἔτι δὲ σφαίρας καὶ ὅπλα καὶ τὸν ἐπιστα[τήσοντ]α τῶν ἐφήβων τοῖς ἐκ φιλολογίας (μαθήμασι) γραμματικόν, δι' [ὧν μὲν] τὸ σῶμα βουλόμενος ἄσκνο[ν] τυγχάνειν, δι' ὧν δὲ τ[ὰς ψυχ]ὰς πρὸς ἀρετὴν καὶ πάθος ἀνθρώπινον προάγεσθαι. Cf. Wörrle 1995:249. Τὰ κάλλιστα are an educational concern in IK 28.1 (Iasos) 98.10 (ἀπό τε τῆς πρώτης ἡλικίας ζηλωτὴς τῶν

To sum up: Agatharchides claimed to be the first to introduce the south into history—or at least into historiography. To do this, he had to give a truthful account, based on a fresh summary or interpretation of old material. At one point he tells us exactly what the prerequisites of history were. He excuses himself for not having written an account of some islands, people, and substances (Phot. 110.460b), only to continue: ὁ δὲ καὶ τοῖς κατὰ μέρος πράγμασιν ἐντετευχώς, καὶ λόγοις κατεσκευασμένοις ἱστορίας ἀξίοις, καὶ προαίρεσιν ἔχων δυναμένην δόξαν πόνῳ θηρεύειν, οὐκ ἀφέξεται. It is one thing to study τὰ κατὰ μέρος πράγματα, but this is not the end of it: if you want to be an historian, you have to toil to reach a stylistically adequate account based on the detailed knowledge of the subject. History still is very much a part of literature, and a historian of any consequence had to condense detailed accounts written without any awareness of the larger subjects into a work of literature—and at least Photius had the highest praise for our author in this regard. Questioned about his place in historiography Agatharchides would have answered that there was a lot of material in the writings of travelers and other people with a special knowledge of foreign lands and customs, that history was different from geography and ethnography pure and simple, and that nobody had cared enough to introduce this material into history.

V. Universal History

Agatharchides, aware of the larger subjects, wanted more than to write κατὰ μέρος or to explore a hitherto unknown section of the world—universal history was one of the main themes of the day, and a history in 49 books, comprising the affairs of Asia and Europe has to be explained in terms of universal history.[97] There were two varieties:[98] one aimed at giving an account of all events (and their relation to each other) in a

καλλίστων γενόμενος ἀνέστραπται ἐν τῶι γυμνασίωι φιλοπονῶν καὶ φιλομαθῶγ καὶ ἐπὶ τὰ κάλλιστα ἐπιδιδοὺς ἑαυτόν); *Claros* 1.1.1 (col. 1.1–4: ἔτι τὴν ἀπὸ τῶν ἐφήβων ἔχων ἡλικίαν προσεδρεύων τῶι γυμνασίωι καὶ τὴν μὲν ψύχην τοῖς καλλίστοις συντρέφων μαθήμασιν).

[97] Alonso-Núñez 1997:60.
[98] Schepens and Bollansée 2004:63–64.

specific period of time (Polybius[99]). Agatharchides was more interested in the other variety: to write the history of mankind from the earliest beginnings. Some historians had tried this, for instance Ephorus, whom Polybius regarded as his only predecessor,[100] even if Ephorus' concept was different.[101] Ephorus started his history with the return of the Heraclids,[102] and he omitted the early days, "because the evidence is unsatisfactory."[103] This skepticism was not shared by Ephorus' immediate successors: Zoilus of Amphipolis, an orator and philosopher, wrote a history in three books, starting with the theogony and ending with Philip II,[104] while his pupil, Anaximenes of Lampsacus, wrote 12 books of history from the theogony to the death of Epaminondas in 362 BC, continuing with another work, *Philippika*.[105] He separated the history of his own times from universal history, but—more important still—he included the barbarians (the Persians?) in his universal history.[106] This

---

[99] Walbank 1972:67. This kind of universal history made sense only after the history of the east and the west had become intertwined, i.e., after Rome's intervention in Greek affairs.

[100] Polyb. 5.33.2 (*FGrH* 70 T 7) τὸν πρῶτον καὶ μόνον ἐπιβεβλημένον τὰ καθόλου γράφειν. Polybius knows, of course, that there had been other authors (Jacoby, *FGrH* 83 calls them "Anonymoi des Polybius") with the same pretension, 5.33.1: καίτοι γ᾽ οὐκ ἀγνοῶ διότι καὶ πλείους ἕτεροι τῶν συγγραφέων τὴν αὐτὴν ἐμοὶ προεῖνται φωνήν, φάσκοντες τὰ καθόλου γράφειν κτλ. These authors also claim (5.33.5) πάσας ... τὰς κατὰ τὴν Ἑλλάδα καὶ βάρβαρον περιειληφέναι πράξεις.

[101] Polybius may have thought Ephorus' description of the development of the Persian or Macedonian empire similar to his Roman history (Momigliano 1984:86), but he may have meant Ephorus' separate treatment of geography, which resembled his own, too. Cf. Strabo 8.1.1 p332 (*FGrH* 70 T 12): οἱ δ᾽ ἐν τῇ κοινῇ τῆς ἱστορίας γραφῇ χωρὶς ἀποδείξαντες τὴν τῶν ἠπείρων τοπογραφίαν, καθάπερ Ἔφορός τε ἐποίησε καὶ Πολύβιος.

[102] Diod. Sic. 4.3, cf. 16.76.5 (*FGrH* 70 T 10).

[103] Brown 1973:112, alluding to *FGrH* 70 F 110.

[104] *FGrH* 71 T 1: ῥήτωρ δὲ ἦν καὶ φιλόσοφος, ἔγραψε μέντοι τινὰ καὶ γραμματικά ... ἱστορίαν ἀπὸ θεογονίας ἕως τῆς Φιλίππου τελευτῆς βίβλια γ᾽.

[105] *FGrH* 72 T 4: τὴν πρώτην τῶν Ἑλληνικῶν ἀνέγραψεν ἀρξάμενος ἀπὸ θεογονίας καὶ ἀπὸ τοῦ πρώτου γένους τῶν ἀνθρώπων ... περιέλαβε δὲ πάσας σχεδὸν τάς τε τῶν Ἑλλήνων καὶ βαρβάρων πράξεις ἐν βύβλοις δώδεκα.

[106] Lehmann 1990:197 conjectures that Anaximander was not alone in separating universal history and contemporary history: "Könnte man nicht vielleicht dieses sehr komplexe Werk [sc. by Theopompus], auch mit seinem Titel, besser verstehen, wenn man hier eine Hinwendung Theopomps zu Herodot, und zwar eine ziemlich enge Hinwendung an das Paradigma des herodoteischen Werkes annimmt, und zwar in dem Sinne,

tendency must have increased in the times of and after Alexander the Great, including the valiant efforts of local historians[107] and chronographers, who—if they had scientific ambitions like Eratosthenes—started only with the fall of Troy.[108]

Agatharchides struggled with his aim to write the history of mankind from the beginning and his belief that there was no secure knowledge about the origin of the gods or the actions of the heroes.[109] The theogony, even the return of the Heraclids was no viable starting-point for his work. Only a poet like Hesiod could tell the story of the earliest beginnings.[110] Was this the end of this variety of universal history? Some Greek and Roman historians and antiquarians thought so, among them the great Varro.[111]

Agatharchides had an ingenious idea: he omitted the mythical past altogether. The place of the theogony and the heroic age is taken by the origins of civilization and the development of mankind from an almost

---

daß eine Kombination eines systematischen Teiles, eines Oikoumene-Überblicks mit einem zeitgeschichtlichen Prozeß vorgenommen worden ist?" Alonso-Núñez 1990:173–199 provides a different approach.

[107] Dieuchidas is the best example for this, *FGrH* 485 T 1: ὃς τὴν ἀρχὴν τοῦ λόγου ἐκ τῆς Ἑλλανίκου Δευκαλιωνείας μετέβαλεν.

[108] Geus 2002:315–316.

[109] He would have agreed with the remark on the (other) Greek attempts to write universal history in Momigliano 1984:77–78: "But the majority of these patterns had their origins in what we can loosely call mythical or philosophical imagination of the Greeks rather than in the empirical collection and critical interpretation of past events called *historia.*"

[110] Phot. 8.444b: οὐδ᾽ Ἡσιόδῳ μέμφομαι δηλοῦν τολμῶντι θεῶν γένεσιν.

[111] Censorinus, *DN* 20–21: *et si origo mundi hominum notitia venisset, inde exordium sumeremus. nunc vero id intervallum temporis tractabo, quod* ἱστορικόν *Varro appellat. hic enim tria discrimina temporum esse tradit: primum ab hominum principio ad cataclysmum priorem, quod propter ignorantiam vocatur* ἄδηλον, *secundum a cataclysmo priore ad olympiadem primam, quod, quia multa in eo fabulosa referuntur,* μυθικόν *nominatur, tertium a prima olympiade ad nos, quod dicitur* ἱστορικόν, *quia res in eo gestae veris historiis continentur.* Christian authors shared this notion (and knew everything about the theogony to be wrong), e.g. Iulius Africanus, *Chron.* F 34 Wallraff: μέχρι μὲν τῶν ὀλυμπιάδων, οὐδὲν ἀκριβὲς ἱστόρηται τοῖς Ἕλλησι, πάντων συγκεχυμένων, καὶ κατὰ μηδὲν αὐτοῖς τῶν πρὸ τοῦ συμφωνούντων ... οὗ δὴ χάριν τὰς ἐνδοξοτάτας, καὶ μυθώδεις ἐπιλεξάμενος ἱστορίας, μέχρι τῆς πρώτης ὀλυμπιάδος ἐπιδραμοῦμαι κτλ. Their way of reconciling tradition with belief was euhemerism: see Iulius Africanus F 24 Wallraff.

animal-like status to the heights of political structures.[112] Agatharchides used the southern tribes as an example for this development, and perhaps he felt entitled to do so, since some people fixed human origins in Ethiopia (Diod. Sic. 3.2.1: ἱστοροῦσι πρώτους ἀνθρώπων ἁπάντων γεγονέναι—a passage by some attributed to Agatharchides). On the other hand, there are some indications that he believed men to have appeared spontaneously in all places on earth.[113]

Agatharchides was not the first to try to give some account of the cultural development of early man. The question had been put in different ways since the pre-Socratics,[114] and the answers differed: there were optimists perceiving a story of human progress from primitive beginnings, there were pessimists perceiving a constant change for the worse as man was estranged from nature, i.e., from his natural way of life; others still, like Dicaearchus, took a position in the middle. Agatharchides knew these authors and their solutions, knew also the solution offered by mythology—the myth of the ages—and counted it among the untrustworthy stories of mythology (Phot. 7.443a). There is some discussion in regard to the question, if Agatharchides was a Peripatetic, a Platonist, an Epicurean and so forth—based mostly on his stand in this question. I do not want to add to this debate now, because another argument is more important to the subject.

"Antike Kulturentstehungslehre ist immer philosophische Spekulation; denn eine empirisch vorgehende anthropologische Wissenschaft, gar ein Fach 'Vor- und Frühgeschichte', gab es nicht."[115] Therefore many representation of early man took the shape of a myth or of a "once upon a time" fairy tale.[116] Such an approach could not find the approval

---

[112] Thus proving Momigliano 1984:85 wrong: "But even if we were much better informed we would hardly find cultural developments as one of the central themes of Greek historical research. More specifically, we would not find universal histories built on schemes of cultural development." Momigliano's view is in keeping with the generally bad name Hellenistic universal histories acquired. On this, see recently Wirth 2005:363.

[113] See Diod. Sic. 3.20.2 on the fish-eaters, quoted below in text after n119; cf., too, Phot. 59.453b: πᾶσι τοῖς περιοίκοις ἄβατος, οὐκ ἀπ' ἀρχῆς σπανίσασα ἀνθρωπίνου γένους.

[114] The early ideas are newly discussed by Utzinger 2003:97–229 *passim*; for later writers see Spoerri 1959; Cole 1967; Blundell 1986.

[115] Bees 2005:16.

[116] Utzinger 2003:126–127: "Die Einleitung … 'es war einmal' … scheint ein Topos in

of Agatharchides, and it is one of his great accomplishments to find a way out of this dilemma. He used the ethnographic material that he found in his (bookish) exploration of the south to get rid of the necessity of a purely speculative reconstruction of the origins of civilization and society: his reconstruction of this historical epoch could be checked with the help of eyewitness accounts. Such a use of contemporary, but archaic ways of life to form a picture about an older state of mankind is not new: Thucydides introduced it, and he did not remain alone.[117] But Agatharchides was the first to use this method for an overview of human development as part of universal history—and this is, of course, the reason why fish-eaters could claim a part in history.

VI. Ethnography and History

Agatharchides describes the tribes of the south—and we have to notice at the beginning, that this description matches exactly the stages of cultural development. Our excerpts start with a description of the fish-eaters, and they end with the civilization of Arabia Felix. This sequence is one of the strongest arguments for the deliberate intention of providing a complete picture of the different stages of human development. It is therefore not surprising that Agatharchides presents us an overall picture according to this development—and some contradictory information is not included. We are therefore less concerned with a representation of the fish-eaters as they lived at every coast of the Red Sea, the Persian Gulf, and the Indian Ocean,[118] but with the way Agatharchides perceived them.

---

solchen Urzeitschilderungen gewesen zu sein." Utzinger provides all the necessary references and reminds us that Protagoras chose to tell a myth, because it was expected to be more charming (Pl. *Prt.* 320c: δοκεῖ τοίνυν μοι, ἔφη, χαριέστερον εἶναι μῦθον ὑμῖν λέγειν). Cf. Utzinger 237n10 on Cic. *Inv. Rhet.* 1.2.

[117] Thuc. 1.5.3, 6.6 etc.; Arist. *Pol.* 1252b20–27; Theophrastus F 584A5.5, 21.4 Fortenbaugh, Huby, Sharples, Gutas (= Porph. *Abst.* 2.5.5, 21.4).

[118] The purely ethnographical approach is given by Longo 1987. Diod. Sic. 3.18.1 distinguishes between the way of life of the fish-eaters within and beyond the straits, but Phot. 40.449a does not. In Diod. Sic. 3.22 the fish-eaters of Babylonia use bow nets to catch the fish brought in by the tide. They are also the first to exhibit any idea of long-term supplies

The fish-eaters occupy the largest place in his history—neither because of the excerptor's special interest or the chance of transmission—but because Agatharchides chose to describe them more fully than all the other tribes: none of them represented life at such an early, primitive stage, as was duly emphasized.[119] One group caused special wonder for him. They lived in a completely inaccessible place, blocked by cliffs on the one side and—lacking the knowledge of proper boats and rafts—by the sea on the other side (Diod. Sic. 3.20.2): τοιαύτης δὲ ἀπορίας περὶ αὐτοὺς οὔσης, ὑπολείπεται λέγειν αὐτόχθονας αὐτοὺς ὑπάρχειν, ἀρχὴν μὲν τοῦ πρώτου γένους μηδεμίαν ἐσχηκότας, ἀεὶ δ᾽ ἐξ αἰῶνος γεγονότας, καθάπερ ἔνιοι τῶν φυσιολόγων περὶ πάντων τῶν φυσιολογουμένων ἀπεφήναντο.[120]

The implication about the other fish-eaters is most interesting: all of them live in the same way—and if the autochthonous group did not learn its way of life from others, then their διάθεσις—and by implication also that of all the other fish-eaters—was close to the very origins of human behavior. Nature created under the same circumstances the same set of behavior and the same way of life.

The life of the fish-eaters differed not much from the life of animals, and Agatharchides confirms the old idea of their life being θηριωδής:[121] the fish-eaters procured their food in the same way as the seals—and live in some kind of close co-operation with them.[122] They eat like

___

of food; on the problems of this chapter, which has no correspondence in Photius, see n55 above.

[119] Phot. 31.448b starts: τοῦτο δὲ τὸ γένος ἔχει μὲν οὔτε πόλεις οὔτε χώρας οὔτ᾽ ἄλλης ἐντέχνου κατασκευῆς ὑπογραφὴν οὐδεμίαν. Diod. Sic. 3.18.7: οὗτος μὲν οὖν ὁ βίος, καίπερ ὢν παράδοξος, ἐκ παλαιῶν χρόνων τετήρηται τοῖς γένεσι τούτοις.

[120] This time, Diodorus seems to have retained more of the original text than Phot. 46.451a: τούτων δὲ ὑφεστώτων, φησί, λοιπὸν εἰπεῖν ὡς αὐθιγενές εἰσι, μνήμην τοῦ πρώτου σπέρματος οὐ λαβόντες, ἀεὶ δὲ ὑπάρχοντες, ὃν τρόπον ἔνιοι τῶν καλουμένων ὡρίσαντο φυσικῶν. On autochthony as an ethnographic topos, see Trüdinger 1918:75n4, 109; on spontaneous generation, Blundell 1986:62–65. Most Stoics believed the first generation of human beings to be parentless: Censorinus, *DN* 4.10 (*SVF* 1.124); Origen, *C. Cels.* 1.37 (*SVF* 2.739). Cornutus, *ND* 39.15–40.4; Sext. Emp. *Math.* 9.28.

[121] O'Brien 1985:264–277. The animal-like behavior of early man is also emphasized by his nakedness, his lack of clothing: Diod. Sic. 3.8.2, 5 (Hutter 2002:51).

[122] Diod. Sic. 3.18.7. This is a form of πεφύρμενος βίος, used to describe an early stage of human history by Anaxagoras, 59B1 DK; Archelaus, 60A4 DK, see Lämmli 1962:63–71.

animals and they live in caves like animals do;[123] their way to the distant sources of water is compared with a train of cattle,[124] and they lead a life without any hint of *ratio* or *societas*.[125]

The fish-eaters possess no language, every expression is inarticulate; gestures are the only means of communication.[126] Even songs—with other people one of the earliest ways of tradition and one of the earliest forms of group-memory[127]—are inarticulate and without any social function. Communication about emotions precedes communication about everyday matters.[128] For mere need, gestures are enough.

Many different theories had been proposed on the origins of language before Agatharchides wrote, and some of them—as Epicurus did, for instance (*Ep. Hdt.* 75–76)—took the evolution of language as a paradigm of cultural evolution in general.[129] Gesture came before

---

Epicurus declared such a compact (σύμβολον τοῦ συμφέροντος) possible between men (*Sent. Vat.* 32; Lucr. 5.1019–1020), not between men and animals.

[123] Phot. 36.450a: τοῖς φωλεύουσι τῶν θηρίων τὴν αὐτὴν διάθεσιν λαμβάνουσι; 43.450b.

[124] Diod. Sic. 3.17.3: ἡ δὲ ὁδοιπορία τούτων παραπλήσιος γίνεται ταῖς ἀγέλαις τῶν βοῶν.

[125] As would have been expected, had Agatharchides followed the ideas of the Stoa. On the Stoa's theory about the origins of culture, see Bees 2005:23–25, where he reminds us that the early Stoa did not value the concept of χρεία as an explanation of any development, that Sen. *Ben.* 4.18.3 declares the superiority of man over beasts on the grounds of their *ratio* and *societas*, and that the Stoics believed in a consortium even at the earliest origins of society.

[126] Diod. Sic. 3.15.5: μετὰ βοῆς; Phot. 37.450a: πρὸς ᾠδαῖς ἀνάρθροις; Diod. Sic. 3.18.6 (discussing their ἀπάθεια): διὸ καί φασιν αὐτοὺς διαλέκτῳ μὲν μὴ χρῆσθαι, μιμητικῇ δὲ δηλώσει διὰ τῶν χειρῶν διασημαίνειν ἕκαστα τῶν πρὸς τὴν χρείαν ἀνηκόντων; Phot. 41.450b: ὅθεν (φησὶν ὁ συγγραφεύς) ἔγωγε νομίζω μηδὲ χαρακτῆρα εὔγνωστον ἔχειν αὐτούς, ἐθισμῷ δὲ καὶ νεύματι, ἤχοις τε καὶ μιμητικῇ δηλώσει διοικεῖν πάντα τὰ πρὸς τὸν βίον.

[127] Norden 1923:116 with references.

[128] Diod. Sic. 3.17.1: εὐωχούμενοι πανδημεὶ μεθ᾽ ἱλαρότητος καὶ ταῖς ἀνάρθροις ᾠδαῖς ἀλλήλους ψυχαγωγοῦντες. A certain problem is presented by Diod. Sic. 3.40.9 (no parallel in Photius): παρὰ δὲ τοῖς πλήσιον κατοικοῦσιν Ἰχθυοφάγοις παραδέδοται λόγος, ἐκ προγόνων ἔχων φυλαττομένην τὴν φήμην, ὅτι κτλ. Gera 2003:189–190 tends toward a rational explanation: the observers could not understand the meaning of the gestures and sounds made by the fish-eaters, but they had language and emotion—because there is no human society without language. This may be true or not, but the observation is only valuable to someone studying the fish-eaters and does not concern the use Agatharchides made of them.

[129] For the details, see Verlinsky 2005:56–100, esp. 88–89 on Agatharchides and Lucretius.

language in some theories,[130] and Epicurus thought that words originated spontaneously through utterances caused by emotion, mostly by misery.[131] This concurs with Agatharchides' own observations: language and emotion were connected, since need was taken care of through gestures, emotion lay at the root of language—and since the fish-eaters were ἀπαθεῖς, they could not create any sounds reproducing emotions. Even Aristotle, who believed that man was endowed with speech to indicate the good and the bad, would have found his ideas supported by the findings of Agatharchides, since the fish-eaters do not distinguish between just and unjust.

No language means, *inter alia*, no society. There are no social structures; there is no private property, even the fish are ἕτοιμον θήρημα καὶ τροφή (Phot. 32.449b), and—of course—women and children belong to everybody (Phot. 31.449a).[132] The fish-eaters form a πλῆθος, but they do not do so voluntarily or forced by the superior power of some individual, but only by chance.[133]

The fish-eaters possess no technology—not even to catch fish: they use only what nature supplies them with (Diod. Sic. 3.15.3, 19.2). There are no tools, there are no provisions, and the fish are not cooked, but eaten raw, which is an important cultural marker.[134] In short, there is no τέχνη of any kind.[135] Their effortless life, ἀσχολία, is the result of their very simple form of food supply—and the simplicity of their food is the main reason why they are healthier than other people—

---

[130] E.g. Diod. Sic. 1.8.3–4; Vitr. *De arch.* 2.1.1; Lactant. *Div. inst.* 6.10.13–14; cf. Pl. *Cra.* 422e–423b.

[131] Lucr. 5.1022–1023.

[132] The comparison with animals is noted by Diodorus, perhaps on his own, but perhaps copying Agatharchides, 3.15.2: παραπλησίως ταῖς τῶν θρεμμάτων ἀγέλαις.

[133] Diod. Sic. 3.15.5, where they are acting καθάπερ ἀφ' ἑνὸς κελεύσματος—but only καθάπερ, and because of the circumstances.

[134] Phot. 31.448b: οὔτ' ἄλλης ἐντέχνου κατασκευῆς ὑπογραφὴν οὐδεμίαν; Diod. Sic. 3.15.7: τεχνικῆς μὲν ὅπλων κατασκευῆς οὐδὲν ἔχοντες; on the preparation of food: Phot. 34.449b.

[135] According to Bees 2005:21, Philo, *De aeternitate mundi* 130 proves that Zeno thought τέχναι to be necessary for any survival, that therefore man must have used τέχναι as an expression of his *ratio* from the beginning on—an argument controverted by Agatharchides' portrayal of the fish-eaters.

and perhaps they lived even longer.[136] The analogy of man and beast, both being supplied by nature with all what is necessary, seems to be in direct contradiction to Epicurean doctrine, which saw men as disadvantaged by nature, a "Mängelwesen" (Lucr. 5.222–234). According to Agatharchides, the difference between man and animal was originally not great enough to warrant the Epicurean view.[137]

All of this seems to convey the picture of a primitivistic golden age—man living in harmony with nature, without any needs, without any desire, greed or rivalry, without any laws, and completely different from the ways of life in modern times (Phot. 49.451b):[138] ὅτι τῆς ζωῆς ἡμῶν ἡμῖν ἐφεστώσης ἔν τε τοῖς περιττοῖς καὶ τοῖς ἀναγκαίοις, τὰ εἰρημένα γένη τῶν ἰχθυοφάγων τὰ μὲν ἄχρηστα περιγεγράφασιν ἅπαντα, φησί, τῶν δὲ καθηκόντων οὐδὲν ἐλλείπουσι, τῇ θείᾳ πρὸς τὸ ζῆν ὁδῷ βραβεύοντες πάντες, οὐ τῷ παρασοφιζομένῃ ταῖς δόξαις τὴν φύσιν. Some examples follow: the fish-eaters know no office, therefore no rivalry; they know no greed, do not want to harm an enemy, they do not sail the sea, and therefore they do not measure distress by the accidents of their life: ἀλλὰ μικρῶν δεόμενοι μικρὰ καὶ πενθοῦσι, τὸ μὲν ἀρκοῦν κτώμενοι, τὸ δὲ πλέον οὐ ζητοῦντες. Now Agatharchides turns to a general maxim: ἐνοχλεῖ δ' ἕκαστον οὐ τὸ ἀγνοούμενον, εἰ μὴ πάρεστιν, ἀλλὰ τὸ βουλητόν, ὅταν ὑστερίζῃ τοῦ καιροῦ τῆς ἐπιθυμίας σπευδούσης. οὐκοῦν ἐκεῖνος, πάντ' ἔχων ἃ θέλει, εὐτυχήσει κατὰ τὸν τῆς φύσεως λογισμόν, οὐ κατὰ τὸν τῆς δόξης. νόμοις δὲ οὐ δικαιοῦνται· τί γὰρ δεῖ προστάγματι δουλεύειν τὸν χωρὶς γράμματος εὐγνωμεῖν δυναμένου;

---

[136] Phot. 39.450a: καὶ νοσήμασι μὲν διὰ τὴν ἁπλότητα τῆς διαιτῆς σπανίοις περιπίπτουσι, τοσούτῳ δ' ἀφαιροῦσιν ἀπὸ τοῦ χρόνου τῶν ἐτῶν, ὅσῳ περ ἀπονωτέραν τῶν λοιπῶν ἔχουσι τὴν ἀναστροφήν; Diod. Sic. 3.17.5: νόσοις δὲ διὰ τὴν ἁπλότητα τῆς τροφῆς σπανίως περιπίπτοντες, ὀλιγοχρονιώτεροι δὲ πολὺ τῶν παρ' ἡμῖν ὄντες (cf. 3.29.4). The idea of θηριώδης δίαιτα as a reason for illness and death was known since the fifth century, e.g. Archelaus, 60A4.5–6 DK (Utzinger 2003:150–151).

[137] Bees 2004:116–117 remarks that a difference between man and beast that is only gradual indicates as a connection with a post-Aristotelian Peripatos.

[138] Diodorus omitted this paragraph altogether, but Mazza 2002:64 compares Diod. Sic. 2.48.

Is this unreserved praise? Is not the depicted way of life rather barbaric, a far cry from paradise lost or the picture of the noble savage?[139] A positive evaluation omits at least some differences between the fish-eaters and other, more civilized men: moderation is not a virtue for them,[140] and they have only a physical perception of pleasure and pain, and therefore are unable to distinguish between good and evil, honorable and disgraceful.[141] Since the fish-eaters know only physical pain, they know no pity or compassion. And though Agatharchides held some kind of ἀλυπία as a good thing,[142] he almost refused to believe the stories about their complete insensitivity to pain—bodily or emotional:[143] even when their children and women are slaughtered, the fish-eaters remain unmoved. If happiness is the elimination of distress resulting from needs, then the fish-eaters can stay happy even in the face of the fate of their fellow-men, because a relation with other human beings is not considered a need in a group without structures and without any need of cooperation or teamwork—and they do not need such a society, because nature presents them with everything

[139] The fish-eaters have much in common with the Homeric Cyclopes, since they lack most skills, do not work the land, cook or build, live in caves and not in houses, are indifferent to the suffering of others, and have almost no social bonds.

[140] Concerning food, Phot. 34.449b: οὐ πρὸς μέτρον καὶ σταθμόν, ἀλλὰ πρὸς τὴν ἑκάστου βούλησιν καὶ χάριν.

[141] Phot. 31.449a: ἔτι δὲ ἡδονῆς μὲν καὶ πόνου φυσικὴν ἔχοντες γνῶσιν, αἰσχρῶν δὲ καὶ καλῶν οὐδὲ τὴν ἐλαχίστην εἰσφερόμενοι ἔννοιαν.

[142] Phot. 63.454b: οὕτω, φησί, ταῖς κηδείαις καταχρῶνται νουνεχῶς, εἴπερ μὴ λυπεῖν ἑαυτοὺς ἐπὶ τοῖς ἀλυπήτοις συνέσεως σημεῖον; 40.450a: φέρουσι δὲ ἀλύπως ἅπερ αὐτοῖς ἀπ' ἀρχῆς ἡ τύχη παραδέδωκεν. Longo 1987:43 noted the criticism in the depiction of the fish-eaters' ἀπάθεια.

[143] Phot. 41.450a–b: ὅτι τοὺς ἐν τοῖς εἰρημένοις τόποις οἰκοῦντάς φησι πρὸς τοῖς εἰρημένοις ἔτι μηδὲ πρὸς τὰ μέγιστα τῶν παρ' ἡμῖν δεινῶν ὁμοίαν ἡμῖν ἔχειν τὴν ἔννοιαν. οὔτε γὰρ σίδηρον κατ' αὐτῶν ἐπαιρόμενον φεύγειν, οὔτε προπηλακισμῷ ἐρεθίζεσθαι, οὔτε τοὺς μὴ πάσχοντας τοῖς πάσχουσι συναγανακτεῖν· ἀλλ' εἴ τι γένοιτο περὶ αὐτοὺς ἐξ ἀλλοφύλων τοιοῦτον, βλέπουσι μὲν οὗτοι ἀτενῶς εἰς τὸ γινόμενον καὶ τὰς κεφαλὰς πυκνὰ διανεύουσι, τῶν δὲ εἰθισμένων ἀνθρώπῳ πρὸς ἄνθρωπον οὐδὲ τὴν ἐλαχίστην διδόασιν ἔννοιαν. ὅθεν (φησὶν ὁ συγγραφεύς) ἔγωγε νομίζω μηδὲ χαρακτῆρα εὔγνωστον ἔχειν αὐτούς, ἐθισμῷ δὲ καὶ νεύματι, ἤχοις τε καὶ μιμητικῇ δηλώσει διοικεῖν πάντα τὰ πρὸς τὸν βίον. This might entail the belief that fish-eaters had no soul, because it is near to the opinion of Dicaearchus F 15 Mirhady (8d Wehrli; Cic. *Tusc.* 1.41): *Dicaearchum vero cum Aristoxeno ... omittamus, quorum alter ne condoluisse quidem umquam videtur, qui animum se habere non sentiat, alter etc.* Cf. ad loc. Sharples 2001:148n22.

they need[144]—and since they do not care about their dead, they return to the eternal cycle of life (Phot. 45.450b–451a; Diod. Sic. 3.19.6).

An historian intent on the depiction of πάθος to raise the consciousness of his public to human suffering, valuing sympathy and compassion, cannot have considered this way of life favorably. Life according to nature demanded too high a price. Agatharchides was no primitivist. In his mind, mankind did not deteriorate, however slowly, from a state of natural grace. And of course, as a Greek, he believed, almost as a matter of course, in the intellectual superiority of the Greeks over the southern barbarians (even if they reached a state of higher civilization).[145]

Turtle-eaters, root-eaters, fiber-eaters, and seed-eaters follow, even if they are still very close to the fish-eaters. They have the first tools (Phot. 47.451a–b), even if only μέρμιθες, and whatever the turtles themselves furnished to build huts and boats. The root-eaters use stones to prepare their food (Phot. 50.451b), and live in peaceful co-existence with each other (Diod. Sic. 3.22.2). Only the next group, the fiber- and seed-eaters, use their crude instruments, i.e., sticks, for strife and warfare (Phot. 51.452a). All of these tribes lived without any social organization, without any food shortage, possessing children and females in common.

Even more advanced were the hunters, who are described in different groups according to their prey. They use different weapons, conduct their hunt in bands, and exercise their youths in the use of the bow (Diod. Sic. 3.25.5); they are also the first to use fire (52.452a–b), and they know warfare, because they are attacked by their neighbors (Phot. 57.453a; Diod. Sic. 3.28.6). The κυναμόλγοι may be described as hunters, too, even if their dogs are their tools. This is an example for the use of animals by man (Phot. 60.453b–454a), in direct opposition to the πεφύρμενος βίος some fish-eaters led with the seals. The hunters

---

[144] Diod. Sic. 3.16.4: ἀνεκλείπτως γὰρ καὶ διὰ παντὸς ἑτοίμοις χρῶνται ταμιεύμασιν, ὡς ἂν τοῦ Ποσειδῶνος τὸ τῆς Δήμητρος ἔργον μετειληφότος.

[145] Diod. Sic. 3.6.3: κατὰ μὲν τοὺς ἐπάνω χρόνους ὑπήκουον οἱ βασιλεῖς τοῖς ἱερεῦσιν, οὐχ ὅπλοις οὐδὲ βίᾳ κρατηθέντες, ἀλλ᾿ ὑπ᾿ αὐτῆς τῆς δεισιδαιμονίας τοὺς λογισμοὺς κατισχυόμενοι. κατὰ δὲ τὸ δεύτερον Πτολεμαῖον ὁ βασιλεὺς τῶν Αἰθιόπων Ἐργαμένης, μετεσχηκὼς Ἑλληνικῆς ἀγωγῆς καὶ φιλοσοφήσας, πρῶτος ἐθάρρησε καταφρονῆσαι τοῦ πράγματος.

seem to have some kind of organization, but it is not formalized in any way.[146]

The nomads are already divided into tribes. They have chieftains (tyrants, dynasts), therefore a basic social hierarchy, and the wife of the chieftain belongs to him only: women and children cease to be common and parentage is known. Songs are learned from the parents, implying traditions and the creation of identities in the group (Phot. 63.454a). They have started to cook, even if it is only milk they cook, and this is by all accounts an important cultural marker (61.453b–454a). Conflicts and quarrels in the group are mentioned, but also its special respect for the old women, prescribed by tradition (νόμιμον γάρ ἐστιν, Diod. Sic. 3.33.4). They are the first for whom burial rituals are described (Phot. 63.454a–b). Finally, the nomads use their weapons not only against animals, but also against people: they fight battles over pasturages—which seemed more acceptable to Agatharchides than the reasons for which the Greeks go to war.[147]

The Psylli took the next step and left family communism behind: they differentiated between legitimate and illegitimate children (Plin. *HN* 7.14 and Ael. *NA* 16.27 = *FGrH* 86 F 21a, b). The Libyans, then, are divided in peasants and nomads (Diod. Sic. 3.49.2), both groups having kings, and they are said to lead a life not completely wild, but not completely according to the standards of human civilization either. Finally, there is a third group, without king or justice, living as robbers—but knowing nevertheless leaders, oaths, solid encampments, knowing therefore a social organization, too.

The process of civilization comes to an end with Ethiopians[148] and the Arabs, especially the Sabaeans. They are rich through gold and

---

[146] Diod. Sic. 3.31.4 (no exact parallel in Photius) closes this section with the following remark: τὰ μὲν οὖν τελευταῖα γένη τῶν πρὸς μεσημβρίαν οἰκούντων ἐν μορφαῖς ἀνθρώπων τὸν βίον ἔχει θηριώδη. All during the account the different people are called barbarians—but can we be sure that this was still derogatory?

[147] This is a general remark, but it can be construed also as a criticism of his own time (and its rulers).

[148] Diod. Sic. 3.5–7: the Ethiopians possess not only kings, but also an elaborate religion, army, bureaucracy—here the differences in τὰ νόμιμα are highlighted. In 3.8–10 Agatharchides describes Ethiopian tribes which are still uncivilized, ταῖς μὲν ψυχαῖς παντελῶς ὑπάρχουσιν ἄγριοι καὶ τὸ θηριῶδες ἐμφαίνοντες.

incense, but also through agriculture. For the first time, exchange with other people is mentioned (Phot. 96.458a). They are experienced in war, build houses, are governed by a hereditary king—and they are the first group to exhibit a trace of religion.[149] With the Sabaeans we have reached a stage of civilization that can be compared to the *poleis* of Greece, and the social and political development of mankind can be studied from now on without recourse to ethnography. Other people on the Arabian Peninsula worship the gods in the same form as did the Greeks—at least their worship could be represented in this form.[150] In Ethiopia, the importance of the priests and the gods is stressed (Diod. Sic. 3.5.1, 6.1),[151] the rule of the king is governed by τὸ δεδογμένον νόμιμον and τὸ ἔθος—implying the existence of strong ancestral traditions.[152]

Unfortunately, we have no real idea how the changes between the different stages of society came about—in Agatharchides' thought. The fragments offer us only some hints on why a certain group lived in a certain form: in the case of the fish-eaters there is "habit" fashioned "over the long space of time" or "a need imposed by necessity because of stress of circumstances,"[153] and he believes that "need teaches every-

---

[149] There is an old oracle (Phot. 100.459a), and it might be deemed typical that the first mention of religion is a mention of its political form and political implications; cf. Utzinger 2003:129 on this concept in early accounts of the origins of civilization.

[150] They used letters, too (Diod. Sic. 3.42.4), which could be found on an altar served by an old couple, διὰ βίου τὴν ἱερωσύνην ἔχοντες. He continues with a πανήγυρις πενταετηρική, in the course of which hecatombs were sacrificed to the gods (3.43.1–2).

[151] Including the political aspects of religion: see Diod. Sic. 3.5.1 on the election of kings (οἱ μὲν γὰρ ἱερεῖς ἐξ αὐτῶν τοὺς ἀρίστους προκρίνουσιν κτλ.).

[152] Agatharchides is interested in the strangeness of these traditions and customs, implying many differences to current Greek practices, but in regard of emotions and συμπάθεια, he presents us also with a strong contrast to the life of the fish-eaters. Diod. Sic. 3.7.2: ἄτοπον γὰρ εἶναι τὸ συμπενθεῖν μὲν καὶ συλλυπεῖσθαι καὶ τῶν ἄλλων ἀγαθῶν ἁπάντων τε καὶ κακῶν κοινωνεῖν τὴν βέβαιον φιλίαν, τῆς δ' εἰς τὸ σῶμα λυπῆς ἄμοιρον γίνεσθαι.

[153] Diod. Sic. 3.18.7: οὗτος μὲν οὖν ὁ βίος, καίπερ ὢν παράδοξος, ἐκ παλαιῶν χρόνων τετήρηται τοῖς γένεσι τούτοις, εἴτε ἐθισμῷ διὰ τὸν χρόνον εἴτε ἀναγκαίᾳ χρείᾳ διὰ τὸ κατεπεῖγον ἡρμοσμένος. Dihle 1984:26n1 asserts that χρεία always meant *usus*, but never meant *egestas*: "Soll gesagt werden, daß Not und Mangel es waren, die den Weg der Praxis und Übung wiesen, erscheinen Ausdrücke wie ἀναγκαίᾳ χρείᾳ"; he refers to Hollerbach 1964. I am not sure if this distinction is generally true. Cf. for instance Phot. 96.458a: οἷς ἀποβλέπει πᾶς ὁ βίος οὐ πρὸς τὴν φύσιν, ἀλλὰ πρὸς τὴν χρείαν. Diodorus uses χρεία quite

thing to nature, which suitably accommodates existing resources to the desired use."[154] Need and stress of circumstances are fashioned by the climate and the natural environment: a way of living is determined by the place one lives in, and this place and its circumstances are a product of fortune[155] or nature.[156] People get used to their way of living and, given the chance, sometimes even refuse to change it.[157] What does this tell us about the possibilities of evolution? It seems that a group staying in its given environment could learn certain basic skills (if necessary),[158] but could not develop much further, had to stay always in the same cycle of life and death,[159] if there were no exogenous incentives to change.[160]

---

often in the sense of "necessity," at least in his paraphrase of Agatharchides, e.g. 3.15.7, 18.5, 19.2: τῆς κατὰ φύσιν χρείας αὐτοδίδακτον τέχνην ὑφηγουμένης.

[154] Diod. Sic. 3.15.7: πάντα γὰρ ἡ χρεία διδάσκει τὴν φύσιν, οἰκείως τοῖς ὑποκειμένοις καιροῖς ἁρμοζομένην πρὸς τὴν ἐκ τῆς ἐλπίδος εὐχρηστίαν. Photius ignores this part, and Bommelaer 1989:19n3 believes therefore that it is a thought of Diodorus himself; but Photius omitted most of Diod. Sic. 3.15. Different opinions about χρεία in this passage are summed up by Utzinger 2003:157n333.

[155] Phot. 40.450a: φέρουσι δὲ ἀλύπως ἅπερ αὐτοῖς ἀπ᾽ ἀρχῆς ἡ τύχη παραδέδωκεν. 98.458b: οἱονεὶ φθονούσης τοῖς ἁδροῖς ἐπιτεύγμασι τῆς τύχης καὶ παραπλεκούσης τἀγαθῷ τὸ βλαβερόν, ὅπως μηδεὶς εἰς τέλος ἐξυβρίζων τιτανῶδες καὶ κατεγνωκὸς τοῦ θείου τὸ φρόνημα λαμβάνῃ τῶν ἀγαθῶν εὐτυχούντων. For the mixture of good and bad in the natural surroundings of a tribe, cf. 89.457b.

[156] Diod. Sic. 3.21.5: ὥστε δοκεῖν τούτοις τὴν φύσιν δεδωρῆσθαι μίᾳ χάριτι πολλὰς χρείας· τὴν γὰρ αὐτὴν αὐτοῖς εἶναι τροφήν, ἀγγεῖον, οἰκίαν, ναῦν.

[157] Ptolemy is unable to convince a tribe to change its way of life (Phot. 56.453a): πολλὰ καὶ θαυμαστὰ αὐτοῖς ὑπισχνούμενος, οὐ μόνον οὐκ ἔπεισεν, ἀλλ᾽ οὐδ᾽ ἂν τὴν ὅλην ἀλλάξασθαι βασιλείαν πρὸς τὸν ἐνεστῶτα βίον εἰπόντων ἀπόκρισιν ἤκουσεν. Gozzoli 1978:68 calls this "il primo tentativo di opporsi alla civilizzazione." Phot. 66.455a: ἀλλ᾽ ὅμως τοσαύτης οὔσης τῆς τοπικῆς διαστάσεως, ἀνυπέρβλητον ἔχουσι πρὸς ἀλλήλους οἱ ἄνθρωποι τῶν τε βίων καὶ τῶν ἐθῶν καὶ τοῦ ἀέρος τὴν διαφοράν, ὥστε μηδὲ πιστεύεσθαι παρ᾽ ἑτέροις τὰ παρ᾽ ἄλλοις συνήθη τε καὶ ὁμολογούμενα, μηδὲ στέγειν ὅλως δύνασθαι ὧν χωρὶς ἕτεροι οὐδὲ ζῆν ἂν ἕλοιντο. οὕτως ἔχει τι φίλτρον μέγα πᾶσα συνήθεια, καὶ νικᾷ τὴν ἀπὸ τοῦ περιέχοντος δυσχέρειαν ὁ χρόνος ὁ τὴν πρώτην δεξάμενος εἰς τὸν βίον ἡλικίαν.

[158] Diod. Sic. 3.15.7 (see n154 above), 19.2: τῆς κατὰ φύσιν χρείας αὐτοδίδακτον τέχνην ὑφηγουμένης. The meaning of φύσις in this passage is disputed: see Utzinger 2003:157n333.

[159] Phot. 39.450a: καὶ τούτῳ κύκλῳ διὰ βίου γίνεται, πρὸς ἀσχολίαν καὶ μέριμναν οὐδενὸς ἀποβλεπόντων αὐτῶν πράγματος. Diod. Sic. 3.19.6: διὸ καὶ τὴν ἰδίαν ταφὴν τροφὴν τῶν ἰχθύων ποιούμενοι κυκλούμενον ἰδιοτρόπως τὸν βίον ἔχουσι παρ᾽ ὅλον τὸν αἰῶνα.

[160] Agatharchides seems to acknowledge such incentives, because in Diod. Sic. 3.43.5 he relates the change in the Nabataean way of life after the Ptolemaic trade offered them the possibility of successful piracy.

Moving to a new physical surrounding could result in a change of society, because the new environment forces man to develop technical skills and more advanced social forms. If Agatharchides thought along those lines, it explains both why he does not tell us anything about divine or human intervention in the development of culture, and also why there are still groups of people in an early stage of society. And he may have had another reason for silence on this point, namely that the change in itself was not observable for him: he could only be a witness to different societies in different stages of development. Therefore change was only a matter of conjecture, whereas the state of society was a matter of description.

VII. Dicaearchus

We have seen that the ideas of different stages of human life and of a certain progress—or perhaps regress—in human history are not new: Protagoras, Plato, Aristotle and others come to mind. To what extent was Agatharchides' way of composing his history and solving his problems original to him, and how far did he depend on others? To assess his originality in the discussion of early human history, we will take a short look at Dicaearchus of Messana, who was nearer in times to Agatharchides than Aristotle and his predecessors.[161]

The resemblances are clear, even though we possess only fragments of Dicaearchus' βίος Ἑλλάδος. Dicaearchus was one of the people who believed that mankind had existed forever,[162] and who believed in a development of mankind in three or four different stages, as Varro and Porphyry tell us in their summaries (F 54–56 Mirhady [48–51 Wehrli]). In the beginning was a golden age, *cum viverent homines ex iis rebus, quae inviolata ultro ferret terra*, and then the pastoral and agricultural life followed, and perhaps Dicaearchus counted the present as his own stage in the development of the human race.[163] He has at least some

---

[161] Interest in Dicaearchus has grown somewhat during the last years. Cf. Wehrli 1968; id. 1983:535–539, and above all Fortenbaugh and Schütrumpf 2001.

[162] F 53 Mirhady (47 Wehrli; Censorinus, *DN* 4.2).

[163] F 54 Mirhady (48 Wehrli; Varro, *Rust.* 2.1.5): *ibi processerunt longe, dum ad nos perveniret.*

notion of chronological progress, because the later epochs are given with precise dates.[164]

Because of the bias of our sources we know more about Dicaearchus' conceptions of the first stage of human history than we know of his other stages. His earliest stage of human life is very similar to the life of the fish-eaters: early man has no τέχνη, lives as a vegetarian while the plants grow of their own accord. Therefore man is at leisure, lives free from labors and care, and is quite healthy as a result of his diet.[165] War came into being only with the νομαδικὸς βίος, and then people started to search for things that appeared useful—and got always nearer to the third stage, the agricultural life. We do not really know how Dicaearchus pictured the further development, if he had any ideas on it, how important the influence of the συνετοί and νομοθετικοί had been in his mind.[166] We just notice that he mentioned the Chaldaei and other eastern people, and that there is an astonishing similarity to the beginning of Diodorus' *Bibliotheke*.[167]

There is some discussion whether Dicaearchus used a primitivist approach or whether he was—like Aristotle—a believer in teleological progress. Both answers and a middle way have found their defenders.[168] Again, something else should be more interesting to us: are there differences between Dicaearchus' and Agatharchides' pictures of human development?

To start with two minor points (though not to Porphyry): the earliest stage of society Agatharchides depicts is not vegetarian—the

---

[164] F 59–61 (58a, 55–56 Wehrli); Ax 2001:283n14.

[165] F 56A Mirhady (49 Wehrli; Porphyry, *De abst.* 4.2.3–6). I give some excerpts: αὐτόματα μὲν γὰρ πάντα ἀφύετο, εἰκότως· οὐ γὰρ αὐτοί γε κατεσκεύαζον οὐθὲν διὰ τὸ μήτε τὴν γεωργικὴν ἔχειν πω τέχνην μηθ' ἑτέραν μηδεμίαν ἁπλῶς. τὸ δ' αὐτὸ καὶ τοῦ σχολὴν ἄγειν αἴτιον ἐγίγνετο αὐτοῖς καὶ τοῦ διάγειν ἀνεὺ πόνων καὶ μερίμνης, εἰ δὲ τῇ τῶν γλαφυρωτάτων ἰατρῶν ἐπακολουθῆσαι δεῖ διανοίᾳ, καὶ τοῦ μὴ νοσεῖν. οὐθὲν γὰρ εἰς ὑγίειαν αὐτῶν μεῖζον παράγγελμα εὕροι τις ἂν ἢ τὸ μὴ ποιεῖν περιττώματα ... ἀλλὰ μὴν οὐδὲ πόλεμοι αὐτοῖς ἦσαν οὐδὲ στάσεις πρὸς ἀλλήλους· ἆθλον γὰρ οὐθὲν ἀξιόλογον ἐν τῷ μέσῳ προκείμενον ὑπῆρχεν.

[166] Cf. White 2001:195–236 on Dicaearchus' *principes sapientium* and their connection to Ninos and Sesostris in the βίος.

[167] Ax 2001:295–296.

[168] See the articles by Saunders 2001 (esp. 241–249), Schütrumpf 2001 (esp. 262–267), and Ax 2001 (esp. 283–296).

fish-eaters devour all kinds of animals.[169] Agatharchides' next stage included hunting as a prelude to pastoralism: Dicaearchus does not mention hunts. More important is the way Dicaearchus depicts his earliest society: he firmly believes that even the earliest men had formed a society.[170] Contrary to that, Agatharchides knows of almost no social relations among early men, but believes in a development over time. Dicaearchus' humans know emotion, which Agatharchides discards for his first stage, because neither love nor need formed any attachment between early men: both were absent.

Lastly, Dicaearchus did not write a history—neither according to usual standards, nor according to the methods deemed necessary by Agatharchides. Even if Dicaearchus wrote about a stretch of time reaching from the first humans to the fourth century,[171] there is no reason to believe that he addressed what was commonly regarded as history in antiquity.[172] The fragments, especially F 62.65–77 Mirhady, concern almost exclusively topics belonging to "Kulturgeschichte."[173] So even if Agatharchides started with the same kind of material, he moved on and did not stay with it, as Dicaearchus did.

Being no historian, Dicaearchus was under no obligation to adhere to strict methodological criteria. How did he know about the early stages of mankind? A first answer is given by him: καὶ ταῦτα, φησίν, οὐχ ἡμεῖς, ἀλλ' οἱ τὰ παλαιὰ ἱστορίᾳ διεξελθόντες εἰρήκασιν (F 56A Mirhady [49 Wehrli]; Porph. *Abst.* 4.2.7). He does not specify what kind of writers he has in mind, but it is quite clear that he started with Hesiod, even

---

[169] Vegetarianism was one of the signs of the golden age, e.g. Gatz 1967:165–171; Schütrumpf 2001:270 justly emphasizes that this idea goes back to Plato, and that vegetarianism in Dicaearchus is not to be explained as a deformation made by Porphyry (271: Aristotle did not care to ponder this early stage), since it is also attested by F 56 B Mirhady (50 Wehrli; Jer., *Adv. Iovinian.* 2.13 [= *PL* 23.315–316]: *nullum comedisse carnes, sed universos vixisse frugibus et pomis*).

[170] Porph. *Abst.* 4.2.6 mentions φιλία (F 56 A Mirhady [49 Wehrli]).

[171] Ax 2001:295–296 raises the question of universal history in this regard, and Schütrumpf 2001:256–257 points out that the βίος Ἑλλάδος contained material concerning the fourth century (F 77 [64 Wehrli]).

[172] Strasburger 1982:965–1016.

[173] Of course, Cicero calls him ἱστορικώτατος (*Att.* 6.2.2; F 79 Mirhady; 20 Wehrli), but Mirhady's translation "most given to enquiry" seems to get the point. A good comparison for the topics treated by Dicaearchus is now Reinhard 2004.

if he had some kind of reservations about him.[174] These reservations are not too strong, as his only moderate criticism of Homer indicates (F 63 Mirhady [61 Wehrli]). Dicaearchus still believes in a kernel of truth in the old poets—as did most of his contemporaries.[175] Therefore Dicaearchus began with the exegesis of a myth, using more or less the same reasoning as Hecataeus of Miletus did in grappling with the mythical tradition. And other fragments of Dicaearchus show clearly that he was prepared to take Greek mythology at its face value: Heracles and Cadmus are described as acting, Teiresias, Apollo and the other gods appear—whereas gods are not present in Agatharchides, neither as agents of history nor as givers of gifts. The most important difference between Agatharchides and Dicaearchus was therefore the use of evidence—distinguishing the historian from the philosopher.

Even if Agatharchides had no great problems accepting the principal truth of the earlier ideas on the development of the human race, he still differed in his methodological approach to the problem. Whereas his predecessors, Dicaearchus included, had used the old myths and poets to construct an optimistic or pessimistic idea of human development, he had looked for palpable truth, had looked for the missing proof.

The same happened also in another sphere: we learned, by the way, that Agatharchides confirmed or rejected current philosophical thinking on the origins of civilization and, for instance, on the origin and evolution of language. These passages were always used to confirm

---

[174] F 56 A: ὃ δὴ καὶ τοὺς ποιητὰς παριστάντας χρυσοῦν μὲν ἐπονομάζειν γένος [Hes. *Op.* 116–120 is cited]. ἃ δὴ καὶ ἐξηγούμενος ὁ Δικαίαρχος τὸν ἐπὶ Κρόνου βίον τοιοῦτον εἶναι φησιν, εἰ δεῖ λαμβάνειν μὲν αὐτὸν ὡς γεγονότα καὶ μὴ μάτην ἐπιπεφημισμένον, τὸ δὲ λίαν μυθικὸν ἀφέντας, εἰς τὸ διὰ τοῦ λόγου φυσικὸν ἀνάγειν.

[175] Cf. e.g. Wehrli 1983:537; Saunders 2001:247: "Pretty obviously, in the text which Porphyry has in front of him, Dicaearchus is engaging in the old game, a constant habit of the Master, of assuming that myth and poetry, as well as common reputable opinions, ἔνδοξα, and the work of early philosophers, contain some kernel of truth, which one often proceeds to winkle out." Schütrumpf 2001:261: "Dikaiarch las Hesiod als ein aufgeklärter, moderner Mann, der den Mythos, wenn überhaupt, dann nur in einer naturwissenschaftlich erklärten Form akzeptierte und seine Übertreibung auf sinnvolle Verhältnisse zurechtstutzte"; 275: "Aber er las Hesiod als ein wissenschaftlich gebildeter Mann, der im Mythos den vorwissenschaftlichen Ausdruck durchaus richtiger Einsichten sah und die mythologische Übertreibung auf die natürlichen Gründe zurückführte."

that he was (or was not) a Peripatetic, a Stoic, an Epicurean.[176] But it was not his agenda to side with one of the current philosophical schools: the theories of the philosophers were not based on the observation of different societies, but on their observations of Greek society, on the easily assessable differences of vocalization in men and beast, on extrapolations from their findings in these matters. Based on this kind of material, the philosophical schools of his time had developed different theories in accordance with their general suppositions. This was not Agatharchides' idea of a proof—and in discussing actual specimens of early societies, he found that none of the different theories on the origin of civilization was completely true. As a consequence, he similarly adopts and contradicts Peripatetic, Stoic, and Epicurean ideas, even if he found Epicurus more often right than the others.[177]

VIII. End

Agatharchides' world knew its east and west, north and south, and accepted all of it as part of the *oecumene*—realizing the new intellectual possibilities opened by the widening geographical range. He looked from the West to the East, and in doing so, he recognized the basic unity of human history. What he observed in his study of Arabia and the Red Sea could be used to confirm or refute the ideas of current theories on the origin and the further history of civilization.

Thucydides and others had used the different stages of civilization observable in their times to form an idea of past behavior and past stages of development. The fact that different stages were observable at the same time is explained with recourse to the different environments, and this fact provided the chance to look at the origins of mankind without

---

[176] He is called an eclectic by, e.g., Leopoldi 1892:54–60, who nevertheless insists that most of his philosophical ideas are Peripatetic, and by Fraser 1972:547, remarking that Agatharchides' formal allegiance must have been to the Peripatos.

[177] Cf. Verlinsky 2005:88n85: "I suppose that Agatharchides is parodying Epicurean ideas, presumably pointing to occurrences which contradict the generalities of cultural development assumed by Epicurus." I disagree only with the word "parodying." In Diod. Sic. 3.20.2, Agatharchides even cites the pre-Socratics: καθάπερ ἔνιοι τῶν φυσιολόγων περὶ πάντων τῶν φυσιολογουμένων ἀπεφήναντο (Theophr. *Hist. pl.* 3.1.4 calls Anaxagoras and other pre-Socratics φυσιόλογοι when writing against the idea of spontaneous generation).

invoking the stories of Greek, Egyptian or Chaldaean mythology—as Hesiod, Plato and many others were forced to do. Ethnology became thus a part of history, providing direct access to times otherwise lost and a certain knowledge of developments that could not be obtained through the historian's usual sources. To reach this aim, Agatharchides had to turn to the life of the common people—not the least because an upper class was itself a phenomenon only developing in the course of the process of civilization described by Agatharchides.

Agatharchides succeeded in furnishing historical proof and secure knowledge in a field that until now had defied any proof and knowledge—as he amply demonstrated in his criticism of poetry (and of certain contemporary attempts at universal history). He used the observations and the knowledge of eye-witnesses[178]—and if historians nowadays believe that some groups described are rather animals (chimpanzees, for instance) than men, this goes only to show that Agatharchides and his eye-witnesses were predisposed to see what they knew (or believed to know) according to the tales of Herodotus and to the theories of the origin of civilization.

Agatharchides' brand of universal history may have led to a sometimes awkward literary composition of his 49 books, perhaps prone to digressions that cannot be easily recognized nowadays and a bit awkward, because for some reason he could not start with the fish-eaters since he followed another overriding principle of composition. But it advanced knowledge in its field, and some later historians followed his ideas—starting with Posidonius, then down to even the late nineteenth and early twentieth century, when ethnography was supposed to give us some ideas about a life according to nature.[179]

---

[178] In our eyes, Agatharchides' approach may have been flawed because he relied solely on written evidence, but I believe that it was a singular improvement for his age and that we have to look at his conceptual progress.

[179] One important step backwards was taken by Diodorus, who insisted on the inclusion of myth in universal history (1.3.2), and whose approach to the matter did not depend on Democritus or Hecataeus of Abdera, but presented the common knowledge and assumptions of his times (Spoerri 1959), thereby indicating how far the inclusion of human prehistory in universal history had progressed, and how extraordinary Agatharchides' improvement had been for his time.

It seems to me that this was creative historical writing, and that Alexandria—contrary to what Peter Fraser thought—developed this creative writing.

FRIEDRICH-SCHILLER-UNIVERSITÄT, JENA

Bibliography

Alonso-Núñez, J. M. 1997. "Approaches to World History in the Hellenistic Period: Dicearchus and Agatharchides." *Athenaeum* 85:57–67.

Altheim, F., and R. Stiehl. 1964. *Die Araber in der alten Welt* I. Berlin.

Ameling, W. 1996. "Pausanias und die hellenistische Geschichte." In *Pausanias historien: huit exposés suivis de discussions: Vandoeuvres-Genève, 15–19 août 1994*, ed. J. Bingen, 117–166. Geneva.

Ax, W. 1991. "Sprache als Gegenstand der alexandrinischen und pergamenischen Philologie." In *Geschichte der antiken Sprachtheorie*, ed. P. Schmitter, 275–301. Tübingen.

———. 2001. "Dikaiarchs *Bios Hellados* und Varros *De vita populi Romani*." In Fortenbaugh and Schütrumpf 2001, 279–310.

Battazzato, L. 2003. "Agatarchide di Cnido e i commenti ai poeti: testimonianze sulla formazione degli scoli ad Euripide e su Elena in Stesicoro." *Lexis* 21:279–302.

Bees, R. 2004. *Die Oikeiosis-Lehre der Stoa I: Rekonstruktion ihres Inhalts.* Würzburg.

———. 2005. "Die Kulturentstehungslehre des Poseidonios: Wege zu ihrer Rekonstruktion." *A&A* 51:13–29.

Berger, H. 1880. *Die geographischen Fragmente des Eratosthenes.* Leipzig.

Bloch, H. 1940. "Herakleides Lembos and his *Epitome* of Aristotle's *Politeiai*." *TAPA* 71:27–39.

Blundell, S. 1986. *The Origins of Civilization in Greek & Roman Thought.* London.

Bommelaer, B. 1989. *Diodore de Sicile, vol. III.* Coll. Budé 246. Paris.

Bowersock, G. W. 2000. *Selected Papers on Late Antiquity.* Bari.

———. 2004. "Centrifugal Force in Late Antique Historiography." In *The Past before Us: The Challenge of Historiographies of Late Antiquity*, ed. C. Straw and R. Lim, 19–23. Turnhout.

———. 2005. "The East-West Orientation of Mediterranean Studies and the Meaning of North and South in Antiquity." In *Rethinking the Mediterranean*, ed. W. V. Harris, 167–178. Oxford.

Brown, T. S. 1973. *The Greek Historians*. Lexington, MA.

Burstein, S. M. 1989. *Agatharchides of Cnidus: On the Erythraean Sea*. London.

Capelle, W. 1953. "Zwei Quellen des Heliodor." *RhM* 96:166–180.

Clarke, K. 1999. *Between Geography and History: Hellenistic Constructions of the Roman World*. Oxford.

Cole, T. 1967. *Democritus and the Sources of Greek Anthropology*. Cleveland.

Desanges, J. 1998. "De bon usage d'Agatharchide ou de la nécessité de la Quellenforschung." In Geographica Historica, ed. P. Arnaud and P. Counillon, 69–82. Bordeaux.

Dihle, A. 1984. *Antike und Orient: Gesammelte Aufsätze*. Heidelberg.

———. 1994. *Die Griechen und das Fremde*. Munich.

Engels, J. 2004. "Agatharchides' von Knidos Schrift *Über das Rote Meer*." In Ad Fontes: *Festschrift für Gerhard Dobesch*, ed. H. Heftner and K. Tomaschitz, 179–192. Vienna.

Ferrary, J. L. 1988. *Philhellénisme et impérialisme: Aspects idéologiques de la conquête romaine du monde hellénistique, de la seconde guerre de Macédoine à la guerre contre Mithridate*. Paris.

Fortenbaugh, W. W., and E. Schütrumpf, eds. 2001. *Dicaearchus of Messana: Text, Translation, and Discussion*. New Brunswick, NJ.

Fraser, P. M. *Ptolemaic Alexandria*. 3 vols. Oxford.

Frieten, H. F. 1847. De Agatharchide Cnidio. Bonn.

Gatz, B. 1967. *Weltalter, goldene Zeit und sinnverwandte Vorstellungen*. Hildesheim.

Gera, D. L. 2003. *Ancient Greek Ideas on Speech, Language, and Civilization*. Oxford.

Geus, K. 2002. *Eratosthenes von Kyrene: Studien zur hellenistischen Kultur- und Wissenschaftsgeschichte*. Munich.

Gozzoli, S. 1978. "Etnografia e politica in Agatarchide." *Athenaeum* 56:55–79.

Hägg, T. 1975. *Photios als Vermittler antiker Literatur*. Uppsala.

Hollerbach, H. R. 1964. *Zur Bedeutung des Wortes* chreia. Cologne.

Hornblower, J. 1981. *Hieronymus of Cardia*. Oxford.

Hornblower, S. 1994. "Introduction." In *Greek Historiography*, ed. S. Hornblower, 1–72. Oxford.

Immisch, O. 1919. Agatharchidea. Heidelberg.

Jacob, C. 1991. *Géographie et ethnographie en Grèce ancienne*. Paris.

Jacoby, F. 1926. *Die Fragmente der griechischen Historiker, Zweiter Teil*. Berlin.

Keyser, P. T. 2001. "The Geographical Work of Dikaiarchos." In Fortenbaugh and Schütrumpf 2001, 353–372.

Knaack, G. 1907. "Eratosthenes." *RE* 6.1:358–389.

Kunz, M. 1935. *Zur Beurteilung der Prooemien in Diodors Historischer Bibliothek*. Zürich.

Lämmli, F. 1962. *Vom Chaos zum Kosmos: Zur Geschichte einer Idee*. Basel.

Lampe, G. W. H., ed. 1961. *A Greek Patristic Lexicon*. Oxford.

Laqueur, R. 1936. "Timagenes." *RE* 6A.1:1063–1071.

Lehmann, G. A. 1988. "Diskussionsbeitrag." In Verdin, Schepens, and De Keyser 1990, 197.

Leopoldi, H. 1892. De Agatharchide Cnidio. Rostock.

Longo, O. 1987. "I mangiatori di pesci: regime alimentare e quadro culturale." *MD* 18:9–55.

Marcotte, D. 2001. "Structure et caractère de l'œuvre historique d'Agatharchide." *Historia* 50:385–435.

Marincola, J. 1997. *Authority and Tradition in Ancient Historiography*. Cambridge.

Marrou, H. I. 1977. *Geschichte der Erziehung im klassischen Altertum*. Munich.

Mazza, M. 2002. "Il prezzo della libertà: la risposta degli Arabi Nabatei a Demetrio Poliorcete." In Arma virumque: *Studi di poesia e storiografia in onore di Luca Canali*, ed. E. Lelli, 45–66. Pisa.

Meier, C. 1986. "Gedächtnisrede auf Hermann Strasburger." *Chiron* 16:171–197.

Meißner, B. 1992. *Historiker zwischen Polis und Königshof: Studien zur Stellung der Geschichtsschreiber in der griechischen Gesellschaft in spätklassischer und frühhellenistischer Zeit*. Göttingen.

Meister, K. 1973/1974. "Absurde Polemik bei Diodor." *Helikon* 13/14:454–459.

Mirhady, D. C. 2001. "Dicaearchus of Messana: The Sources, Text and Translation." In Fortenbaugh and Schütrumpf 2001, 1–142.

Momigliano, A. D. 1984. *Settimo Contributo alla storia degli studi classici e del mondo antico.* Pisa.

Mortley, R. 1996. *The Idea of Universal History from Hellenistic Philosophy to Early Christian Historiography.* Lewiston, ME.

Müller, C. 1882. *Geographi Graeci Minores.* 2 vols. Paris.

Nicolai, R. 1992. *La storiografia nella educazione antica.* Pisa.

O'Brien, M. J. 1985. "Xenophanes, Aeschylus, and the Doctrine of Primeval Brutishness." *CQ* 35:245–263.

Palm, J. 1955. *Über Sprache und Stil des Diodoros von Sizilien.* Lund.

Pédech, P. 1964. *La méthode historique de Polybe.* Paris.

Peremans, W. 1967. "Diodore de Sicile et Agatharchide de Cnide." *Historia* 16:432–455.

Pfeiffer, R. 1978. *Geschichte der klassischen Philologie von den Anfängen bis zum Hellenismus.* Munich.

Pirenne, J. 1961. *Le royaume sud-arabe de Qataban et sa datation d'après l'archéologie et les sources classiques.* Louvain.

Pohlenz, M. 1965. *Kleine Schriften.* 2 vols. Hildesheim.

Reinhard, W. 2004. *Lebensformen Europas: Eine historische Kulturanthropologie.* Munich.

Reinhardt, K. 1921. *Poseidonios.* Munich.

———. 1953. "Poseidonios." *RE* 22.1:558–826.

Rudberg, G. 1918. *Forschungen zu Poseidonios.* Uppsala.

Runia, D. T. 1998. "Herakleides Lembos." In *Der Neue Pauly* 5:375–376. Stuttgart.

Sacks, K. S. 1990. *Diodorus Siculus and the First Century.* Princeton, NJ.

Sartori, M. 1984. "Storia, utopia, e mito nei primi libri della *Bibliotheca Historica* di Diodoro Siculo." *Athenaeum* 72:492–536.

Saunders, T. J. 2001. "Dicaearchus' Historical Anthropology." In Fortenbaugh and Schütrumpf 2001, 237–254.

Schamp, J. 1987. *Photios: Historien des lettres.* Paris.

Schepens, G., and J. Bollansée. 2004. "Myths on the Origins of Peoples and the Birth of Universal History." In *Historia y mito: El pasado legendario como fuente de autoridad*, ed. J. M. C. Moron, F. J. G. Ponce and G. C. Andreotti, 57–75. Malaga.

Schepens, G. 2005. "Polybius' Criticism of Phylarchus." In *The Shadow of Polybius: Intertextuality as a Research Tool in Greek Historiography. Proceedings of the International Colloquium, Leuven, 21–22 September 2001*, ed. G. Schepens and J. Bollansée, 141–164. Louvain.

Schmitt, H. H. and E. Vogt, eds. 2005. *Lexikon des Hellenismus*. Wiesbaden.

Schneider, G. J. 1880. "*Quibus ex fontibus petiverit Diodorus Lib. III capp. 1-48.*" In *Symbolae Joachimicae: Festschrift des königlichen Joachimsthalschen Gymnasiums*, vol. 1, 221–254. Berlin.

Schütrumpf, E. 2001. "Dikaiarchs βίος Ἑλλάδος und die Philosophie des 4. Jhs." In Fortenbaugh and Schütrumpf 2001, 255–277.

Schwartz, E. 1893. "Agatharchides." *RE* 1.1:739–741.

Sharples, R. W. 2001. "Dicaearchus on the Soul and on Divination." In Fortenbaugh and Schütrumpf 2001, 143–173.

Spoerri, W. 1959. *Späthellenistische Berichte über Welt, Kultur und Götter.* Basel.

Staab, G. 2004. "Athenfreunde unter Verdacht: Der erste Asianist Hegesias aus Magnesia zwischen Rhetorik und Geschichtsschreibung." *ZPE* 148:127–150.

Strasburger, H. 1982. *Studien zur alten Geschichte.* 2 vols. Hildesheim.

Susemihl, F. 1891, 1892. *Geschichte der griechischen Literatur in der Alexandrinerzeit.* 2 vols. Leipzig.

Tarn, W. W. 1929. "Ptolemy II and Arabia." *JEA* 15:9–25.

Theiler, W. 1970. *Untersuchungen zur antiken Literatur.* Berlin.

Thesleff, H. 1961. *An Introduction to the Pythagorean Writings of the Hellenistic Period.* Åbo.

———. 1965. *The Pythagorean Texts of the Hellenistic Period.* Åbo.

Urías Martínez, R. 1993. "La historia a través del mundo: Agatárquides de Cnido y la 'Nueva Historia' de Posidonio." *Habis* 24:57–67.

Utzinger, C. 2003. *Periphrades aner: Untersuchungen zum ersten Stasimon der sophokleischen Antigone und zu den antiken Kulturentstehungstheorien.* Göttingen.

Véïsse, A.-E. 2004. *Les "revoltes égyptiennes:" Recherches sur les troubles intérieurs en Égypte du règne de Ptolémée III à la conquete romaine.* Louvain.

Verdin, H. 1983. "Agatharchide et la tradition du discours politique dans l'historiographie grecque." In *Egypt and the Hellenistic World:*

Proceedings of the International Colloquium, Leuven, 24-26 May 1982, ed. E. van 't Dack, P. van Dessel, and W. van Gucht, 407–420. Louvain.

———. 1990. "La vérité des historiens et celle des poètes: La témoignage d'Agatharchide de Cnide." In Verdin, Schepens, and De Keyser 1990, 1–15.

———, G. Schepens and E. De Keyser, eds. 1990. *Purposes of History: Studies in Greek Historiography from the 4th to the 2nd Centuries BC. Proceedings of the International Colloquium, Leuven, 24-26 May 1988.* Louvain.

Verlinsky, A. L. 2005. "Epicurus and his Predecessors on the Origin of Language." In *Language and Learning*, ed. D. Frede and B. Inwood, 56–100. Cambridge.

Wachsmuth, C. 1891. "Pentadenbände der Handschriften klassischer Schriftsteller." *RhM* 46:329–331.

Wagner, E. A. 1901. *Agatharchides und der mittlere Peripatos. Erster Teil.* Leipzig.

Walbank, F. W. 1979. *A Historical Commentary on Polybius.* Vol. 3. Oxford.

———. 1972. *Polybius.* Berkeley, CA.

———. 1985. *Selected Papers: Studies in Greek and Roman Historiography.* Cambridge.

Wehrli, F. 1968. "Dikaiarchos." *RE* Suppl. 11:526–534.

———. 1983. "Der Peripatos bis zum Beginn der Kaiserzeit." In *Die Philosophie der Antike III,* ed. H. Flashar, 459–599. Basel.

White, S. A. 2001. "*Principes sapientiae*: Dicaearchus' Biography of Philosophy." In Fortenbaugh and Schütrumpf 2001, 195–236.

Wilson, N. G. 1994. *Photius—The* Bibliotheca. London.

Wirth, G. "Geschichtsschreibung A." In Schmitt and Vogt 2005, 360–368.

Woelk, D. 1966. *Agatharchides v. Knidos:* Über das Rote Meer. Freiburg.

Wörrle, M. 1995. "Vom tugendsamen Jüngling zum 'gestreßten' Euergeten: Überlegungen zum Bürgerbild hellenistischer Ehrendekrete." In *Stadtbild und Bürgerbild im Hellenismus,* ed. M. Wörrle and P. Zanker, 241–250. Munich.

Zecchini, G. 1990. "La storiografia lagide." In Verdin, Schepens, and De Keyser 1990, 213–232.

Zimmermann, K. 1999. *Libyen: Das Land südlich des Mittelmeers im Weltbild der Griechen.* Munich.

3

METIS IN ROME
A GREEK DREAM OF SULLA

Andrea Giardina

I.

In a passage of his *Consolatio ad Marciam*, Seneca cites several exemplary cases to prove that the evil that befalls the happiest of men is not necessarily the one perceived as the greatest. He begins with a man who was the happiest of all, a man whose very name contained the notion of happiness: Lucius Cornelius Sulla Felix. The loss of a son, says Seneca, did not make him any less wicked, or less determined in persecuting his enemies and fellow citizens. Seneca then utters a famous judgment which has mesmerized and puzzled both ancient and modern commentators: *Sed istud inter res nondum iudicatas abeat, qualis Sulla fuerit*, "Who was Sulla?"—says Seneca—"This question still ranks among unsolved problems." Significantly, his statement appears to be connected in the text with the mention of Sulla's spontaneous resigning of his dictatorship.[1]

Seneca's often repeated words never seem to elicit surprise. On the contrary, they appear to reflect an incontrovertible fact, a widely accepted opinion: Sulla was a mysterious character, and his life story contains an impenetrable enigma. What is really enigmatic, however, is Seneca's statement. In his time, copies of the 22 books of Sulla's *Memoirs* were easily available for consultation (even Plutarch was able to draw extensively on them). So the question inevitably arises as to why, after

---

Translated by Federico Poole.

[1] Sen. *Dial.* 4 (= *Consolatio ad Marciam*) 12.6.

having written so much about himself, and hence having indubitably given his own version of the act—the decision to resign at the peak of his power—which more than any other caused him to come across as an indecipherable personality, the man still appeared so mysterious.

II.

We do not know what exact time in his life Sulla had reached in his autobiography when his death cut it short. In the twenty-first book, Sulla wrote the sentence, reported by the grammarian Priscianus: *ad summam perniciem rem publicam perventurum esse.*[2] He was evidently referring to the events which had preceded his final victory in the civil war and his assuming of the dictatorship; events about which it would have been indeed reasonable to say that the Republic was on the edge of the abyss.[3] It is unthinkable that Sulla would have referred to the Republic as having come *ad summam perniciem* during the time when he was dictator, or during his subsequent withdrawal to the country after having consolidated the state. It is plausible that he began narrating his actions as dictator in the same book; unless the sentence *ad summam perniciem rem publicam perventurum esse* stood at the end of the book, as a transition to the following one. At any rate, that period of his life was certainly narrated in the twenty-second and last book, which was left unfinished and was completed by Sulla's freedman Epicadus after the dictator's death.[4] The sentence *ad summam perniciem rem publicam perventurum esse* can hardly refer to events preceding the civil war (e.g., the Social War, or the circumstances which led to the march on Rome), because in the tenth book Sulla mentioned an event following the first phase of the battle of Chaeronea.[5]

---

[2] Prisçian. 9 p476 H. (= *HRRel* fr. 20, p203).

[3] Pascucci 1975:291; Lewis 1991:517 points out an interesting parallel in Vell. Pat. 2.27.1: *Pontius Telesinus [...] kal. Novembribus ita ad portam Collinam cum Sulla dimicavit ut ad summum discrimen et eum et rempublicam perduceret.*

[4] This is the only possible interpretation of the expression γράφων ἐπαύσατο in Plut. *Sull.* 37.1, which means "stopped writing" and not "concluded:" Pascucci 1975:292, pace Lanzani 1936:290; Calabi 1951:249; Badian 1969:4; Angeli Bertinelli 1997:201; and others.

[5] Plut. *Sull.* 17.2 (= *HRRel* fr. 16, p201).

The only information we have about the contents of the twenty-second book is supplied by Plutarch:

Ὁ δὲ Σύλλας οὐ μόνον προέγνω τὴν ἑαυτοῦ τελευτήν, ἀλλὰ τρόπον τινὰ καὶ γέγραφε περὶ αὐτῆς. τὸ γὰρ εἰκοστὸν καὶ δεύτερον τῶν ὑπομνημάτων πρὸ δυεῖν ἡμερῶν ἢ ἐτελεύτα γράφων ἐπαύσατο· καί φησι τοὺς Χαλδαίους αὐτῷ προειπεῖν ὡς δέοι βεβιωκότα καλῶς αὐτὸν ἐν ἀκμῇ τῶν εὐτυχημάτων καταστρέψαι. λέγει δὲ καὶ τὸν υἱὸν αὐτοῦ, τεθνηκότα μικρὸν ἔμπροσθεν τῆς Μετέλλης, φανῆναι κατὰ τοὺς ὕπνους ἐν ἐσθῆτι φαύλῃ παρεστῶτα καὶ δεόμενον τοῦ πατρὸς παύσασθαι τῶν φροντίδων, ἰόντα δὲ σὺν αὐτῷ παρὰ τὴν μητέρα Μετέλλαν ἐν ἡσυχίᾳ καὶ ἀπραγμόνως ζῆν μετ' αὐτῆς.

Sulla not only foresaw his own death, but may be said to have written about it also. He stopped writing the twenty-second book of his *Memoirs* two days before he died, and he says there that the Chaldaeans foretold him that, after an honourable life, he was to end his days at the height of his good fortunes. He says also that his son, who died a little while before Metella, appeared to him in his dreams, clad in mean attire, and besought his father to put an end to anxious thoughts, and come with him to his mother Metella, there to live in peace and quietness with her.[6]

There is a widespread persuasion that these words were written two days before Sulla's death and expressed a foreboding of its imminence. The dream in which the son beseeches the father to "put an end to anxious thoughts" is commonly regarded as "Sulla's last dream."[7] But this is certainly not true. We shall see how shedding light on this apparently minor point opens a whole new perspective on Sulla's story and our understanding of his self-representation.

---

[6] Plut. *Sull.* 37.1–3 (= *HRRel* fr. 21, p204), trans. Perrin.
[7] Cf., for example, Carcopino 1947:235–237; Schilling 1954:278; Pascucci 1975:292–293; Hinard 1985:264; Hurlet 1993:111.

III.

The widespread opinion that the dream recounted by Plutarch, in which the son urges his father to drop all cares, was Sulla's last dream, the one he had two days before his death, is also based on two other testimonies that are commonly believed to refer to the same event. In the first book of his *Civil Wars*, Appian writes:

> Σύλλας δ' ἐν τοῖς ἀγροῖς ἐνύπνιον ἔδοξεν ἰδεῖν, ὅτι αὐτὸν ὁ δαίμων ἤδη καλοίη· καὶ ὁ μὲν αὐτίκα μεθ' ἡμέραν τοῖς φίλοις τὸ ὄναρ ἐξειπὼν διαθήκας συνέγραφεν ἐπειγόμενος καὶ αὐτῆς ἡμέρας συνετέλει.

> While he was living in the country Sulla had a dream in which he thought he saw his Genius already calling him. Early in the morning he told the dream to his friends and in haste began writing his will, which he finished that day. After sealing it he was taken with a fever towards evening and died the same night.[8]

And Pliny, in the seventh book of his *Historia naturalis*, says:

> Quod ut dissimulaverit et supremo somnio eius, cui inmortuus quodammodo est, credamus ab uno illo invidiam gloria victam [...]

> Although he dissembled the pangs, and although on the evidence of that last dream of his, which may almost be said to have accompanied his death, we believed that he alone vanquished odium by glory [...].[9]

But if we compare these two documents with Plutarch's story, we will realize that they cannot refer to the same dream. In Plutarch, it is the son who appears to the father, in Appian it is the δαίμων. Plutarch says that Sulla put his dream down in writing in the twenty-second book of his *Memoirs*, while Appian states that it was reported orally

---

[8] App. *B Civ.* 1.105, trans. White.
[9] Plin. *HN* 7.138, trans. Rackham.

to his friends on the following morning (Appian clearly distinguishes Sulla's oral account of the dream—ἐξειπών—from his written testament—συνέγραφεν).[10] As to Pliny's brief testimony, it also has nothing to connect it with Plutarch's story. It may, instead, belong to the same tradition that Appian drew upon, which goes back to the additions by the freedman Epicadus.[11] It is plausible, in other words, that the dream told by Sulla to his friends—the one which we can legitimately regard as his "last dream"—included the appearance of the Genius. And that the Genius, in beseeching Sulla to rejoin him (as related by Appian), had told him that his glory would have prevailed over odium among his posterity (as related by Pliny). This detail, however, is of secondary importance, whereas the realization that Plutarch's story has no connection with Appian and Pliny's accounts of Sulla's death has remarkable implications. In fact, there is reason to believe that Plutarch is referring to a whole other event.

IV.

The modes of expression of ancient autobiography are not those of an intimate diary, or the notes that people take of their dreams before the next session with the psychoanalyst. In a diary I can write: "last night I had this dream ...," without attributing any special significance to the dream. But such annotations would not make any sense in the autobiography of a great political figure, written for publication. In a work of this kind, a dream is only recounted when it is regarded as an omen of future momentous events.

Testimonies that certainly draw on Sulla's *Memoirs* clearly bear out this narrative function of dreams. For example, in his narration of the battle of Sacriportus, Plutarch says that before the battle Sulla dreamed of the elder Marius "exhorting his son to beware of the coming day,

---

[10] Calabi 1951:251–252 remarked the differences between Appian and Plutarch's stories, but drew wrong conclusions from her observation; notably that Plutarch had obtained his information about the Chaldaean oracle and Sulla's dream about his son from a "collection of prophecies and portents" (251), and that Sulla, in writing his *Memoirs*, had got no further than the speech he had held after the battle of Porta Collina (301).

[11] Cf. the brief but to the point observations of Keaveney 1983:55n58.

because it would bring disaster." The telling of this dream is followed by the fulfillment of the prophecy, that is, by the slaughtering of Sulla's enemies: "There the Deity fulfilled the words which Sulla had heard in his dreams."[12] One could cite several other examples.[13]

Neither Plutarch nor other authors say that in the twenty-second book Sulla was recounting the hours immediately preceding his death. Plutarch merely says that Sulla "somehow" (τρόπον τινα) wrote about his death in that book, and that he did so by referring to the prophecy of the Chaldaeans, who had predicted his death at the peak of his success,[14] and to his nighttime visions of his son inviting him to withdraw from his cares. For the reasons I have detailed above, we must assume that the last part of Sulla's autobiography dealt with not, as is commonly believed, the hours immediately preceding his death, but the moment when he had decided to give up the dictatorship.[15] This

[12] Plut. *Sull.* 28.4, 6, trans. Perrin. This testimony should be added to the *reliquiae* of Sulla's *Memoirs*, both for the typically Sullan character of the narration, and because it included a direct quotation (Σύλλας φησίν) of the *Memoirs*: 28.8 (= *HRRel* fr. 19, p203). For further proposals for the integration of the fragments gathered by Peter, see Brennan 1992.

[13] Cf., for example, Keaveney 1983:54.

[14] This Chaldaean prophecy should not be confused with the one mentioned by Plutarch (*Sull.* 5.5–6). In the latter case, Plutarch speaks of a "Chaldaean" in the singular, whereas in 37.2 he speaks of "Chaldaeans." Furthermore, in 5.5 he introduces his account of the prophecy with the verb ἱστορεῖται, whereas at 37.2 he explicitly says λέγει. We do not know what the circumstances of the prophecy in 37.2 were. It need not have taken place in the Orient. As regards, more in general, Sulla's first encounter with the Chaldaeans, cf. the acute observation of Keaveney 1983:50: "It is impossible to say whether the seer was the first to implant these notions in Sulla's mind or if he merely confirmed him in opinions he already held. The swaggering self-confidence which Sulla had shown prior to this might suggest that the latter view is the correct one."

[15] This consideration alone is sufficient to give the lie to a bizarre indication by Granius Licinianus 32.14 Fl.: *Data erat Sullae prov[inci]a Gallia Cisalpina*; concerning this problem, see Laffi 2001:219. It also reflects on the role of the freedman Epicadus, who, according to Suetonius, *librum [...] quem Sulla novissimum de rebus suis inperfectum reliquerat ipse supplevit* (*Gram.* 12; compare, for the coincidence of word and substance, with what Suetonius himself, *Iul.* 56.1, affirms regarding A. Hirtius: *Nam Alexandrini Africique et Hispaniensis incertus auctor est; alii Oppium putant, alii Hirtium, qui etiam Gallici belli novissimum imperfectumque librum suppleverit*). Obviously, if Sulla had written the story of his life up to two days before his death very little would have remained for his devoted freedman to complete: just a few lines about his patron's death and the funeral (Peter,

hypothesis also has the merit of suggesting a plausible distribution of subject matter in the last two books of Sulla's *Memoirs*. If the civil war was indeed discussed in the twenty-first book, it is hardly conceivable that all the rest of the dictator's life, until two days before his death, could have been narrated within the space of the twenty-second.[16]

If we accept the—I think inevitable—conclusion that the dream told in Book 22 of the *Autobiography* is not "Sulla's last dream," remarkable possibilities open up. We can now hope to gain knowledge, or at least a glimpse, of how Sulla chose to recount the most extraordinary decision of his life, the decision which more than any other disoriented ancients and moderns alike: his sudden and unexpected resigning of the dictatorship. It is possible that Sulla also gave eminently political reasons for his withdrawal. He may have proudly affirmed that he had defeated the seditious faction that was trying to ruin the country, pacified the Republic, and restored the senate's prestige. At the same time, he may have represented in a "Solonian" style his decision to retire to private life after accomplishing his task. We cannot rule out that he actually cast himself in that mould. What we know for sure, however, is that he gave an oracular and oneiric reason for his decision; indeed, that may have been the only reason he ever gave. In Sulla's *Memoirs*, oracles and dreams often occurred in conjunction[17] and—as we shall see more clearly below—gave rise to a consistent system of existential reference points.

V.

In the twenty-second book of his *Memoirs*, Sulla spoke of the apical moment of his career as the fulfillment of a Chaldaean oracle. The Chaldaeans had also foreseen that there would have been no decline in the

---

HRRel 1² CCLXXI). But if we draw the apparently inevitable conclusion that Sulla did *not* really tell the story of his life until two days before his death, we must also drop the idea that Epicadus' contribution was so insignificant.

[16] Hence the hypothesis that Sulla left "a large lacuna between the end of his fully developed narrative and his final addenda hastily appended only two days before he died:" Lewis 1991:519.

[17] Brennan 1992:108.

last phase of Sulla's life: "he would have died at the peak of his power." To give up power before it wore away and lost its lustre was actually the only way to make the prophecy come true. We all know that sooth-sayers, both ancient and modern, owe their great popularity to the fact that whoever consults them does everything in his or her powers to make their prophecies come true; we cannot rule out that Sulla did the same.[18] Sulla's reference to seeing his son in his dream added overtones of religious feeling to this general atmosphere. Sulla evidently did not interpret his son's appearance as an immediate *omen mortis*, but rather as an invitation to settle down to a peaceful existence, to let himself drift away on the calm sea of old age, in preparation for death.

We are looking at a pious Sulla whom ancient and modern commen-tators have not always been ready to acknowledge. Sulla's religious feelings have been represented as ambiguous, insincere, or opportu-nistic. The doubts of ancient writers about Sulla were largely due to his pretension to call himself Felix, and hence characterize himself as a man blessed with *felicitas* more than any other. They argued that his heinous crimes towards his fellow citizens proved the absurdity of that pretension and, as a consequence, his lack of authentic religious feeling. *Crimen deorum erat Sulla Felix*, wrote Seneca.[19]

In modern times, frequent doubts have been expressed about the sincerity of Sulla's religious feelings. Jérôme Carcopino claims that Sulla used religion as a mere instrument to set up a theocratic monarchy. The truth was that "Sylla n'avait rien du dévot," "il cultivait trop sa propre jouissance pour s'inquiéter beaucoup des dieux," "il s'amusait des fables de la mythologie" and "se moquait, au lieu d'en trembler, des foudres de Jupiter."[20] In a not altogether different vein, Andreas Alföldi argues that Sulla's frequent appeals to the gods to inspire and protect his political action, rather than reflecting sincere religious feelings,

---

[18] Badian 1969:27 does suggest that Sulla's retirement may have been influenced by the Chaldaeans' prophecy, but takes the edge out of his hypothesis by adding "in any case, there was no choice."

[19] Sen. *Dial.* 4 (= *Consolatio ad Marciam*) 12.6. One can sometimes catch glimpses of a different tradition in ancient sources; cf. lately Barden Dowling 2000. On the ancient sources and modern historiography, see mainly Hinard 1985:261–294.

[20] Carcopino 1947:86.

were a mere "zynische Ausbeutung" whose purpose was to fascinate and control the masses.[21]

In these and other similar views, the Machiavellan stereotype of religion as *instrumentum regni* prevails. This aspect of Sulla's personality was so difficult to understand that one scholar even suggested that the frequent allusions to the supernatural in the dictator's *Memoirs* may have depended on the feeble mental health of the author at the time he was writing them.[22] Even when it was not the target of such drastic judgments, Sulla's piety has always been regarded with diffidence,[23] dismissed as a form of superstition, or simply ignored, as in the case of a recent and in other respects valuable biography.[24]

There have indeed been detailed studies on subjects such as Sulla's adoption of the cognomen Felix/Ἐπαφρόδιτος, or the very concept of *felicitas*; but these studies have mainly focused on the semantic scope of these terms (notably in connection with the Greek notion of τύχη) and the propagandistic side of Sulla's actions; an approach which, although valid, has failed to produce an in-depth reconstruction of what we could call Sulla's "religious personality."

Only two modern historians have actually addressed this question. The first is Carolina Lanzani, who in a book written in 1936 defined Sulla's temperament as "mystic," stressing the sincerity and profundity of his religious feelings. The author's methodological weaknesses, frequent naiveté, and emphatic, redundant, often even cloying prose, hindered other scholars from perceiving the importance of the issue she was raising.[25]

The most in-depth existing study of Sulla's piety was recently written by Arthur Keaveney.[26] In spite of the author's overestimation

[21] Alföldi 1976:143.

[22] Balsdon 1951:2.

[23] A typical example is the cautious attitude of Schilling 1954, e.g., 277: "Dès lors, Sylla se considérait (ou *affectait* de se considérer) comme marqué par un caractère sacré" (my emphasis).

[24] Christ 2002.

[25] Another author who argued for the sincerity of Sulla's religious feelings was Valgiglio 1956:154–197; however, he tended to regard it as something that happened late in the dictator's life and was not devoid of ambiguities (170–171).

[26] Keaveney 2005 and esp. 1983.

of the Apolline component in Sulla's piety and consequent underesti-
mation of his devotion to Venus, and in spite of his persuasion that the
dictator's piety, inasmuch as it was "political," was perfectly in line with
the common mentality, Keaveney's investigation is to date the most
complete and successful attempt to bring out the "passionate" Sulla.
His portrait of the dictator is a distinct departure from Sulla's traditional historiographic image.

To address this issue, we need to proceed in two stages. First of all,
we will try to analyze Sulla's self-representation. Only then will we be
able to form an opinion about his religious feelings and their influence
on his political decisions. For the first stage, we can rely on certain data
which—as we shall see—can be combined into a "system." The second,
instead, inevitably leaves wide margins for interpretation, so that any
conclusions we draw will have to rely largely on our intuition.

VI.

In dedicating his *Memoirs* to his disciple Lucullus, Sulla advised him
to have the highest regard for the indications coming from deities at
nighttime: ἔτι δὲ Λευκόλλῳ μὲν ἐν τοῖς ὑπομνήμασιν, ὧν ἐκείνῳ τὴν
γραφὴν ἀνατέθεικε, παραινεῖ μηδὲν οὕτως ἡγεῖσθαι βέβαιον ὡς ὅ τι ἂν
αὐτῷ προστάξῃ νύκτωρ τὸ δαιμόνιον.[27] While his contemporaries and
posterity saw him as cold and calculating, Sulla preferred to represent
himself as a man guided by oracles and dreams, who believed in fateful
coincidences,[28] and was accustomed to act on impulse. The contrast was
clear to Sulla himself. In a passage of his *Memoirs*, also cited by Plutarch,
he made a statement whose importance has completely eluded modern
critics. Plutarch says: ἐν τοῖς ὑπομνήμασι γέγραφεν ὅτι τῶν καλῶς
αὐτῷ βεβουλεῦσθαι δοκούντων αἱ μὴ κατὰ γνώμην, ἀλλὰ πρὸς καιρὸν
ἀποτολμώμεναι πράξεις ἔπιπτον εἰς ἄμεινον ("in his *Memoirs* he writes
that, of the undertakings which men thought well-advised, those upon
which he had boldly ventured, not after deliberation, but on the spur of

---

[27] Plut. *Sull.* 6.6.

[28] In his *Memoirs*, Sulla remarked the coincidence of the kalends of March, when he
seized Athens, with the first day of the month of Anthesterion, when the Athenians
solemnly commemorated the Deluge: Plut. *Sull.* 14.6.

the moment, turned out for the better").[29] Sulla was thus stressing the contrast between the false common opinion that his most successful actions had been the fruit of careful and lucid planning, on the one hand, and the authenticity of his actual way of doing things, based on impulse and his readiness to grasp the καιρός, on the other.[30] Decisions which appeared consistent to Sulla, because they were all inspired by καιρός, for that very reason may have appeared to his contemporaries and posterity as evidence of a contradictory, unstable, and unpredictable personality.[31] At the same time, this inconsistency in behaviour could be interpreted as a form of cunning, as suggested by Gnaeus Papirius Carbo when he declared that in contending with the fox and the lion that coexisted in Sulla, it was the fox that gave him the most trouble.[32] Sulla's cunning must have been a popular theme among his contemporaries for it to be echoed with such emphasis by later tradition: *ad simulanda negotia altitudo ingenii incredibilis* was Sallust's celebrated judgment.[33]

Thus, while Sulla's relationship with καιρός was actually an aspect of his piety, it was one that his contemporaries failed to grasp; and this in spite of the importance Sulla himself granted to it, since it guided his actions in the most difficult and critical circumstances.

VII.

Significantly, Plutarch's subsequent words lead us directly to the issue of the cognomen *Felix*, which Sulla adopted officially immediately after his final victory in the civil war.[34] In 82, a *senatus consultum*

---

[29] Plut. *Sull.* 6.5, trans. Perrin. Significantly, Balsdon 1951:2–3 mentions this passage as evidence for his hypothesis that Sulla was mentally deranged at the time he was writing his *Memoirs*.

[30] We can only guess what Latin term Sulla used in his *Memoirs* to render Plutarch's καιρός. It was probably *occasio*, although *opportunitas* cannot be ruled out. Among the numerous references in *TLL*, s.v. "occasio," col. 331.40, cf. especially Livy 25.38.18: *si in occasionis momento, cuius pratervolat opportunitas cunctatus paulum fueris, nequiquam mox omissam quaeras.* On the evolution of this concept in the Greek world, see Trédé 1992.

[31] Plut. *Sull.* 6.7–8.

[32] Plut. *Sull.* 28.3.

[33] Sall. *Iug.* 95; cf. Zecchini 2002:47.

[34] Cf. Behr 1993:144–170.

declared valid and legal all the measures taken by Sulla in his capacity as proconsul and consul, and ordered that a gilt equestrian statue be erected to him in front of the *rostra* in the Forum. The inscription on this statue is reported by Appian in a Greek translation (Κορνηλίου Σύλλα ἡγεμόνος Εὐτυχοῦς) which we can easily trace back to the Latin original: *Cornelio Sullae imperatori Felici*.[35]

Felix, as Pliny the Elder said, was a *superbum cognomen*.[36] *Superbum* it was indeed, but above all it was original; so original as to disconcert the ancients and draw a host of comments from the moderns, partly because Sulla had called himself in Greek by the unexpected Ἐπαφρόδιτος.

Plutarch's perspective has strongly influenced modern critics' approach to the issue of Sulla's cognomen. As a Delphic priest, Plutarch had a keen interest in the supernatural in the lives of his heroes. He thus devoted much attention to oracles, prodigies, dreams, visions, and fateful coincidences. The cognomen chosen by Sulla could not fail to attract Plutarch's attention. But translating *Felix* into Greek was not an easy matter, because there were several possible synonyms to choose from, all more or less true to the original. One could have used Αἴσιος, or Εὐδαίμων, or again Εὐτυχής; another possible alternative would have been to merely transliterate the name in Greek letters (Φέλιξ) rather than translate it. Plutarch opted for Εὐτυχής, a term designating an individual blessed with good fortune (τύχη). It was a short leap from here to construing Sulla as a devotee of the goddess Fortuna, which Plutarch did as a matter of course. He also duly used εὐτυχία to translate the term *felicitas* as employed by Sulla. He was wrong, but his mistake depended more on his fascination with the theme of Fortune rather than an imperfect understanding of Latin,[37] and on his inability to fully identify with a mentality which even Sulla's contemporaries had perceived as strange.

Plutarch's error has had a long-lasting influence on modern historians, who have generally taken for granted that there existed an important connection between Sulla and Fortuna. Two variants of this opinion exist, but both come to the same conclusion. According to one, Felix

[35] App. *B Civ.* 1.97. *Imperator* is preferable to *dictator*: Balsdon 1951:4n50; Gabba 1967:263.
[36] Plin. *HN* 22.12.
[37] On Plutarch's Latin, see Jones 1971:81–87.

was an attribute of Fortuna, and Ἐπαφρόδιτος a Greek cognomen that was independent of the Latin one. More frequently, historians postulate a substantial equivalence of Aphrodite and Fortuna. Only recently has J. Champeaux finally exposed this misunderstanding, and the goddess Fortuna has hence lost the central role in Sulla's religious world she was long credited with because of an ancient translation error.[38]

Plutarch's mistake is all the more serious because Sulla himself had proposed *Felix* as the equivalent of Ἐπαφρόδιτος, thus making clear that he owed his *felicitas* not to Fortuna, but to Aphrodite. The view that Sulla rendered *Felix* as Ἐπαφρόδιτος because the Roman notion of *fortuna* did not correspond to the Greek notion of τύχη[39] is based on the erroneous opinion that the *cognomen* Felix was connected to the goddess Fortuna. Now, even if this were true, it is hard to see why Sulla would have preferred to translate *Felix* by an epithet formed on the name of Aphrodite, a goddess who was quite distinct from the Roman Fortuna, rather than on that of Τύχη, a goddess who, if not identical with Fortuna, certainly bore much closer resemblance to her.

Everything seems to indicate that it was Latin, not Greek, that Sulla was having trouble with, and that the whole problem arose from the fact that he had decided to allude to Aphrodite in his cognomen while he was still in Greece. Plutarch, who knew Chaeronea well, mentions that the cognomen Ἐπαφρόδιτος frequently recurred on the trophies Sulla erected on the site of the battle,[40] whereas its Latin translation Felix does not appear until late in 82.

Unlike Ἐπαφρόδιτος, which leaves no room for doubt, *Felix* does not imply necessarily and exclusively protection by Venus. But Sulla, if we think of it, had no alternatives: *Venustus* was not an option because it referred exclusively to physical appearance,[41] nor was the Latin trans-

---

[38] Champeaux 1987:216–236. Her analysis of Sulla's *felicitas* is of fundamental importance for our understanding of Plutarch's interpretation and its far-reaching consequences, as well as the weak presence of the goddess Fortuna in Sulla's world. On the "Oriental" aspects of Sulla's *cognomina*, see Fadinger 2002.

[39] Keaveney 1983:46–48; Hurlet 1993:117.

[40] Plut. *Sull.* 34.2. It is impossible to determine exactly when Sulla conceived this predilection for Aphrodite.

[41] Marinoni 1987:202.

literation *Epaphroditus*, which, among other things, did not suit Sulla's communication requirements vis-à-vis Latin-speaking Romans. The Latin term that came closest to Ἐπαφρόδιτος was *Venerius*. This adjective was indeed used by Sulla in the year 80, when he gave the name of *Colonia Veneria Cornelia* to the new colony of Pompeii, which he populated with his veterans. He chose this name to stress the close association of his own person (represented by his family name Cornelius) with a goddess who was especially dear to the heart of the Pompeians.[42] That adjective, however, was suitable for a colony, a legion (like the X *Veneria* instituted by Caesar), or a century of a *collegium*,[43] but not for Sulla's personal name, and this because it contained an unequivocal allusion to the sphere of sexual pleasure. To adopt it would have meant characterizing L. Cornelius Sulla *Venerius*, not as a military and political leader whom Venus protected and guided to victory, but as an individual committed to voluptuous pleasures. The consequences of such a choice could have been very serious indeed, considering that by 82 rumours about Sulla's sexual voracity must have already been widespread.[44] This moral unsuitableness was compounded by a social one. Later epigraphic documents attest to the frequent occurrence of *Venerius* and—even more often—*Veneria* as names of slaves, *cognomina* of freedmen, and family names of servile origin. Even in Sulla's age the slaves of the temple of Venus Ericina were called *Venerii* or *Venerii servi*.[45] Cicero clearly had this sordid implication in mind when he called Verres *homo Venerius* as he denounced one of his many crimes that was connected with this temple.[46]

The cognomen *Felix* offered the undeniable advantage of avoiding both these awkward implications. Therefore we should not say that

---

[42] This association was not grasped by Balsdon 1951:6 in his rather convoluted argumentation. The Pompeian Venus is very different from the one favoured by Sulla: Lepore 2004:161–163.

[43] *CIL* 10.1403 (Herculaneum).

[44] Plut. *Sull.* 2.3, 33.2.

[45] Habermehl 1955. Cf., more in general, Degrassi 1967:262.

[46] The insult *homo Venerius* appears in an account of the execution of a Roman citizen whose possessions were appropriated by Verres, who used them to dedicate a silver Cupid to Venus (Cic. *2Verr.* 5.142).

Ἐπαφρόδιτος was an intentionally unfaithful translation of *Felix*, but that *Felix* was an inevitably generic rendering of Ἐπαφρόδιτος. Generic, but not any less efficacious. By assuming this cognomen immediately after his victory in the civil war, Sulla was celebrating his own *felicitas*, but the implication was that it extended to the exhausted Republic.[47]

The concept of *felicitas* overlapped in many respects with that of *fortuna*, as the following celebrated formula bears out: *quod bonum fortunatum felixque salutareque siet populo Romano Quiritium*.[48] Still, *felicitas* was not synonymous with *fortuna*. Champeaux explains Sulla's choice not to adopt the cognomen *Fortunatus* as depending on the ambiguity of that concept. By choosing *Felix* instead of *Fortunatus*, she argues, Sulla avoided the aleatoric implications of the latter to represent himself, instead, as a man endowed with a stable, intangible, and immutable *felicitas*.[49] But if this were true, we would have to ask ourselves why reliable Felicitas did not take the place of capricious Fortuna not only in Sulla's heart, but in that of all Romans, and why Fortuna enjoyed, instead, a dazzling popularity, both in private and public cult, for as long as paganism lasted. Besides, when a person was given the name "Fortunatus," it was to designate him as someone who was "blessed by Fortune" and not "subject to the whims of Fortune"; someone who was a special protégé of the goddess, not just a casual fellow adventurer. It is out of the question that the name was intended to mean that its bearer was at the mercy of fate. Thus, if Sulla did not choose *Fortunatus*, it is for the simple reason that it was too far removed in meaning from Ἐπαφρόδιτος, and for him this was a crucial consideration.

Modern historians have wondered why Sulla chose to call himself *Felix* and place himself under the protection of Aphrodite. The prevalent view is that it was a reasoned decision prompted by political calculation. Upholders of this thesis maintain that, at least since the victory of Chaeronea,[50] Sulla associated himself with Venus in the hope of gaining a powerful legitimation from the goddess who was the Romans'

---

[47] On the issue of how this notion was received, see Laffi 1967:255–257.

[48] Varro *Ling.* 6.86.

[49] Champeaux 1987:235.

[50] Plut. *Sull.* 34.2.

ancestor; a legitimation that would have stood him in good stead in both the eastern and the western theatre. Now, it is beyond doubt that this consideration had its weight in Sulla's decision. But the question "Why did Sulla choose Aphrodite, and therefore take the name of *Felix*?" conceals an insidious problem of method. With its apparent reasonableness and harmlessness, it actually threatens to put a strong bias on interpretation. This is because the question implies that Sulla made a cold, calculated decision; that we are dealing here with the dictator's careful engineering of his own personal charisma. But things may have gone differently. Maybe it was Aphrodite who chose Sulla.

VIII.

Some historians have cast doubt on the importance of Sulla's privileged relationship with Venus, proclaimed by stably assuming a cognomen referring to her—Ἐπαφρόδιτος in Greek, *Felix* in Latin—on the argument that Sulla was also devoted to other deities, notably Apollo, a goddess from Cappadocia ("whether Semele, Athena, or Bellona," says Plutarch[51]), Mars, Diana, and others as well.[52] But this is like suggesting that to understand a polytheist's authentic inclinations he must appear to us as a monotheist. In fact, Sulla's religious versatility is precisely what we should expect from a man like him in that specific cultural context. Far from being marred, enfeebled, or obliterated by other competing feelings, the inspiration Sulla drew from Venus appears to have been all the more important precisely because it outweighed other inspirations, however strong and vivid they may have been. Furthermore, Sulla's devotion to Venus differed from his devotion to other gods in one important respect, viz., that it was an integral part of an elaborate psycho-religious "system," one which Sulla himself illustrated in his *Memoirs*. As I have stressed above, ancient and modern difficulties in understanding the meaning of this "system" derive not so much from a lack of clarity on Sulla's part, but rather from the originality of the system itself, which one could well describe as "archaic."

---

[51] Plut. *Sull.* 9.4.
[52] Balsdon 1951:7; Keaveney 1983 insists especially on Sulla's devotion to Apollo.

In his inaccurate, but nevertheless invaluable, musings about Sulla's cognomen, Appian recounts an important episode that occurred during the initial stages of the Mithridatic campaign.[53] At that time, the Roman general received a very favourable response from the Delphic oracle:

> Πείθεό μοι, Ῥωμαῖε. κράτος μέγα Κύπρις ἔδωκεν
> Αἰνείου γενεῇ μεμελημένη. ἀλλὰ σὺ πᾶσιν
> Ἀθανάτοις ἐπέτεια τίθει. μὴ λήθεο τῶνδε·
> Δελφοῖς δῶρα κόμιζε. καὶ ἔστι τις ἀμβαίνουσι
> Ταύρου ὑπὸ νιφόεντος, ὅπου περιμήκετον ἄστυ
> Καρῶν, οἳ ναίουσιν ἐπώνυμον ἐξ Ἀφροδίτης·
> ᾗ πέλεκυν θέμενος λήψῃ κράτος ἀμφιλαφές σοι.

Believe me, Roman! Cypris granted great power to Aeneas' line, which is dear to her heart. But be sure to bring yearly gifts to all the gods. And do not forget this: bring gifts to Delphi! There is a goddess at the foot of snow-clad Taurus, in the city of Carian men which they have named after Aphrodite. Dedicate an axe to her, and endless power will be yours.

Sulla sent the goddess a golden wreath and an axe on which the following words were incised:

> τόνδε σοι αὐτοκράτωρ Σύλλας ἀνέθηκ', Ἀφροδίτη,
> ᾧ σ' εἶδον κατ' ὄνειρον ἀνὰ στρατιὴν διέπουσαν
> τεύχεσι τοῖς Ἄρεος μαρναμένην ἔνοπλον.

Sulla *imperator* brought this to you, oh Aphrodite, for in a dream I saw you march at the head of my army and fight with the weapons of Mars.[54]

So, when the oracle urged him to send gifts to the Aphrodite of the town of Aphrodisias in Caria, Sulla complied by sending the goddess an axe bearing an inscription on which he commemorated an apparition of an armed Aphrodite. Some scholars have accordingly deduced that the

---

[53] Keaveney 1983:56; for another hypothesis, see Marinoni 1987:223–226.
[54] App. *B Civ.* 1.97.

Aphrodite of Aphrodisias was an armed goddess. But Aphrodisias has left us no testimony, in writing or art, of such an Aphrodite. It is hence plausible that the Aphrodite "dreamed" by Sulla was a personal version of the goddess evoked by the oracle. We will never know whether the dream was authentic or not,[55] but it certainly played a crucial role in Sulla's system of self-representation.

It is impossible to tell how and where Sulla encountered an armed Aphrodite.[56] It could have happened anywhere. He was so immersed in Greek culture that some scholars have even put forward the absurd hypothesis that his *Memoirs* had been written in Greek. But to whatever year we may date the consulting of the oracle and Sulla's certainly authentic[57] answer, one cannot regard the epithet Ἐπαφρόδιτος as unrelated to the armed Venus in the dream. If the dream was made public prior to Sulla's assuming of the cognomen Ἐπαφρόδιτος, the latter must have necessarily appeared to be connected with the dream. If, vice versa, it was the public adoption of the cognomen after the victory of Chaeronea that preceded the dream, the latter would have necessarily been interpreted as referring to the assuming of the cognomen. The close relationship between these two events seems to be confirmed by a significant coincidence. We know that the trophies erected by Sulla at Chaeronea were dedicated to Ares, Nike and Aphrodite, and we know that on them Sulla bore the cognomen Ἐπαφρόδιτος.[58] Just as the dream was an *omen victoriae* in which Aphrodite was associated with Ares (through a reference to her wearing the "weapons of Ares"), so did the trophies of Chaeronea associate Nike—the victory Sulla had obtained—with Aphrodite and Ares. But, as in the dream, what counted most was the relationship of the Ἐπαφρόδιτος with his goddess.

[55] The authenticity of Sulla's dream lends itself to the same doubts as Constantine's, on which see Harris 2005.

[56] Even if we regarded the dream as authentic, we would have to assume that Sulla had a previous knowledge of the armed Aphrodite; otherwise he could not have dreamt of her.

[57] Independently of its probable origin from Sulla's own *Memoirs*. The *argumentum ex silentio* applied to Plutarch by Marinoni 1987:218–223 to rule out that Appian's account is derived from Sulla's *Memoirs* is not decisive.

[58] Plut. *Sull.* 19.5, 34.2. The reconstruction proposed by Picard 1957:170–181 is very imaginative.

IX.

The Greeks had long known about the Romans' Trojan origins. It was hence natural for the Delphic oracle to invite a powerful Roman general to send gifts to Aphrodite (and even if the oracle had actually been aware of Sulla's predilection for the goddess, that would not have significantly altered the terms of the question). It was equally natural for the oracle to direct him to Aphrodite's sanctuary in a city that was named after her and stood in the same geographical area as Troy. But Sulla's answer added a flare of originality to the event. In dedicating his gift, he did not evoke the canonic type of the Roman Venus, goddess of love and mother of Aeneas, but an eccentric one and, above all, one that was extremely rare; a goddess of victory who was not identifiable *tout court* with the Venus Victrix type.[59]

Armed Aphrodites are extremely rare in ancient art and culture. With the possible exception of two bronze statuettes from the Greek sanctuary of Gravisca, we would search in vain for a single image probably depicting an armed Venus among the thousands of Venuses pictured in sculpture, painting, mosaics, and on coins.[60]

It should be clear that the armed Venus is not, as some authors claim, Venus holding Mars' weapons. That is a charming Venus stripping the god of war of his weapons and about to enter an erotic fray from which she is going to come out the winner. The armed Venus is something else: an iron-clad, martial goddess ("I saw you march at the head of my army and fight with the weapons of Mars," wrote Sulla)—a terrifying and disconcerting Venus.

The armed goddess of the dream was a "personal," Sullan version of Aphrodite, the progenitor of the Romans evoked by the Delphic oracle. It was only natural that Sulla, in presenting himself as the protégé of Venus on coins, would have evoked the canonic type of the goddess, the one familiar to the Greeks and dear to the Romans. But once again he did this in his own fashion, stressing his personal connection with the

[59] Keaveney 1983:61 takes a different view, placing these events within a mainly Apolline framework.

[60] Cf. Flemberg 1991. On Gravisca, cf. Torelli 1977:433.

goddess. On the coins struck by his itinerant mint in the late Eighties, the head of the goddess pictured above the name *L. Sulla* on the obverse is associated with a Cupid bringing Sulla the palm of victory, and the reverse shows the two trophies of the battle of Chaeronea.[61] Venus had never been pictured in this guise on coins before. Sulla intended to emphasize that the granting of Venus' protection depended on his privileged relationship with the goddess. Cupid is there to signify this special connection between Aphrodite and Ἐπαφρόδιτος.[62]

Sulla's Greek dream was an exotic one, and one which we could perhaps characterize as "archaic." The only precise reference we have to a temple of the armed Venus is by Pausanias, who mentions the existence in Sparta of an "ancient temple with a wooden image of Aphrodite armed." This temple was so ancient that another one had been erected above it: "This is the only temple I know that has an upper storey built upon it. It is a sanctuary of Morpho, a surname of Aphrodite [...]."[63]

Aphrodite was a typical goddess endowed with μῆτις, an ancient form of intelligence combining lucid foresight, quick intuition, mimetic perfection, an ability to seize the moment for action, and skill in getting out of tight spots.[64] Because of the inversion in roles, the disquieting Aphrodite evoked by Sulla was no doubt even more endowed with μῆτις.

As a goddess of μῆτις, Aphrodite—and especially the armed Aphrodite—was at the same time a goddess of καιρός, of the fleeting instant, of the opportunity to be grasped. This aspect of the goddess in Sulla's dream can hardly be unconnected with Sulla's own self-portrait as a man of καιρός, who achieved his most remarkable successes by acting, as Plutarch said, "on the spur of the moment."

X.

The above analysis allows us to discern a coherent "system" in the intricate labyrinth of Sulla's life and personality.

---

[61] *RRC* 359. Cf. Martin 1988; Behr 1993:152–153.

[62] Crawford, *RRC* 373 is right to insist on this point.

[63] Paus. 3.15.10, trans. Ormerod.

[64] Detienne and Vernant 1974:278; Loraux 1989:265–267.

Sulla represented himself as a man of καιρός. A man of καιρός is an unpredictable and disconcerting individual endowed with a particular and fearsome form of cunning called μῆτις. This aspect of Sulla's personality was recognized by those of his contemporaries who declared that they feared the fox in him more than the lion. To others, Sulla's καιρός-inspired actions may have seemed to reflect an inconsistent and capricious nature.

Sulla called himself *Felix* and, as his chosen Greek equivalent Ἐπαφρόδιτος bears out, attributed his *felicitas* to the goddess Aphrodite.

His reaction to the response of the Delphic oracle was to remember a dream in which, before a decisive battle, Aphrodite had appeared to him bearing the weapons of Ares. This armed Aphrodite, to whom he dedicated votive objects, was a typical goddess of μῆτις.

In Sulla's actions, dreams and oracles are often connected, and provide helpful indications for rapid and efficient decision-taking.

In the dedication of his *Memoirs*, Sulla advised his disciple Lucullus to have the highest regard for the indications coming from dreams. Nothing, he said, is more important than dreams for the politician. This statement is evidently also a representation of the conduct followed by Sulla himself in his political action.

In his *Memoirs* he attributed his decision to give up the dictatorship to his memory of a Chaldaean oracle, and to a dream where his son had appeared to him.

A man of καιρός knows how to seize the occasion to turn the tables in his favour. But he also knows the right time to call himself out; which is exactly what Sulla did when, to the general astonishment, he withdrew to the countryside.

Istituto Italiano di Scienze Umane (Florence, Rome)

Bibliography

Alföldi, A. 1976. "Redeunt Saturnia Regna. V: Zum Gottesgnadentum des Sulla." *Chiron* 6:143–158.

Angeli Bertinelli, G. 1997. in Plutarco, *Le Vite di Lisandro e di Silla*. Milan.

Badian, E. 1969. *Lucius Sulla the Deadly Reformer*. Sydney.

Balsdon, J. P. V. D. 1951. "Sulla Felix." *JRS* 41:1–10.

Barden Dowling, M. 2000. "The Clemency of Sulla." *Historia* 49:303–340.

Behr, H. 1993. *Die Selbstdarstellung Sullas: Ein aristokratischer Politiker zwischen persönlichem Führungsanspruch und Standessolidarität.* Frankfurt a. M.

Brennan, T. C. 1992. "Sulla's Career in the Nineties: Some Reconsiderations." *Chiron* 22:103–158.

Calabi, I. 1951. "I *Commentarii* di Silla come fonte storica." *MAL* 3:247–302.

Carcopino, J. 1947. *Sylla ou la monarchie manquée.* 2nd ed. Paris.

Champeaux, J. 1987. *Le culte de la fortune dans le monde romain, 2: Les transformations de Fortuna sous la République.* Paris.

Christ, K. 2002. *Sulla. Eine römische Karriere.* Munich.

Degrassi, A. 1967. "Cornelia." In *Scritti vari di antichità* vol. 3, 261–263. Venice and Trieste.

Detienne, M. and Vernant, J-P. 1974. *Les ruses de l'intelligence: La* mètis *des Grecs,* Paris.

Fadinger, V. 2002. "Sulla als *Imperator Felix* und 'Epaphroditos' (= 'Liebling der Aphrodite')." In *Widerstand-Anpassung-Integration: Die griechische Staatenwelt und Rom. Festschrift für Jürgen Deininger zum 65. Geburtstag,* ed. N. Ehrhardt and L.-M. Günther, 155–188. Stuttgart.

Flemberg, J. 1991. *Venus Armata. Studien zur bewaffneten Aphrodite in der griechisch-römischen Kunst.* Stockholm.

Gabba, E. 1967. *Appiani Bellorum civilium liber primus.* Florence.

Habermehl, H. 1955. s.v. "Venerii servi." In *RE* 7 A 1:701–702.

Harris, W. H. 2005. "Constantine's Dream." *Klio* 87:488–494.

Hinard, F. 1985. *Sylla.* Paris.

Hurlet, F. 1993. *La dictature de Sylla: Monarchie ou magistrature républicaine? Essai d'histoire constitutionnelle.* Brussels and Rome.

Jones, C. P. 1971. *Plutarch and Rome.* Oxford.

Keaveney, A. 1983. "Sulla and the Gods." In *Studies in Latin Literature and Roman History* 3, ed. C. Deroux, 44–79. Brussels.

———. 2005. *Sulla: The Last Republican.* 2nd ed. London and New York.

Laffi, U. 1967. "Il mito di Silla." *Athenaeum* 45:177–213, 255–277.

———. 2001. *Studi di storia romana e di diritto*. Rome.

Lanzani, C. 1936. *Lucio Cornelio Silla dittatore: Storia di Roma negli anni 82–78 a.C.* Milan.

Lepore, A. 2004. "Venus Fisica Pompeiana." *Siris* 5:159–169.

Lewis, R. G. 1991. "Sulla's Autobiography: Scope and Economy." *Athenaeum* 79:509–519.

Loraux, N. 1989. *Les expériences de Tirésias: Le féminin et l'homme grec*. Paris.

Marinoni, E. 1987. "Silla, Delfi e l'Afrodite di Afrodisia: Per una interpretazione di Appiano, *B.c.* I 97, 451–55." In *Studi di antichità in memoria di Clementina Gatti*, 193–235. Milan.

Martin, R. T. 1988. "Sulla *imperator iterum*, the Samnites and Roman Republican Coin Propaganda." *SNR* 67:19–45.

Pascucci, G. 1975. "I 'Commentarii' di Silla." *StudUrb(B)* 49:283–295.

Picard, G.-Ch. 1957. *Les trophées romains: Contribution à l'histoire de la religion et de l'art triomphal de Rome*. Paris.

Schilling, R. 1954. *La religion romaine de Vénus, depuis les origines jusqu'au temps d'Auguste*. Paris.

Torelli, M. 1977. "Il santuario greco di Gravisca." *PP* 32:398–458.

Trédé, M. 1992. Kairos. *L'à-propos et l'occasion (le mot et la notion, d'Homère à la fin du IVe siècle avant J.-C.)*. Paris.

Valgiglio, E. 1956. *Silla e la crisi repubblicana*. Florence.

Zecchini, G. 2002. "Sylla selon Salluste." *CCG* 13:45–55.

4

IURE PLECTIMUR
THE ROMAN CRITIQUE OF ROMAN IMPERIALISM

Miriam T. Griffin

G LEN BOWERSOCK HAS TAUGHT US, among other things, to view the Roman empire from the outside in and to look for the cultural coincidences between Greeks and Romans in the time of the late Republic and early Principate. It is therefore with some diffidence that I offer here an investigation into a view of Roman imperialism from the inside out. This Roman point of view certainly incorporates elements of earlier Greek thought and makes contact with the ideas of historians writing in Greek or from a Greek perspective, but it is nonetheless distinctively Roman.

I take my title from Book 2 of *De officiis*, where Cicero discusses the decline of standards in Rome's handling of her *imperium*. He arrives at the topic in a rather indirect way. Having treated in Book 1 the derivation of *officia* or duties from the *honestum*, the honorable or virtuous, he proceeds in Book 2 to discuss duties generated by the *utile* or advantageous—the ultimate aim being to demonstrate that the honorable and the advantageous coincide. Cicero introduces the discussion of the *utile* by arguing that the most advantageous thing one can acquire in life is the support of one's fellow men and that the best way of acquiring their good will is by being loved rather than feared. This is then illustrated by examples of individual tyrants and their fate, including Julius Caesar. Cicero then moves on to Sparta and points out that her unjust command lost her the support of her allies, with the result that she was defeated at the battle of Leuctra (371 BC). Sparta, as ever, suggests Rome and then comes Cicero's nostalgic lament:

Verum tamen quam diu imperium populi Romani beneficiis tenebatur, non iniuriis, bella aut pro sociis aut de imperio gerebantur, exitus erant bellorum aut mites aut neces-sarii, regum populorum nationum portus erat et perfugium senatus, nostri autem magistratus imperatoresque ex hac una re maximam laudem capere studebant, si provincias, si socios aequitate et fide defendissent. Itaque illud patrocinium orbis terrae verius quam imperium poterat nominari.

But as long as the empire of the Roman people was main-tained through benefits and not through injustices, wars were waged either on behalf of allies or about imperial rule; wars were ended with mercy or through necessity; the senate was a haven and refuge for kings, for peoples, and for nations; moreover, our magistrates and generals yearned to acquire the greatest praise from one thing alone, the fair and faithful defense of our provinces and of our allies. In this way we could more truly have been called a protectorate than an empire of the world. (2.26–27).

Then, after discussing the degeneration of Roman imperialism, Cicero comes to its consequences (2.28), the *iure plectimur* ("we are justly punished")—of my title. We shall return to that later.

I. The Code of the Roman Governing Class

First, we should note that Cicero has here given us a sketch of the Roman ideal of imperialism, covering war and acquisition of control, postwar arrangements, and, finally, government and administration. He includes both governmental policy ("the senate," "our") and the conduct of individuals with authority ("magistrates and generals").[1] This latter distinction had already been deployed very effectively by

---

[1] Steel 2001:194 exaggerates in saying that the whole diagnosis is only concerned with personal behavior. The motives given for wars echo 1.38 on just causes for declaring wars and 1.36 on the Fetial procedure; the senate as a *perfugium* alludes to audiences of foreign envoys before the senate, and *patrocinium orbis terrae* expresses metaphorically the relation of the Roman government to its subjects.

Isocrates in his speech *On the Peace*, where he discussed imperialism, notably Spartan imperialism, and the Spartan defeat at Leuctra (96): ἀρχή, he says, fills ἰδιῶται with injustice, lawlessness, and greed, and τὸ κοινὸν τῆς πόλεως with contempt for allies, desire for others' possessions, contempt for oaths, and complaints. It is a distinction that is vital to the actual record of any imperial power, since effective mechanisms to control bad agents and support good ones will only exist if government policy is salutary, while, in reverse, bad conduct by individual agents can undermine even the most salutary policies at the centre. Indeed later in Book 2 of *De officiis*, Cicero will dilate on the third phase of activity, administration of the empire, and show how the governmental policy of controlling extortion had failed through the avarice of Rome's leading men (2.75–77).

Before his discussion of imperialism from the point of view of advantage, Cicero has already outlined in Book 1, in his treatment of justice, the ancestral code of governmental conduct for the first two phases, adducing the Fetial procedure for embarking on a just war and the reception of the defeated *in fidem* (1.35–38). Here the reader is made aware that Cicero is struggling to match the rather legalistic notions of the *mos maiorum* to the demand of moral philosophy that war should only be used as a last resort to maintain peace (Pl. *Leg.* 1.628D; Arist. *Pol.* 1333a35; cf. *Eth. Nic.* 10.7.20). In particular, he finds it hard to justify the destruction of Corinth in 146 BC, for the policy of the Roman *maiores* is said to have been to spare the conquered, except for enemies who have proved themselves monstrously cruel, like Carthage, but Corinth clearly does not fit that exception.[2] In fact, later on in the work he uses the destruction of Corinth as an example of doing something wrong because it seems expedient (3.46). Then again, his own view of how to treat enemies who lay down their arms and seek refuge in the good faith of the general is that we should ensure their protection "even though the battering ram has hammered at their walls" (1.35). This last alludes to the old Roman formula for a surrender that deserves

---

[2] Cicero falls back on its advantageous situation (1.35). The destruction of Numantia could be justified by the consideration mentioned later (1.38) that this was a war for survival, though the claim is dubious.

mercy, but makes it more lenient. We meet it in its traditional form in Caesar's statement to the envoys of the Aduatuci who sued for peace as the Roman siege machines approached: "According to his custom, and not through any merit of theirs, he would preserve their state if they surrendered before the battering ram touched the wall" (*B Gall.* 2.32). Cicero implicitly criticizes Caesar in the interest of giving a rather idealized picture of Roman principles.

And yet, though Cicero is setting higher standards, we need not doubt that there was a Roman code of correct conduct towards enemies and subjects, adherence to which by the government and by individuals governors and agents brought praise, and contravention of which brought blame, if not punishment.[3] Thus, as regards the policy of the government, two famous incidents of the second century BC demonstrate a feeling among some Roman senators, at least, that keeping faith and being honest should be the hallmark of Roman conduct, at least in appearance. When, on the eve of the Third Macedonian War in 171 BC, the king of Macedon was encouraged to negotiate for peace in order to give Rome time to make her preparations for war, Livy reports that the older senators protested against this *nova sapientia*. "It was not," they said, "by pretended flight followed by sudden attacks upon an enemy off his guard, nor with a pride in trickery rather than true valor, that our ancestors waged war. They were accustomed to declare war before they fought it" (Livy 42.47). Then again, the Elder Cato in 167 BC successfully defended before the senate the island of Rhodes which it was proposed to punish for its alleged sympathy for Rome's enemy Macedon: this, it was said, counted as treason, even without overt action. Cato maintained that greed for the riches of Rhodes was the real motive, for wishes and intentions could not be punished unless they issued in action (Gell. *NA* 6.3, *ORF*[2] 8 fr. 167–8).[4] As for the pride of Rhodes, Cato said, "Does that arouse our anger, if someone is

---

[3] Brunt 1978:188–191. Riggsby 2006:158–189 argues for a shared Roman assumption that wars needed to be justified. I have not been able to make systematic use of this interesting book, which only became available when this paper was ready for publication.

[4] Astin 1978:123–124, 128 discusses the relation of Cato's policy to that regarding Lusitania and Carthage (*ORF*[2] 8 fr. 195).

prouder than we?" (fr. 169). The speech was familiar enough at Rome to be discussed by Tiro, praised by Aulus Gellius, and assumed by Livy (45.25.3) to be accessible to his readers in Cato's *Origines*.[5] The institution of a standing court to try cases of extortion in 149 BC and the subsequent efforts to make the law more effective by tightening its provisions and installing more impartial *iudices* shows too that it was felt that Rome's subjects must have some redress, and that it was desirable for the Roman governing class to hold itself to certain basic standards and for the Roman government to enforce them.[6]

As regards individuals in positions of authority, the aristocratic code included, in addition to military glory, the notions of *fides* with regard to Rome's allies, of *clementia* towards the conquered, and of self-restraint, avoiding anger and cruelty in handling those subject to one's authority. "Brave men should be hard on their foes and angry towards them in battle ... but when they conquer, they should be gentle and humane"; so said the Roman commander Flamininus in 197 BC, according to Polybius (18.37.2). It was less a "utilitarian" ethic concerned with the effect of one's conduct on others than an ethic of aristocratic self-respect and honor, though the welfare of the provincials was not completely overlooked.[7] It was still going strong at the end of the Republic. We need only think of the concern Cicero felt that his brother Quintus should bring back a good reputation from his province of Asia, where his governorship had just been extended: a reputation to match that which Cicero felt he had earned in his consulship three years before. "Since so great a theatre has been given for your virtues to display themselves, the whole of Asia, no less, a theatre so crowded, so vast, so expertly critical, and with acoustic properties so powerful that cries and demonstrations echo as far as Rome, pray strive with all your might, not only that you may appear worthy of what was achieved here, but that men

[5] Sallust could assume that his readers would pick up an allusion to Cato's speech in Caesar's contribution to the debate on the fate of the Catilinarian conspirators (*Cat.* 51.5 with McGushin 1977:242; Syme 1964:112–113).

[6] Lintott 1993:97–107, in his succinct history of the court in the Republic and early empire, points to the connection with Rome's reputation.

[7] Cic. Q Fr. 1.1.24: *ut ii qui erunt in eorum imperio sint quam beatissimi.*

may rate your performance above anything that has been seen out there" (*Q Fr.* 1.1.42). Since Asia was a peaceful province, the virtues the older brother spells out are financial honesty, emotional self-control, fairness in dispensing justice, protection of those in his charge, control over the behavior of his staff. Though this letter was clearly intended for wider circulation, Cicero's concern about his brother was real: he makes it clear that Quintus had been criticized for his tendency to anger (7–9) and his manipulation by clever subordinates (17).[8] He was afraid that this could be used as a pretext for prosecution by enemies of the upstart Cicerones.

Then again, Atticus urged that Cicero should bring back a good reputation (*fama*) from governing his province, stressing particularly *abstinentia* and *modestia* (*Att.* 5.9.1, 10.2, 13.1, 14.2, 15.2, 16.3, 21.5 and 7), which Cicero glosses as behaving in accordance with the convictions he voiced in his philosophical work *De re publica* (*Att.* 6.1.8, 6.3.3), where the view that the empire was based on justice had been first attacked, then defended (as discussed below). Cicero wrote repeated descriptions of his own virtuous conduct in his province to influential correspondents. Cato replied that Cicero's reputation for upright government was greater than the traditional celebration of a triumph, which after all gave credit to the gods, not to him (*Fam.* 15.5). No doubt is cast on the existence and power of this code of conduct by the fact that Atticus was later shown to be willing to sacrifice Cicero's integrity to the financial advantage of his friend Brutus (*Att.* 6.2.7–9, 3.5–7), or that Cato was really concerned that a triumph for Cicero would reduce the prospects of one for his brother-in-law Bibulus.[9] For insincerity and hypocrisy of this kind only demonstrate the existence of an acknowledged code of conduct that it is important to be *seen* to uphold.

II. Criticism of Rome's Conduct: Expected Places

The instances cited have included considerable evidence for the violation of the standards that were supposed to be enforced by public

---

[8] See Shackleton Bailey 1965:388.
[9] At least that was Cicero's view (*Att.* 7.2.7, 3.5).

opinion and the courts. Therefore it is not surprising to find that Rome was often criticized by outsiders for hypocrisy in her claims to wage just wars only in defense of herself and her allies: even Cicero admits that the notion of a *iustum bellum* could include wars fought not only *de imperio* (which could include defending the empire[10]) but *de gloria* (*Off.* 1.38). Polybius, writing primarily for a Greek audience, records the kind of criticisms Greeks made.[11] Thus the Macedonians, trying to recruit allies, represented Rome's first venture into imperialism, the acquisition of the province of Sicily (Cic. *2Verr.* 2.2), in this way:

> It was to help the city of Messana that they first crossed into Sicily; the second time was in order to liberate Syracuse, oppressed by the Carthaginians. Both Messana and Syracuse, together with the whole of Sicily, are now in their hands, and they have reduced it to a tax-paying province subject to their rods and axes (Livy 31.29.6, derived from Polybius).

Polybius himself gives his own view that the first war did not violate Rome's treaty with Carthage, but that the mercenary war had no reasonable pretext or motive and was contrary to all justice, a mere act of opportunism (3.26.6–28.2).

Then there are the motives adduced by the Greeks, according to Polybius, for the destruction of Carthage. Two groups cited defended Rome, but the other two felt that the Romans had departed from the principles by which they had won their supremacy: they had moved from a policy of *parcere subiectis*, as Virgil was to call it, to complete extermination, and from a policy of good faith and straightforwardness to deceit and fraud (36.9–11). The mirror image of this is the criticism of Roman aggression in the east, penned by a historian from the western part of the empire. Pompeius Trogus, of the tribe of the Vocontii in southern Gaul, whose family had held Roman citizenship for three generations and served in many Roman campaigns, wrote

---

[10] The defensive aspect of wars for empire is brought out by Cicero at *Off.* 2.26 where, in the phrase *bella aut pro sociis aut de imperio,* he associates them with wars to defend Rome's allies.

[11] Walbank 1972:3–4.

universal history in Latin, probably primarily for an audience in the western provinces.[12] He puts in the mouths of Rome's enemies a number of attacks on Roman imperialism (28.8–14, 29.2–4). The most telling is that of Mithridates, who ends a lengthy oration cataloguing Roman abuses and broken promises: *atque ut ipsi ferunt conditores suos lupae uberibus altos, sic omnem illum populum luporum animos inexplebiles sanguinis atque imperii divitiarumque avidos ac ieiunos habere* ("They themselves say that their founders [Romulus and Remus] were suckled by a wolf. Therefore, as a people, they all have the souls of wolves, insatiable for blood, greedy and starving for empire and wealth" [38.4–7]).[13]

Criticism also came from Romans, as we saw, in the senatorial debates about Macedon and Rhodes. This is not surprising. Deliberative oratory deploys arguments that will move the audience to adopt the policy being advocated by the speaker, and so it appeals, for support of the policy, to the accepted code which it claims is being violated. So, when Cicero is urging passage of a tribunician bill appointing Pompey as general to conduct the war against Mithridates, he argues that, unlike most Roman governors they have seen, who extort money and treasure from their subjects and let their soldiers run wild, the inhabitants of the eastern empire now "at last begin to believe that those self-controlled Romans of legend had actually existed" (*Leg. Man.* 40–41). "Words cannot express," he continues, "how bitterly we are hated among foreign peoples, owing to the wanton and outrageous conduct of the men whom we have in recent years been sending to govern them" (65). The same aim of persuasion explains the criticism of Roman conduct in Cicero's official letters to the senate from Cilicia, in which he is trying to induce them to send more soldiers. "The auxiliary forces furnished by our allies," he writes, "*because of the cruelty and injustice of our rule*, are either so feeble that they cannot give us much help, or so alienated from us that nothing can be expected from them or entrusted to them"

---

[12] Alonso-Núñez 1987:57–58.

[13] Trogus uses indirect speech for this very long and powerful attack, as he disapproved of the rendering of speeches in direct speech by historians like Sallust and Livy (38.3.11). Whether or not he endorses the sentiments of the speech, it represents an attitude plausible to his readers.

(*Fam.* 15.1.5) Cicero may have been trying, as Shackleton Bailey suggests ad loc., to exploit the mood set by Cato when he tried to prevent honors being voted to Caesar by denouncing him in the senate for attacking and killing Germans during a truce, impious behavior that could bring down divine wrath. And Cicero was also hinting at the misconduct of his predecessor Appius Claudius, who would soon be brought to trial.

Cicero in his speeches, according to Catherine Steel, "sees Roman imperialism in terms of individual magistrates: what is at issue is what specific men have done or will do, and when things go wrong they go wrong because of individual misbehaviour and immorality."[14] The conduct of individuals is even more specifically targeted in forensic speeches than in deliberative ones. The existence of courts where misconduct towards Rome's subjects could be prosecuted meant that there must be speeches of accusation, and they would naturally seek to show that the individuals prosecuted had violated the code of acceptable conduct. It is difficult to use such forensic speeches as evidence for genuine Roman concern, since some of these cases were for the accusers a continuation of internal politics by other means, while others were occasioned by provincial complaints taken notice of by highly placed Romans who had some connection with the individuals or the province affected, as Cicero claims was the case with his prosecution of Verres (*Div. Caec.* 66–67; *Off.* 2.50). Moreover, the juries of senators, or of senators and equites, could also be moved by such considerations. Yet, if the jury was not likely to be shocked into conviction by the accused's treatment of Rome's subjects, would a talented orator like Cicero have urged them to deter, by convicting the present miscreant, rampant misconduct by Roman governors, describing it as the cause of lamentation and mourning throughout the empire (*2Verr.* 3.207)?[15]

[14] Steel 2001:190–191.

[15] Whether or not any of the second *actio* was actually delivered by Cicero, it was largely composed before the proceedings ended abruptly, and the techniques and arguments used are similar to those of speeches actually delivered in court (Frazel 2004:128–142; cf. Powell and Paterson 2004:56–57). Brunt 1978:160–161 argued that, in general Cicero's speeches, both when delivered and when published, appealed to the sentiments of their original audiences.

III. Criticism of Roman Conduct: Less Expected Places

Philosophy

The appearance of Roman self-criticism in Cicero's works of moral philosophy makes it hard to deny the existence of real unease. Cicero was writing his philosophical works when it was clear that the Republic was in crisis. His principal discussions of Roman imperialism, in *De re publica* and *De officiis*, occur in works that describe what was good about the Republic in its heyday and how it could be regenerated by a fusion of Greek philosophical precepts with the traditional values of the Roman statesmen of the past. In *De re publica*, written in the late fifties, Cicero is primarily concerned with explaining the excellence of Rome's constitution and the training and dedication of her statesmen in the past; in *De officiis* he prescribes a code of conduct for Romans active in public life, making it clear that the *mos maiorum* effectively got there even without philosophy. Yet, in the first work, we find a debate about whether Rome's acquisition of the empire was just or unjust, while the second makes clear, as we said, that even the conduct of the *maiores* was pretty ruthless.

We see here the particularly unsettling effect of Greek philosophy in the person of Carneades, the head of the Skeptical Academy, who came to Rome as part of an embassy in 155 BC. He took the opportunity to give lectures demonstrating the impossibility of certain knowledge. He argued on one day in favor of the proposition that there is such a thing as natural justice, and on the next that there is no such thing, men being governed entirely by self-interest, which he called *sapientia*. The result of such "wisdom" is the acquisition of "riches, power, resources, honors, commands, rule, for individuals or peoples" (3.24 = Powell 3.18). Such moral questioning was bad enough, but Carneades made things worse by using the Roman empire as an example, showing that it was such wisdom, rather than justice, that had led to Rome's increasing her territory, her wealth, and her control of other peoples. Fragments of his argument remain in *De re publica* and in the Christian fathers, Cicero inverting the order of the two lectures in order that the last word should go to the argument that the Roman empire *was* founded on justice. What survives of this lecture in defense concerns the *iustum bellum* (*Rep.* 3.33–5), the policy of defending allies, and the Aristotelian idea that there are natural rulers and natural subjects to whose advantage it is to be ruled (3.36–7).[16]

Historians

However, the most scathing, and the most surprising, denunciations of Roman imperialism are found in the works of the Roman historians or in quasi-historical works like Caesar's *commentarii*.[17] Even the already-quoted Macedonian denunciation of Rome's invasion of Sicily, though ascribable to Polybius, is in fact found in Livy, who took it over with relish (31.29.6). Many of these indictments, like those in the philosophical writers, are aimed at the total project of empire, not just at bad conduct by individuals or at a particular cynical policy. Thus Sallust gives, in the *Catiline,* a similar picture to Cicero's of the original justice and integrity with which Rome ruled, preferring benefits to fear and pardon to vengeance, but points out that growing *ambitio* and then *avaritia* led to harshness and extortion (*Cat.* 9.4–5, 10.6, 12.5). It is not only Rome's abuses that are lambasted. The whole idea that being ruled by Rome can be beneficial is called into question. Thus Caesar regularly represents the Gauls as fighting for their ancestral freedom against servitude (*B Gall.* 3.8.4, 5.29.4, 7.1.1–4, cf. 8.1.3), and he gives it as his own view that all men by nature desire liberty and hate the condition of slavery (3.10.3). A Roman officer is made to say that Gaul resented the humiliations she had received and regretted her past military glory (5.29.4). Most telling is the rhetoric of the Gallic chieftains, who are said to call on their followers *Galliam in libertatem vindicare* (7.1.6, cf. 76.2), a familiar political slogan of the Romans themselves, to be used by Caesar of himself in the *Bellum Civile* (1.22.5) and, later, to be accorded a place of honor in the first chapter of Augustus' *Res Gestae*. One of these chieftains, Critognatus, gives a passionate indictment of Roman rule:

[16] See Arist. *Pol.* 1327b13–21, 1334a.
[17] See now Riggsby 2006:133–155 on the genre of the *Bellum Gallicum*.

Romani vero quid petunt aliud aut quid volunt, nisi invidia
adducti, quos fama nobiles potentesque bello cognoverunt,
horum in agris civitatibusque considere atque his aeternam
iniungere servitutem? Neque enim ulla alia condicione bella
gesserunt. Quod si ea quae in longinquis nationibus geruntur
ignoratis, respicite finitimam Galliam, quae in provin-
ciam redacta iure et legibus commutatis securibus subiecta
perpetua premitur servitute (7.77).

But the Romans—what else do they seek or desire than to
follow where envy leads, to settle in the lands and states
of men whose noble report and martial strength they have
learnt, and to bind upon them a perpetual slavery? For this is
the fashion in which they have waged wars. And if you do not
know what happens in distant countries, look at Gaul next
door. It has been reduced to a province, its rights and laws
have been changed, and it is crushed beneath the Roman
axes in everlasting slavery.[18]

Then there is Roman hypocrisy, which is well exposed by Ariovistus,
the German leader invited into Gaul by a Gallic tribe at odds with
Rome's allies the Aedui. Only the year before he had been made, with
the support of Caesar himself as consul, *socius et amicus populi Romani*
(*B Gall.* 1.35), but now Caesar, as part of his defense of the Aedui, was
ordering him to leave Gaul. Ariovistus says that he is not so uncivilized
or so naive (*neque tam barbarum neque tam imperitum*) as not to know
that the Romans and the Aedui had not supported each other in recent
conflicts: he was right to suspect that Caesar, under the pretext of this
connection, had brought his army into Gaul in order to crush him (*B
Gall.* 1.44.9–10). He has already (1.44.5) exploded the treasured Roman
euphemism, *amicitia populi Romani*:

---

[18] On Critognatus' oration in direct speech, the longest in the *Bellum Gallicum*, see now
Riggsby 2006:104, cf. 89–91, who points out that though the speech is introduced as being
of singular and nefarious cruelty (*B Gall.* 7.77.3) because of its suggestion of cannibalism,
this does not affect its credibility on the subject of true vs. apparent *virtus*. He also argues
for its success as a speech by Roman standards (118).

Amicitiam populi Romani sibi ornamento et praesidio, non detrimento esse oportere, idque se ea spe petisse. Si per populum Romanum stipendium remittatur et dediticii subtrahantur, non minus libenter sese recusaturum populi Romani amicitiam, quam appetierit.

The friendship of the Roman people ought to be a distinction and a protection to him, not a damaging loss, and he had sought it with that hope. If, through the actions of the Roman people, his tribute were to be withdrawn and his captives returned, he would renounce the friendship of the Roman people as earnestly as he had sought it.[19]

This exposure of what Roman friendship really means can be matched by Sallust's exposure in the *Iugurtha* of what it really means to be even a hereditary *socius et amicus*. Coming to Rome to appeal for help after being driven from his share of his father's kingdom by his adopted brother Jugurtha (13), Adherbal pleads that it would be becoming to the majesty of the Roman people to defend him against wrong (14.7), for his father Micipsa maintained "that those who diligently cultivated your friendship undertook an arduous duty indeed, but were safe beyond all others" (14.12).[20] It is possible for us to defend Rome's policy in Numidia, since this civil war had been brought about by Micipsa's own arrangements; and Adherbal himself acknowledges (14.20) that Jugurtha had friends in Rome, the historian himself having shown us that he had served with distinction at Numantia (7.4). But Sallust goes out of his way to describe Adherbal's cause as *bonum et aequum* (15.3) and to ascribe the senate's leniency towards Jugurtha to bribery (15.2, 16.1). Then, for his *Histories*, Sallust constructs a letter of Mithridates (4.69 M. = McGushin 4.67) that is a match for the speech in Pompeius Trogus, calling the Romans *latrones gentium* ("plunderers of all the nations"). Mithridates

---

[19] Christ 1974 shows how Caesar himself brings out the contradiction between the Roman interpretation of friendship with the Aedui, which involves Rome in obligations, and their interpretation of friendship with Ariovistus, which involves only him in obligations.

[20] Lintott 1972:634.

gives a long recital of the progress of Rome's *cupido profunda imperi et divitiarum* ("deep-seated desire for dominion and riches") via pacts of friendships which are then abandoned or betrayed (5–9).

Tacitus' *Agricola* contains probably the most famous of the great barbarian speeches composed by Roman historians. This is the address by Calgacus, "preeminent in valor and birth" (29), to the assembled tribes before the battle of Mons Graupius. All the themes mentioned so far are found here: Rome's increasing greed and abuse of power; the preferability of self-rule over being ruled by others; the cynical distortion of language that Rome employs. Calgacus warns his people that they cannot escape Roman *superbia* by obedience or self-restraint (*per obsequium et modestiam*, 30.4):

> Raptores orbis, postquam cuncta vastantibus defuere terrae, mare scrutantur: si locuples hostis est, avari, si pauper, ambitiosi, quos non Oriens, non Occidens satiaverit: soli omnium opes atque inopiam pari adfectu concupiscunt. Auferre trucidare rapere falsis nominibus imperium, atque ubi solitudinem faciunt, pacem appellant (30.5).

> Looters of the world, now that earth is failing to satisfy their all-devastating hands, they probe even the sea: if their enemy have wealth, they have greed; if he be poor, they are ambitious. Neither East nor West has glutted them; alone of mankind they covet with the same passion poverty and wealth. To plunder, butcher, steal, these things they misname empire, and where they make a desert they call it peace.

Tacitus, it has been argued, presents a picture of Britain as the repository of Old Roman Values. "Britain in its pristine state, as represented by Calgacus at Mons Graupius, is the location of true *eloquentia* and *virtus*," and, of course, of *libertas*.[21] Certainly the reply of Agricola is no match in length and power for this diatribe, especially as Calgacus uses some of the Romans' own rhetorical tricks to great effect, complaining of the *superbia* of the enemy and appealing to the *virtus*

---

[21] Clarke 2001:107.

of his people's *maiores* (32.4, 30.3). Moreover, Agricola has earlier been shown implementing the cynical Roman policy of enervating subjects prone to war by introducing them to the softening effects of civilization: urban life and the delights of education. The historian's famous line, *idque apud imperitos humanitas vocabatur, cum pars servitutis esset* ("The innocent natives gave the name of 'culture' to what was part of their enslavement." [21.2]) prompted one editor of the *Agricola* to remark, "The attitude of Tacitus, himself an administrator, towards the policy of conquest by assimilation is remarkable."[22]

Even the speech that Tacitus gives to the Roman commander Petilius Cerealis in his *Histories*,[23] usually cited as the classic defense of Roman imperialism, has a sinister subtext. Cerialis offers the Gauls a stark choice of *obsequium cum securitate* or *contumacia cum pernicie* (*Hist.* 4.74.4), making clear that *libertas* is not an option (73.3).[24] Moreover, it is chilling to hear the Roman commander urge that no one intent on *servitium* and *dominatio* fails to use the specious name of *libertas* (4.73), in the context of German interference in Gaul: we cannot but recall Caesar's telling Ariovistus that the Roman senate wanted Gaul to be free (*B Gall.* 1.45).

IV. Origins and Explanations of Roman Self-Criticism

It remains to try and explain this powerful vein of Roman self-criticism. One need not assume that any of these Roman authors wished to give up the delights of imperialism: indeed, Caesar clearly counted on getting away with murder because of the glory and booty he secured for Rome, while Tacitus makes clear his contempt for a Princeps like Tiberius who was uninterested in expanding the empire (*Ann.* 4.32: *princeps incuriosus proferendi imperi,* cf. *Agr.* 13.2).[25] Even Cicero assumed that it was the

---

[22] R. M. Ogilvie, in Ogilvie and Richmond 1967:228.

[23] Bastomsky 1988 argues that the Roman commander, while ostensibly supporting Roman imperialism, is criticizing it.

[24] Nor does he offer any middle ground between *abrupta contumacia* and *deforme obsequium*, such as Tacitus' hero Marcus Aemilius Lepidus was to offer Roman senators in the *Annals* (*Ann.* 4.20, cf. *Agr.* 42.4).

[25] For Caesar's imperialist aims and the approval of them by his Roman contemporaries, see Brunt 1978:178 = 183. Even in the *Agricola* 14 (cf. *Ann.* 14.29) Tacitus praises governors of Britain who added territory and disparages those who did not (see Mattern 1999:171n34).

duty of those in authority *quibuscumque rebus vel belli vel domi poterunt, rem publicam augeant imperio, agris, vectigalibus* ("by whatever means they can, whether in war or at home, to increase the republic in power, in territory, and in revenues"), just as their ancestors had (*Off.* 2.85).

If Cicero's critique is partly explained by the philosophical doubts stirred by Carneades, that of the historians can be partly explained by the example of Thucydides. He had made Pericles describe the Athenian empire as being like a tyranny, the product of ruthless ambition, and the object of hatred (2.63), though he still showed enthusiasm for the Periclean policies that had brought it to its peak. He makes it clear that the Athenians regarded wealth as a prime motive of empire (1.75, 2.64.3).[26] Like Thucydides on his native Athens, the Roman historians stress ruthless ambition and greed in Rome's exercise of imperial power, and the dislike of Rome's imperial subjects for slavery. But there are significant differences in the criticism. The Roman historians lay more stress on their *patria*'s imperialist deceit and hypocrisy, which is more prominent in Thucydides' Spartans (e.g., 3.32.2, 68.4)[27] than in his Athenians, who are shockingly honest in their rhetoric. The Roman historians insist on Roman decadence and luxury, and they show a greater tendency to let the subjects have their say, evincing their determination to free themselves. This last is all the more striking as the adversaries we have been considering are barbarians, whereas Athens was dominating her fellow-Greeks.

Commentators have tended to treat the speeches as "rhetoric," i.e., literary embellishment, or as the conscientious reporting of "what was thought,"[28] or as a portrayal of Rome' adversaries as "so Roman that they traditionally bring out the best in their Roman counterparts."[29] Yet none of these explanations does justice to the statements *in propria*

---

[26] See Hornblower 1991:ad locc.

[27] Hornblower 1991:246, 454, 462–463.

[28] Fuchs 1938, cf. Balsdon 1979:182. See Riggsby 2006:327n18 on the view that a Roman author would not want to disfigure his text with a substandard speech.

[29] Liebeschuetz 1961:138 thinks "Tacitus introduced the theme of liberty into the British section of the *Agricola* because it provided an issue which could be used to dramatize his hero's achievements there," military and apparently civil (Liebeschuetz 1961:136–137); Cf. Martin 1981:44; Clarke 2001:109, though it is not really her view (see below n45).

persona made by these historians, nor to the vehemence of Roman self-criticism in the speeches and the emotional, not just intellectual, sympathy with which the resentment of the conquered is presented.[30] The last of the explanations mentioned above is perhaps the most plausible. And yet Plutarch, who in his *Life* of Caesar made use of the *commentarii* (22.2) and certainly enhances Caesar's success by stressing the power of his enemies in numbers and ferocity (15.3, 18.1, 19.2, 20.3 and 4, 25.2, 27.2), does not make use of such rhetoric: there are no barbarian speeches and no exposure of Roman hypocrisy. Another Greek writer, Cassius Dio, who also used the *commentarii* for his account of the Gallic war (38.36–46),[31] gives a more balanced account,[32] to which one might think that generating sympathy for the enemy might contribute. But he allows Ariovistus only a few lines, in which he is more explicit (and hence less effective) than in Caesar's account about his claim to equality and less telling in his exposure of Roman methods: it is Dio himself who accuses Caesar of deliberately provoking him to give a pretext for war (38.34.5–6). We need to try again to explain the vehemence of Roman self-criticism in the Roman historians.

Both Cicero in his philosophical works and the Roman historians set themselves didactic purposes, addressing both the *honestum* and the *utile* (Tac. *Ann.* 4.33.2). Certainly, one can see in this Roman self-criticism the latter, pragmatic, ingredient. The Romans were aware that they held down a large empire with relatively few forces and administered

[30] There have been attempts to show that Caesar deliberately sabotaged the freedom rhetoric of the Gauls and Germans (Rambaud 1966:311–324) or of the non-friendly Gauls and Germans (Barlow 1998), and Martin 1981:44 finds it incompatible with the eulogistic purpose of the *Agricola* that Tacitus could have been endorsing what he made Calgacus say, though he admits that Tacitus often shows ambivalence of judgement. See also Mattern in n42 below. But on Caesar, see n18 and Riggsby 2006:117, while Liebeschuetz 1961:137 points out that in the *Agricola*, "Neither in the case of Calgacus, nor in that of some of the other barbarian leaders, does Tacitus insert any disparaging comments about the speaker which might detract from the effect of the speech, in the way in which he was to detract from the more moving speech of a leader of mutinous legionaries," i.e., *Ann.* 1.16.

[31] Millar 1964:55.

[32] Dio shows Caesar in serious military difficulty (40.6.3), behaving more harshly towards Vercingetorix than the spectators would like, who show pity (40.41, cf. Plut. *Caes.* 27.5 who is less sympathetic), and notes that Vercingetorix was counting on their earlier good relations.

it only with the help of local leaders. It was necessary to prevent revolt, if possible, and the best way to prevent unrest was to secure and retain loyalty and good will. As Cicero wrote from his province of Cilicia, at that time under threat from a Parthian invasion:

> Mihi ut in eius modi re tantoque bello maximae curae est ut, quae copiis et opibus tenere vix possumus, ea mansuetudine et continentia nostra, sociorum fidelitate teneamus (*Fam.* 15.3.2, cf. 15.4.14).

> In such a situation and in the face of such a serious war, my main concern is that what we can hardly retain by troops and resources, we should retain by our mildness and self-restraint and the loyalty of our allies.

This was written to Cato the moralist, but we have already seen that in his letter to the senate asking for more troops, Cicero expected that body to accept the link between the ruthlessness of the previous governor and current problems of control. Then, in *De officiis*, he follows his lament about the crescendo of extortion laws and their failure with the frightening thought that Rome only retains her empire by the weakness of others, not through her own *virtus* (2.75). Given the context, namely, the growth of *avaritia*, Cicero must mean that Rome no longer controls her subjects through good will based on just conduct.[33] As Diodorus Siculus was to say, "to rule subjects equitably and creditably—that is much the best way to maintain and extend an empire" (34/35.33.5).

This is more hard-headedness than high-mindedness, and it helps to account for the willingness of Romans to prosecute each other for misconduct in the provinces, for breaches of faith, for cruelty, and for financial corruption. Bad government on the part of a few, they realized, could endanger the profits of the rest. As was said by Thomas Babington Macaulay, historian and classicist, of Warren Hastings, the

---

[33] Cf. Diod. Sic. 36.3.1 where the king of Bithynia tells Marius that he cannot send military support because the majority of the Bithynians have been seized by tax farmers and are in slavery in the Roman provinces, and the senate's counter measures fail in Sicily because the governor there succumbs to bribery, cf. Dio Cass. 27.93.

ruthless Governor General of India, who was tried in the eighteenth century before the House of Lords for High Crimes and Misdemeanours: "The rules of Justice, the sentiments of humanity, the plighted faith of treaties, were in his view as nothing, when opposed to the *immediate* interests of the State. This is no justification, according to the principles either of morality or, of what we believe to be identical with morality, namely far-sighted policy." Macaulay himself had just returned from India. He knew what he was talking about.

Cicero agreed too with the last point, that the *honestum* and the long-term *utile* were here identical. Indeed, the passage just mentioned from Book 2 of *De officiis* suggests a more general *moral* decline in the phrase: "through the weakness of others, not through our own *virtus*" (2.75). The context may be *avaritia*, as we said, but is there not also a hint that Rome no longer has the military virtues needed to defend her empire, because those virtues have been undermined by wealth and luxury, the fruits of extortion? We mentioned that, in contrast to Thucydides, the Roman writers lay more stress on the softening up of moral fibre through wealth and luxury. Thucydides, who sees in the customs of barbarians and people in the remote parts of Hellas what had been the past habits of the Greeks, thinks that things have improved with the elimination of piracy, brigandage, and tyranny, and with progress in the arts and the sciences (1.1–17). However, the idea that degeneration leads to loss of empire also has roots in the Greek tradition. We can hardly embark here on a full exploration, but one important ingredient, the notion of a succession of world empires, each acquired through qualities of excellence and lost through degeneration, can be traced back to Herodotus (1.95–130) and Ctesias (Diod. Sic. 2.21, 23, 24.4) where it was picked up by the writers of the Roman period, Polybius and Diodorus writing in Greek and Pompeius Trogus in Latin (7.1.4, 12.3.8–12, 4.1).[34] The potent idea that imperialism carries

---

[34] Momigliano 1982:77–103. The bare notion of the mutability of fortune fed the anti-Roman propaganda of the last century of the Republic which expressed eastern hopes that Rome too would fall, and called forth tears from Scipio, fearing that Rome would follow Troy, Assyria, Media, Persia, Macedon, and Carthage (Polyb. 38.21; Diod. Sic. 32.24; App. *Lib.*132).

the seeds of its own destruction is already present in the telling last chapter of Herodotus (9.122) where the Persian King Cyrus reacts negatively to a suggestion that the Persians, now that they rule a great territory and a great number of subjects, should move to a bigger and more fertile land. If they do, he says, they must be prepared to be no longer the rulers but the ruled, for "from soft countries come soft men."[35]

The Elder Cato had worried about Rome's being carried away by excessive power and prosperity; he noted that many people feared reduction to servitude by her if she had no one left to fear (*ORF*[2] 8 fr. 163–4). It may be symptomatic of the effect on a Greek intellectual of his close ties to Rome that Posidonius,[36] while valuing (like Thucydides) the progress of these arts of civilization (Sen. *Ep.* 90), also celebrates the Romans' pristine frugality, hardiness, and piety, apparently alluding to later decline (*FGrH* 87 F 59 = F 265–267 E-K).[37] Possibly drawing on Posidonius, Diodorus, a Sicilian who claimed to read Latin but wrote in Greek and who wrote and resided in Rome ca. 56–30 BC (1.4.2–4), describes the warnings of Scipio Nasica about the effects of destroying Carthage, Rome's only effective rival, and frequently marks the moral deterioration of the Romans after that event, seeing a consequent increase in avarice, greed, and cruelty in the way she ruled her subjects (e.g., 34/35.33, 5.26.3). He also exhibits a particular strain of admiration for warlike barbarians, which, though it ultimately has its roots in Greek appreciations of plain-living barbarians, also chimes in with Cato's glorification of Sabine austerity and hard work (*ORF*[2] 8 fr. 128): thus the Spanish chieftain Viriathus exhibited many of the qualities of simplicity and toughness that make a good warrior, and could claim to have a kind of self-taught virtue (Diod. Sic. 33.7.5),[38] as Pompeius Trogus was to say

---

[35] That Herodotus is not just applying environmental determinism in a purely biological sense, as is found in Hippoc. *Aer.* 1.126, 7.102–3, but takes account of custom and lifestyle, here the enervating effects of wealth on a military people, is shown by Thomas 2000:108–111.

[36] Momigliano 1975:35–36 argues that Polybius was explaining to Greeks and Romans why the Romans were bound to win, while Posidonius took the Roman victory for granted and spoke out to remind the Roman rulers of their errors and misdeeds.

[37] Yarrow 2006:196.

[38] On these ideas, see Strasburger 1965:47–48; Malitz 1983:90–94, 122–124, 426–427. The

of the Scythians (2.5.14–15).[39] The same mix of potentially conflicting attitudes is found in Cicero, whose admiration for the useful arts and material progress, perhaps taken over from Panaetius (*Off.* 2.15), does not dim his concern for the deleterious effects of wealth and luxury. Trogus too, writing under Augustus in the Greek historical tradition but in the Latin language, attached to his native Gallia Narbonensis as well as to his Roman citizenship,[40] was to celebrate the austerity of the ancient Romans (28.2.7–10, 31.8.8–9) and lament its corruption through wealth (36.4.12), while approving the civilizing effects of the Greeks of Massilia on the Gauls (43.4.1–2) and later of Augustus' conquest on the Spaniards (44.5.8). Augustan ideology inherited and developed the ambiguous mix. In Livy's portrayal of Rome's founder, his virtues of simplicity and self-sufficiency come from his rustic background, but he founds a great city that challenges the ascendancy of the country-side. As Vergil put it: *Hanc olim veteres vitam coluere Sabini, / hanc Remus et frater, sic fortis Etruria crevit / scilicet, et rerum facta est pulcherrima Roma* (*G.* 2.532–534).

A recent study of Livy by Gary Miles points to two explanations of this curious mixture of attitudes: first, "imperialist nostalgia," a modern conception pointing to a denial of responsibility for the destruction of a previous simpler society by asserting regret for it, or, second, an attempt to cope with violent social change by reasserting "traditional values."[41] Yet, again, neither of these ideas does justice to the vehemence of Roman self-criticism, voiced by writers who were themselves engaged in the running of the empire. A better explanation lies in the Roman consciousness that it was precisely those qualities of courage, austerity, and independence that had first made them rulers. When Caesar writes, "The Belgae are the bravest of all because they are furthest from the culture and civilization of our province,

---

question of how far Diodorus derives from Posidonius (given that he clearly used him for the Sicilian slave revolt, as is shown by the similarity of Athenaeus 12.59 quoting Posidonius to Diod. Sic. 34.34) is now heavily disputed: see Yarrow 2006:116–117, cf. 103; Griffin 1985:568–570.

[39] See Alonso-Núñez 1987:66–67.

[40] Yarrow 2006:346–347.

[41] Miles 1988:137–178, esp. 172–176.

and since they are least often visited by merchants introducing the commodities that make for effeminacy"(*B Gall.* 1.1), we know that he is thinking of the effect of those amenities and luxuries on the Romans themselves. So was Tacitus, when he wrote about the Gauls and Britons losing valor along with liberty (*Agr.* 11.4) and described the softening up policies of Agricola: perhaps his observations were not after all so remarkable an attitude for a Roman administrator and general (above, p99). Seneca says that if once the brave and strong, but impetuous, barbarians acquire discipline, while still remaining strangers to wealth and excess, "we Romans shall have to return to our ancient ways" (*De Ira* 1.11.4). Perhaps the barbarians are already "more Roman than the Romans." Arminius is made to forswear the use of treachery against the Romans (*Ann.* 1.59.3), just as Tiberius is to do against him (2.88). Tacitus has the British leaders reverse the usual Roman rhetoric, claiming that they have *constantia*, the Romans only *impetus* (*Agr.* 15.4). The German chieftains, like Calgacus, impute *superbia* to the Romans (*Ann.* 2.15.3) and appeal to the virtue of their own ancestors (2.10, 1.59 [*antiqua*]).[42]

Those ancient ways, those pristine warrior qualities, the Romans were losing to the wealth and power that went with imperialism (Sall. *Cat.* 9–10, 12.5). There were other costs of imperialism too. The famous lines of Anchises about Rome's destiny being to govern hint at a choice to be made: others will shape finer statues of bronze and portraits in marble; others will speak more eloquently and chart the heavenly bodies with science (Verg. *Aen.* 6.847–850). Yet Cicero thought the Romans could match even Greek philosophy, and Vergil carefully omits literature in his comparison of artistic achievement. He probably thought his poem could stand comparison with both of Homer's epics.

Cicero thought there was a far more serious cost than culture. In the passage of *De officiis* with which we started, after his description of the degeneration of the Roman empire from a *patrocinium orbis terrae* in

---

[42] The use of the inverse of Roman rhetoric by the barbarians is noted by Mattern 1999:175–176, but she takes this to be a way of indicating the arrogance of the enemy making boasts that are only appropriate to Romans. Riggsby 2006:126–132 discusses the blurring of the Roman/non-Roman line by Caesar in *Bellum Gallicum*, relating it to his political vision of broadening the franchise and extending the boundaries of Italy.

the days of our ancestors, Cicero goes on to explain the consequences. He cannot say, as the parallel with Sparta would suggest, that Rome by losing the good will of her subjects has lost her empire, because she patently had not. In fact, the empire stood at its greatest extent since its inception. When he says at 2.28 that Caesar's recent treatment of Massilia affords an "example to oppressed and devastated nations abroad of the loss of empire (*exemplum amissi imperii*)," he means of the loss of empire we deserve to experience. But his phrase, "We are justly punished" points to a different loss: it means the loss of Republican freedom. As he says in the next chapter (2.29), "The republic we have utterly lost. And we have fallen into this disaster—for I must return to my proposition—because we prefer to be feared than to be held dear and loved. If these things could happen to the Roman people when they ruled unjustly, what ought individuals to think?"[43]

What is the connection, then, that Cicero sees between the excesses of imperialism and the loss of political freedom? "If we had not tolerated the crimes of many men going unpunished, such extreme licence would never have come into the hands of one man" (*Off.* 2.28). The latest commentary suggests that Cicero is interpreting Caesar's victory as divine punishment for the treatment of Rome's allies.[44] But this cannot be right. For one thing, Cicero has just said, when discussing our greatest sources of support and injury, that the gods cannot do harm (2.12): he is, in fact, taking in this work the Stoic view of a totally beneficent god. What Cicero means is that general lawlessness and self-indulgence in the provinces led to lack of discipline and self-restraint at home too. Greed and ambition and the resulting inequalities of wealth and power endangered the oligarchic equality and solidarity of the governing class, on which the Republic rested. Caesar acquired an enormous army and heaps of booty in Gaul because standards had become so lax: with these he could and did seize power because he had

---

[43] Steel 2001:94 comments on the "strained logic" of this passage, accounting for it by Cicero's emphasis on the immorality of individual governors "inasmuch as fleecing the provincials, although an excellent example of personal depravity, could not be said to have led directly to the fall of the Republic."

[44] Dyck 1996:405. *Pis.* 85 shows that Cicero could talk of divine vengeance for misconduct in war. See the view of Cato, above, p93.

no self-restraint, and, with Roman moral fibre gone, no one could really stand up to him. Even after his death, many imitated him (*Off.* 2.38: *a quo quidem rei familiaris ad paucos, cupiditatum ad multos improbos venit hereditas,* cf. *Phil.* 8.9). Cicero had already put the threat into Laelius' mouth as a prediction in *De re publica.* There, after something about Asia (probably the wealth of Asia acquired through the legacy of Attalus), Tiberius Gracchus is said to have violated the *iura ac foedera* of Rome's allies. "If this habit of lawlessness begins to spread and changes our rule (*imperium*) from one of justice to one of force, so that those who up to the present have obeyed us willingly are held faithful by fear alone, then ... I am anxious for the permanent stability of our *res publica,* which might live on for ever, if the principles and customs of our ancestors were maintained" (3.41, cf. 5.2). Writing not long after, Diodorus says that the Social War and the civil war of Marius and Sulla were caused by the abandonment of a frugal and austere style of life for luxury and licence after the destruction of Carthage (37.2.1, 37.2.12). The two spheres of domestic politics and foreign policy were inextricably linked. Cicero blames the proscriptions for hardening the Romans to cruelty to their own citizens, which then made nothing seem unjust towards allies (2.27), that unjust treatment then leading to civil war and the dictatorship with further confiscation and intimidation. How far the Romans had sunk, he shows by the word *plectimur,* which comes to mean "to punish" because whipping is the common way to punish slaves. The irony of Roman imperialism was that those who had acquired and ruled the empire became subjects themselves.

Cicero's lament looks forward to the imperial writers like Lucan and Florus, who also traced the civil strife in which the Republic perished to the enhanced ambition and excessive prosperity brought about by imperial expansion (Florus 1.47.8; Luc. 1.84–114). Imperial writers like Lucan contrasted barbarian freedom with their own loss of liberty (Luc. 7.432–441) or, like Tacitus, drew parallels between the threat to barbarian freedom and the loss already sustained by the Roman senators.[45] The idea is expressed in modern institutional terms by Fergus

[45] Liebeschuetz 1961:138–139 thinks the drawing of the parallel in the *Agricola* is unconscious but real "because a Roman senator's experience of subjection to an emperor

Millar: "The evolution of monarchy in Rome could be described ... as the importation into the city of the attributes and functions of a supreme and permanent provincial governor."[46]

That consequence was already clear with Caesar's victory. Cicero himself is credited with a witticism that brings the point home. I mean the famous encounter between Cicero and a Greek he knew from his days as governor of Cilicia (*Fam.* 13.67). This Greek, Andron of Laodicea, had come to seek an audience with Caesar the Dictator and, seeing Cicero, greeted him. Cicero asked why he had come to Rome. "Oh," said Andron, "I have come on an embassy to Caesar to ask for the freedom of my city (*de libertate patriae*)." Quick as a flash, Cicero replied, "Well, if you succeed with him, you might put in a plea for us too."[47]

SOMERVILLE COLLEGE, UNIVERSITY OF OXFORD

Bibliography

Alonso-Núñez, J. M. 1987. "An Augustan World History: The *Historiae Philippicae* of Pompeius Trogus." *G&R* 34:56–72.

Astin, A. 1978. *Cato the Censor.* Oxford.

Balsdon, J. P. V. D. 1979. *Romans and Aliens.* London.

Barlow, J. 1988. "Noble Gauls and the others in Caesar's Propaganda." In *Julius Caesar as Artful Reporter*, ed. K. Welch and A. Powell, 139–170. London.

Bastomsky, S. J. 1988. "Tacitus, *Histories* IV, 73–74." *Latomus* 47:412–416.

Brunt, P. A. 1978. "Laus Imperii." In *Imperialism in the Ancient World*, ed. P. D. A. Garnsey and C. R. Whittaker, 159–191 and 319–330. Cambridge. Repr. in Brunt, P. A. 1990. *Roman Imperial Themes.* 288–323. Oxford.

---

lies behind every part of the work," but cf. Clarke 2001:106–109, who regards the parallels as intentional.

[46] Millar 1977:17.

[47] Macrob. *Sat.* 2.3.12: *quippe ab Androne quodam Laodiceno salutatus, cum causam adventus requisisset comperissetque—nam ille se legatum de libertate patriae ad Caesarem venisse respondit—ita expressit publicam servitutem* "ἐὰν ἐπιτύχῃς, καὶ περὶ ἡμῶν πρέσβευσον." Cic. *Att.* 14.1.2 might suggest the encounter took place in Caesar's waiting room.

Christ, K. 1974. "Caesar und Ariovistus." *Chiron* 4:251–291.

Clarke, K. 2001. "An Island Nation: Re-reading Tacitus' *Agricola*." *JRS* 91:94–112.

Dyck, A. R. 1996. *A Commentary on Cicero, De Officiis*. Michigan.

Frazel, T. D. 2004. "The Composition and Circulation of Cicero's *In Verrem*." *CQ* 54:128–142.

Fuchs, H. 1938. *Der geistige Widerstand gegen Rom in der antiken Welt.* Berlin.

Griffin, M. 1985. Review of J. Malitz, *Die Historien des Poseidonios. Gnomon* 57:568–570.

Hornblower, S. 1991. *A Commentary on Thucydides. Vol. I: Books I–III.* Oxford.

Liebeschuetz,W. 1961. "The Theme of Liberty in the *Agricola* of Tacitus." *CQ* 16:126–139.

Lintott, A. W. 1972. "Imperial Expansion and Moral Decline in the Roman Republic." *Historia* 21:626–638.

———. 1993. *Imperium Romanum.* London and New York.

McGushin, P. 1977. *C. Sallustius Crispus,* Bellum Catilinae: *A Commentary.* Leiden.

Malitz, J. 1983. *Die Historien des Poseidonios.* Munich.

Martin, R. H. 1981. *Tacitus.* London.

Mattern, S. 1999. *Rome and the Enemy.* Berkeley, CA.

Miles, G. B. 1998. *Livy: Reconstructing Early Rome.* Ithaca, NY and London.

Millar, F. 1964. *A Study of Cassius Dio.* Oxford.

———. 1977. *The Emperor and the Roman World.* London.

Momigliano, A. 1975. *Alien Wisdom.* Cambridge.

———. 1984. "The Origins of Universal History." In *Settimo contributo alla storia degli studi classici,* 77–103. Rome.

Ogilvie, R. M. and Richmond, I. 1967. *Cornelii Taciti* De Vita Agricolae. Oxford.

Powell, J. and Paterson, J. 2004. "Introduction." In *Cicero the Advocate,* ed. Powell and Paterson, 1–57. Oxford.

Rambaud, M. 1966. *L'art de la déformation historique dans les Commentaires de César.* Paris.

Riggsby, A. 2006. *Caesar in Gaul and Rome.* Austin, TX.

Shackleton Bailey, D. R. 1965. *Cicero's Letters to Atticus*, vol. 1. Cambridge.

Steel, C. E. W. 2001. *Cicero, Rhetoric, and Empire.* Oxford.

Strasburger, H. 1965. "Poseidonios on Problems of the Roman Empire." *JRS* 55:40–53.

Syme, R. 1964. *Sallust.* Berkeley, CA.

Thomas, R. 2000. *Herodotus in Context.* Cambridge.

Walbank, F. 1972. *Polybius.* Berkeley, CA.

Yarrow, L. M. 2006. *Historiography at the End of the Republic.* Oxford.

5

THE SURVIVAL OF THE SOPHISTS

CHRISTOPHER JONES

THERE HAVE BEEN THREE CROPS of public speakers. The first
spoke without written texts, that of Themistocles,
Pericles, and the orators contemporary with them. The
second spoke with texts, that of Demosthenes, Aeschines,
Isocrates, and with them the established group of ten rhetors.
These crops came about in Athens. But a third crop of these
is a gift of fortune to Asia, that of Polemo, Herodes, Aristides,
and the orators who existed in those times. The third crop,
by which I mean that which came from Asia, produced that
wise and wonderful man, Aristides. He was among the most
famous, and much more, and very sober and superior to
money, as he himself has said in his speech *In Defense of the
Four.*

This summary history of Greek rhetoric comes from Sopater, the
fourth century writer on Aristides.[1] It is immediately obvious how
different Sopater's emphases are from those of Philostratus in his *Lives
of the Sophists*: there is no Second Sophistic, but a "third crop"; this third
crop, even Herodes Atticus, comes from Asia; and its representative at
the center of Sopater's interest is Aristides, who is praised in terms that
might surprise: "wise," "wonderful," "sober" (*sōphrōn*) and above material considerations.

Sopater may serve as the starting-point for studying the after-life
or the survival of the sophists of the Second Sophistic down to the fifth

---

[1] *PLRE* 2.1020, Sopater 2; M. Winterbottom, *Neue Pauly* 11.720, Sopatros 1.

century, with some glimpses beyond. By such a study, I hope in the first place to connect two of Glen Bowersock's interests, his seminal work on Greek sophists in the Roman empire, and his many studies of Late Antiquity, of which in this context it is appropriate to mention that most sophistic of Roman emperors, Julian.

I will argue that Philostratus' concept of a Second Sophistic did not find much echo in antiquity, however much it pinpoints a real phenomenon in Roman imperial history and however useful it is as an analytical tool. His *Lives of the Sophists* survived not as a critical essay on rhetoric, but as a quarry for biographical information; in other words, it became a kind of technical treatise. By the same token, his relative valuation of those he called "sophists" did not establish itself as canonical. When a canon of the Second Ten Orators was finally formed, it did not follow Philostratus, and conversely orators greatly admired by Philostratus, such as Herodes Atticus, soon lost ground to others whom he admired less, such as Aristides. I shall try to follow this process of re-evaluation, so far as it can now be followed, and then try to account for it, and in particular for the predominance of Aristides.

If Philostratus did not impose his views on posterity, that is in part because he was a snob. For him two cities counted above all, Athens and Smyrna; the two others of the "big three" of Asia, Ephesus and Pergamum, come in tied for a distant third. Athens and Smyrna had many links in common, among others the belief that Smyrna was a colony of Athens, and institutions such as the hoplite general. For Philostratus, Smyrna excels all cities of Ionia as a shrine of the Muses, "like the bridge of a musical instrument."[2] His king of sophists is Herodes Atticus, educated in Smyrna and the dominant figure of second-century Athens. Philostratus addresses his preface to a Gordian whom he calls a descendant of Herodes, and his account of Herodes occupies a central position in the work, besides being the longest of the *Lives*. The next longest is Polemo, the leading sophist of Smyrna, who spoke at the dedication of the Olympieion in Athens. Leaving aside his sophists with the reputation of philosophers, almost all Philostratus'

---

[2] Hoplite general: Jones 1990:70–71. "Bridge:" *VS* 1.21, p29.26 K.

subjects are in some way tied to one of these two cities. Of the few exceptions, most come in for more or less harsh criticism: Varus of Perge, Hermogenes of Tarsus, Heliodorus the "Arab." His two Italian sophists, Aelian and Apsines, were both pupils of Pausanias, who in turn studied with Herodes.

Even Ephesus fares comparatively poorly. Philostratus seems to identify it with what he calls the "Ionian" style, as when Isaeus rebukes Dionysius of Miletus with the words, "Young man from Ionia, I did not teach you to sing." Similarly Onomarchus of Andros "caught the Ionian manner as one might ophthalmia" because of his island's proximity to Ephesus.[3] Among a group of sophists whom Philostratus passes over as unworthy of mention is a certain Soteros. It took an inscription, now in the British Museum, to reveal that Soteros taught in Ephesus and attracted pupils from as far away as Ancyra and Pisidian Antioch. The verse inscription that these pupils composed in his honor states that he had twice received and twice obeyed a call, an academic *Ruf*, from Athens to Ephesus. One wonders if this slight to Athens might have added to Philostratus' irritation. Ephesus might also have seemed too Roman, too commercial, when compared to what Philostratus approvingly calls the "quiet" (*hēsuchia*) of Athens.[4]

Even Pergamum gets remarkably little attention. The inscriptions of Pergamum, notably those of the Asclepieium edited by Christian Habicht, show that Aristides was by no means the only sophist who contributed to the city's intellectual life. For Philostratus, Pergamum is mainly interesting as a city where sophists such as Polemo and Aristides went for medical cures. The only native Pergamene whom he records is the consular Aristocles, who was a friend of Herodes and also taught a sophist of Smyrna, Euhodianus.[5]

Bernadette Puech's recent collection of inscriptions relating to rhetors and sophists shows how much of what might be called "retail sophistry" remains unknown to us, the little masters who taught in

---

[3] Isaeus: *VS* 1.20, p26.30 K. Onomarchus: *VS* 2.18, p101.21 K.

[4] Soteros: *VS* 2.23, p107.2 K. Inscription: *SEG* 13.506; Merkelbach-Stauber 1998–2004:1.317, 03/02/31 Ephesos; Puech 2002:455–458. "Quiet:" *VS* 2.21, p104.31 K.

[5] Asclepieium: Habicht 1969. Aristocles: *VS* 2.3, p74.7 K. Euhodianus: *VS* 2.16, p100.18 K.

Chaeronea or Mylasa.[6] But no epigraphical evidence was needed to recall that there were some sophists who enjoyed high reputations in their own day and later, and yet never found admission to Philostratus' catalog. For example, it almost entirely omits two islands, Lesbos and Rhodes. Of Lesbos he only says vaguely that Dionysius of Miletus had once taught there. Lucian by contrast mentions a certain Lesbonax of Mytilene, a "true gentleman" (*kalos kai agathos*), who called panto-mimes or "dancers" *cheirisophoi*, "hand-wise." Arethas of Caesarea, writing about the year 900, comments on this reference: "He means that Lesbonax of whom several wonderful declamations (*meletai*) survive, rivaling those of Nicostratus and Philostratus who were conspicuous among the more recent sophists, and especially his love letters, which drip with great verbal charm." Some of these declamations were also available to Photius in the ninth century, and three of them still exist, of a remarkably pure Attic style. This Lesbonax may belong to a well-known family of Mytilene that included Potamo, the famous rhetor of the age of Augustus, and another Lesbonax known to Strabo.[7]

Something similar is true of Rhodes, which Philostratus mentions only in connection with the last years of Aeschines. A Rhodian sophist from Lindos is honored in a long and detailed inscription of about 100 CE, which says that he was outstanding among the Greeks for his culture. Rhodes also provides two of the students who honored the sophist Soteros of Ephesus, whom Philostratus dismisses as a "toy of the Greeks" (*athurma tōn Hellēnōn*). Several inscriptions of the island mention an Aurelianus Nicostratus, probably of the early third century. He received a chair (presumably in Rome) from "the greatest emperor," and was in charge of the Guild of Artists of Dionysus at Rome, as was one of Philostratus' minor sophists from Smyrna, Euhodianus.[8]

---

[6] Puech 2002.

[7] Dionysios: *VS* 1.22, p38.28 K. Lucian: *Salt.* 69. Arethas: schol. Lucian p189.11 Rabe. Possible relatives of Lesbonax: *PIR*[2] L 159, 160. His works: Kiehr 1907.

[8] Antipater of Rhodes: Jones 2007. Students of Soteros: above, n4. Soteros in Philostratus: *VS* 2.23, p107.2 K. Nicostratus: *PIR*[2] A 1427 (identifying him with a homonym from Macedonia, on whom see below); Puech 2002:367–369 (rightly disjoining the two). Euhodianus: *VS* 2.16, p100.5 K.

A Nicostratus mentioned by Philostratus appears to be a different person from the Rhodian one. He too is from an area slighted by the author, Macedonia, and similarly is a much more conspicuous figure than Philostratus' account might suggest. The *Suda* says of him that he was "numbered among the select second Ten Rhetors, a contemporary of Dio Chrysostom and Aristides," and that he composed an encomium of Marcus Aurelius. The reference to the "Second Ten" shows that this Nicostratus belonged to a very select group whom later generations singled out in distinction to the famous Ten of the classical era. The names of the others are not known for certain, but must surely have included Aristides. We might guess that this new canon was drawn up in the fourth or fifth century, the age of what is sometimes called the "third sophistic" of Libanius, Himerius, and others.[9]

Philostratus' critical judgments on the sophists of the Second Sophistic therefore seem not to have been accepted by later generations, however much they turned to him for biographical information. The reason is perhaps that he belonged to a tradition of public declamation, especially of the improvised kind. Through informants such as Damianus of Ephesus, he was in touch with the birth of this tradition in the mid-first century; and as his closing paragraph shows, he had no idea that the tradition was coming to an end, or at least was to suffer an eclipse as the Greek city began to be transformed in the later third century.

Even before Philostratus wrote his *Lives*, a different set of criteria can be seen forming, and these were to place the conscious art of a practitioner such as Aristides above the improvisatory skills so admired by Philostratus. An example of this preference for the written over the spoken is that opinionated curmudgeon, Phrynichus. His only fully extant work, the *Selection of Attic Words*, can be dated to the 160s or 170s.[10] This amusing little treatise contains a random selection of words and forms over which contemporaries, and sometimes the ancients

[9] Macedonian Nicostratus: *Suda* N 404 and other references in *PIR*[2] A 1427 (see n8 above). Pisidian inscription: *SEG* 32.1302; Merkelbach-Stauber 1998–2004:2.406, 16/61/04 Antiochia; Puech 2002:178–180. "Second Ten:" Jones 1982:266.

[10] *PIR*[2] P 398. The *Eclogae*: Fischer 1974.

too, commonly fell into error, for example the accusative plural νῆας instead of ναῦς. The contemporary who receives the most criticism is Favorinus of Arelate, one of Philostratus' "sophists who were thought to be philosophers."[11] He is accused of "sweeping up expressions from the street-corner"; one of his choices made Phrynichus "hide his face" in shame. True, he is a "man of importance" (*anēr logou axios*) and "[someone] thought to be the first of the Greeks," though these compliments sound heavily ironic. Phrynichus' other favorite target is Polemo, whom Philostratus places second in importance only to Herodes, though he also criticizes other of the biographer's heroes, such as Lollianus, Antiochus of Aegae, and Alexander the Clay Plato.

Phrynichus has two overriding criteria: is a word Attic, that is, do the Athenians use it? And: is it truly ancient? Here he sets the bar high, deploring those who think that a precedent in Menander is enough to prove a word Attic, whereas one in Aristophanes is. (It might be wondered whether "Phrynichus" is a professional name, taken in tribute to the several homonymous Attic poets.) It is striking that practically all the sophists who fail Phrynichus' test of correct Atticism are also ones whose sophistic works have not survived to us. Of Favorinus' speeches, as opposed to his scientific works, one survives in a third-century papyrus, and two as stowaways in the corpus of Dio Chrysostom. Two rather overheated declamations of Polemo survive, while his technical treatise on physiognomy is extant entire in Arabic and abbreviated in a late antique summary. "Lollianus" is the name of the author of a Greek novel known from papyrus, but the novelist is usually thought different from the sophist. The case is the same with Heliodorus, the author of the *Aithiopika*, who is usually differentiated from Philostratus' "Arab," though the identification has its attractions.[12] Of the others criticized by Phrynichus, such as Alexander the

---

[11] Philostr. *VS* 1.8, pp8.23–11.16 K. On his life and career, *PIR*² F 123 and now Amato 2005:1–37. "Street corner:" Phryn. *Ecl.* 161. "I hid my face" (*enekalupsamēn*): *Ecl.* 213. "Man of importance" (*anēr logou axios*): *Ecl.* 216. "First of the Greeks:" *Ecl.* 228.

[12] Favorinus: see n11 above. Polemo (M. Antonius P.): *PIR*² A 862; Puech 2002:396–406. Declamations: Reader 1996 Lollianus (Publius Hordeonius L.): *PIR*² H 203; Puech 2002:327–330; on the identification of the author, Henrichs 1969. Heliodorus: Philostr. *VS* 2.32, pp124.4–125.16 K: the ongoing debate about the date of Heliodorus (third or fourth

Clay Plato, nothing survives at all. This sample of sophists is very limited, but it already suggests that Phrynichus is a more accurate barometer of later preferences than Philostratus. Once the majority of sophists were reduced merely to writing, to what a later age would call "cold print," then the magic that they exercised as performers was lost, and it was their value as examples of correct Greek that counted most. This is also true of Philostratus' hero, Herodes Atticus: he survives, if at all, only in the speech entitled in the sole manuscript *On Policy* (περὶ πολιτείας), a rather arid declamation drawing on an imaginary political situation in fifth-century Thessaly.[13]

By contrast with their declamations, the technical treatises written by some of Philostratus' sophists did survive. Apart from Polemo on physiognomy, there survive full or abbreviated versions of the works of Hermogenes, whom Philostratus regards almost as a figure of fun, a child prodigy who lost his talent in adulthood; "he died at a great age, when he was thought no better than the average (*heis tōn pollōn*), for he was despised when his art deserted him."[14] So also with Pollux of Naucratis: Philostratus admits that he was an excellent "critic," that is, an expert in linguistic usage, but his actual declamations were mediocre, so that it was difficult to say whether he was "educated" or "uneducated."[15] Apsines of Gadara, whom Philostratus praises for his memory and precision, again lives on only in his technical works.[16] The writings of Favorinus that lasted for several centuries, though these too are now lost, are a non-rhetorical collection of anecdotes, the *Jottings* (*Apomnēmoneumata*), and the similar collection called the *Miscellaneous History* (*Pantodapē Historia*).[17] Aelian's survival is very similar. Philostratus observes that he did not trust his ability to declaim, and so "devoted himself to writing and won admiration for that" (τῷ

---

century) usually ignores the old identification (going back to the sixteenth century) with Philostratus' sophist.

[13] Albini 1968.

[14] *VS* 2.7, p83.21 K.

[15] *VS* 2.12, p96.3–9 K.

[16] *VS* 2.33, p127.4 K.

[17] Mensching 1963. On the survival of Favorinus see now Amato 2005:211–214.

ξυγγράφειν ἐπέθετο καὶ ἐθαυμάσθη ἐκ τούτου).[18] What has come down is not declamatory at all, his two collections of curiosities and natural wonders, together with what seems to modern taste a rather insipid collection of "rustic letters." The first presumably appealed to a taste common in all ages for tid-bits and tattle about famous men, as did the similar collections of Favorinus: the second provided later readers for models in the writing of letters, an essential activity in societies where verbal persuasion had to be effected at a distance and not only face to face.

By contrast, the great survivors among Philostratus' sophists are Dio Chrysostom, if Philostratus' classification of him is accepted, and Aelius Aristides. There is also Philostratus' own family, though scholars in later antiquity as well as in modern times have had difficulty in attributing the various works that have come down under the name. Dio clearly survives in the first place because of his perceived excellence of style, which by the fourth century had brought him the nickname of "Golden Mouth" (*Chrysostomos*); in addition, the high moral tone of his philosophical works no doubt commended him to Christian readers. The author of the *Sophists* and the *Life of Apollonius* presumably survives because of his subject matter, since for Byzantine readers his *Sophists* were a continuing source of information about the history of rhetoric, and his *Apollonius* was a mixture of travel, miracle, and rhetoric, besides commemorating a sage who never ceased to fascinate later ages.

Aristides is a special case, and his afterlife would require a separate study, for which only the outlines can be given here. Philostratus' notice of him is slightly dismissive. On his view, Aristides' *Sacred Tales* are a good exercise in how to talk even on the most everyday subjects; his *Monody on Smyrna* led Marcus to rebuild the city after the earthquake of 178 (again, Philostratus' obsession with Smyrna shows through); the biographer quotes at length criticisms of certain declamations (as it happens, none of these particular ones has survived), while praising others as models of their kind. Philostratus' final verdict on Aristides is that "he was the most skilled of the sophists and excellent in devising

---

[18] VS 2.31, p123.10 K.

ideas, but as a result averse to improvisation, since the wish to produce everything only after thinking it out takes away spontaneity."[19] There is no mention of the works that dominated later criticism of this author, notably the gigantic anti-Platonic treatises *In Defense of the Four* and *In Defense of Rhetoric*. Nor does Philostratus notice the prose-hymns that Aristides counted as among his major contributions to the sophistic genre, or the speeches to cities such as Rome, Rhodes, and Smyrna that so interest modern historians of the Roman Empire.

In fact, Aristides' pre-eminence had begun to emerge well before Philostratus. Phrynichus' surviving *Selection of Attic Words* has already been mentioned, but another, much larger work of his survives only in an epitome and the summary of Photius. This is his *Sophistic Preparation* in 36 books, the whole collection being dedicated to Commodus, though each book had a separate and non-imperial addressee, with some addressees getting more than one book. The *Suda* may be right in making him a Bithynian, since the names of the addressees point to a context in western Asia Minor, perhaps Pergamum. Thus the first book had an Aristocles as the addressee, probably the Pergamene sophist and Roman consular Claudius Aristocles, and another book had a Rufinus, who could be the celebrated builder of the temple of Zeus Asclepius or a later member of his family. In one of the books, dedicated to a certain Menodorus, Phrynichus said that he had just been reading the works of Aristides, and he praised them highly. Some critics, it appears, thought Aristides less great than his reputation, but (I quote) "envy issuing from certain people attacked Aristides too, as it did many others conspicuous for their *paideia*." (We are reminded of the criticisms reported by Philostratus).[20] The comparison of Aristides with Demosthenes was one that Aristides himself did nothing to discourage, and a first cautious hint of it comes from his contemporary, Hermogenes of Tarsus, who after comparing a passage in Aristides with

[19] *VS* 2.9, pp86.22–89.31 K. For Aristides and Smyrna see now Franco 2005.

[20] The *Sophistic Preparation*: Phot. *Bibl.* cod. 158, 2 pp115–119 Henry; on Aristides, 101a16, p117 Henry; cf. *PIR*[2] P 398. *Suda*: Φ 764. Aristocles: *PIR*[2] C 789. Rufinus: *PIR*[2] C 1637; note his son or grandson, ibid., 1638. On his role in the building of this temple, Habicht 1969:11–14.

a similar one in Demosthenes adds: "I do not say this as if [the example in Aristides] is better than what Demosthenes said (for I would be out of my mind to say that), but that the latter has more verisimilitude than the former."[21] This tendency was to culminate in the fourteenth century with Theodoros Metochites' formal *syncrisis* of the two masters.[22]

Late Antiquity shows two streams of critical opinion about Aristides, sometimes joining in the same person. The prevalent one is of admiration; thus for Eunapius he is the "divine (*theios*) Aristides," and Libanius, on receiving a portrait of him from a friend, sat down beside it, so he tells us, reading one of the author's works. At the same time, he asked the portrait whether it really resembled the author of the writings. He concluded that the answer was positive, (I quote) "so heavenly (*theoeidē*), beautiful, and superior to the common run they all are." For Sopater of Athens, the author of the extant *Prolegomena*, Aristides is a "wise and wonderful man," and the only other sophists that he names are Herodes and Polemo. There are now four identified papyri of Aristides, all of the fifth or sixth century: significantly, one is of the *Sacred Tales*, one of the treatise *On the Four*, and two of the *Panathenaicus*.[23]

At the same time, Aristides provoked opposition in late antiquity, not for his style but for his ideas. Though modern readers are perhaps not used to thinking of Aristides as having ideas, Philostratus noticed them as one of his conspicuous features, and they certainly stirred much debate later, especially among devotees of Plato. Porphyry wrote a work in no less than seven books against Aristides. The sixth-century Platonist Olympiodorus either used this work, or drew on his own reading of Aristides when answering him in his commentary on the *Gorgias*.[24] Libanius, despite his admiration for his "divine" predecessor, wrote his *Defense of the Pantomimes* in direct answer to Aristides' lost work against them.[25] At least one professional advocate entered the

---

[21] Hermogenes p353.26 Rabe.

[22] Gigante 1969.

[23] Eunapius: *VS* 14.2, p81.11 Giangrande. Libanius: *Ep.* 1534, 11.553.20 Förster. Papyri: *P. Bingen* no. 24, pp128–130.

[24] Porphyry: *Suda* Π 2098. Olympiodorus: Behr 1968; *PLRE* 2.800, Olympiodorus 5.

[25] Molloy 1996.

lists: this is Sergius of Zeugma, sophist, rhetor, and praetorian prefect under Anastasius, who wrote a work *In Defense of the Advocates* (*dikologoi*) *against Aristides*. This title seems mysterious, since Aristides commonly attacks rival sophists, but nowhere in the extant corpus attacks forensic speakers.[26]

The reasons for this eventual triumph of Aristides are various, and no doubt not all applied all the time. An obvious one is his style, Attic but not hyper-Attic. The beauty of this was much more evident to those for whom Greek was a living language than it is to us, and of course it is totally lost in translation. Thus in Photius' *Library*, Aristides fills three whole codices, amounting to about 120 Budé pages.[27] The first codex is a long extract from the *Panathenaicus*, which Photius prefaces by observing that the speech contains "a selection of nouns, verbs and periods, but also of ideas artfully and beautifully arranged" (νοημάτων εἰς δεινότητα καὶ κάλλος διεσκευασμένων). Thus for Photius Aristides' mastery was both stylistic and logical, and in fact a later scholiast has adorned the subsequent extracts with annotations that comment not on the language but on the logic.[28]

That leads to another of Aristides' attractions for later generations: his vigorous and closely sustained defense of rhetoric. It is no accident that, apart from the *Panathenaicus*, the other works extracted by Photius are what he regards as a corpus of four treatises concerned with Plato's *Gorgias*, in modern texts the two books *In Defense of Rhetoric*, the treatise *To Capito*, and the *Defense of the Four*. Rhetoric continued to be a concern of Byzantium throughout its history,[29] and Aristides' defense not only gave it new models, but also defended it against its most influential critic.

A final reason is more elusive, but not less powerful, and that is Aristides' perceived moral character. Sopater spoke of him as "wise (*sophos*), wonderful (*thaumasios*), sober (*sōphrōn*), and superior to money (*kreittōn tōn chrēmatōn*)." This austere character, celibate and

---

[26] *Suda* Σ 246; *PLRE* 2.994, Sergius 7.
[27] Cod. 246–248, 7 pp8–126 Henry.
[28] Thus pp43, 48, 53 Henry.
[29] See for example Kennedy 1983.

childless, lived for his art, or what he calls *logoi*, a term of which "liter-ature" is only a pale translation. In a moving passage of his work *On those who Blamed him because he Did Not Declaim*, he says:[30] "Alone of the Greeks that I know of, not for the sake of wealth, of reputation, of honor, of marriage, of influence, not of any advantage at all did I turn my mind to literature, and as a disinterested lover of that, literature has honored me. Others have found pleasure in the company of boys, others in visiting the baths as much as possible, others in drinking to excess; some have been dazzled by horses and dogs, and indeed some in their pursuit of leisure have deserted literature. But for me litera-ture has every name and every power. I have made this my children, my parents, my actions, and my relaxations, everything." This puritan-ical side of Aristides also emerges from the sustained attack on Cynics that closes the *Defense of Rhetoric*, and in the speech attacking satirical comedy. Such a personality might well have made him sympathetic to Christian readers, just as they could have found what he says about his rivals confirmed in the pages of Philostratus.

The last word may go to a Byzantine epigrammatist, usually dated to the sixth century, Thomas Scholasticus:[31]

> Ῥητορικῆς φιλέω τρεῖς ἀστέρας, οὕνεκα μοῦνοι
> πάντων ῥητήρων εἰσὶν ἀρειότεροι·
> σεῖο πόνους φιλέω, Δημόσθενες· εἰμὶ δὲ λίην
> καὶ φιλαριστείδης καὶ φιλοθουκυδίδης.

> I love three stars of speaking, who alone
> For every other speaker set the tone.
> As much as I love you, Demosthenes,
> I love Aristides and Thucydides.

HARVARD UNIVERSITY

Bibliography

Albini, U., ed. 1968. [*Erode Attico:*] ΠΕΡΙ ΠΟΛΙΤΕΙΑΣ. Florence.

---

[30] *Or.* 33.19–20, p232.15–24 K.
[31] *Anth. Gr.* 16.315; *PLRE* 3B.1320–21, Thomas 23.

Amato, E., ed. 2005. *Favorinos d'Arles: Œuvres*. Paris.

Behr, C. A. 1968. "Citations of Porphyry's *Against Aristides* preserved in Olympiodorus." *AJP* 89:186–199.

Fischer, E., ed. 1974. *Die Ekloge des Phrynichos*. Berlin and New York.

Franco, C. 2005. *Elio Aristide e Smirne*. Rome.

Gigante, M., ed. 1969. *Teodoro Metochites: Saggio critico su Demostene e Aristide*. Milan.

Habicht, C. 1969. *Die Inschriften des Asklepieions*. Berlin.

Jones, C. P. 1982. "A Family of Pisidian Antioch." *Phoenix* 36:264–271.

———. 1990. "Heracles at Smyrna." *AJN*, 2nd series, 2:65–76.

———. 2007. "A Forgotten Sophist." *CQ* 57:328–331.

Kennedy, G. A. 1983. *Greek Rhetoric under Christian Emperors*. Princeton.

Kiehr, F. 1907. *Lesbonactis Sophistae quae supersunt*. Leipzig.

Merkelbach, R., and J. Stauber, eds. 1998–2004. *Steinepigramme aus dem griechischen Osten*. 5 vols. Stuttgart.

Mensching, E., ed. 1963. *Favorin von Arelate: Der erste Teil der Fragmente, Memorabilia und Omnigena Historia*. Berlin.

Molloy, M. E., ed. 1996. *Libanius and the Dancers*. Hildesheim, Zürich and New York.

Puech, B. 2002. *Orateurs et sophistes grecs dans les inscriptions d'époque impériale*. Paris.

Reader, W. W. 1996. *The Severed Hand and the Upright Corpse: The Declamations of Marcus Antonius Polemo*. Atlanta.

6

HIMERIUS' ORATIONS TO HIS STUDENTS

ROBERT J. PENELLA

THE CORPUS OF HIMERIUS, the Athenian sophist of the fourth century, includes many orations to his students. When I say "orations to students" here, I do not mean instructional lectures—for example, on issue theory (*staseis*) or style theory (*ideai*)—which he doubtless gave in his school. Nor do I mean *meletai* or declamations, those imaginary compositions on mythological or historical topics or fictitious court-room speeches, to which I shall return below. Rather, I mean orations on topics arising out of the actual life of the school. These orations were fully elaborated rhetorically,[1] and in delivering them Himerius took his student audience as seriously as he would have taken any extra-scholastic audience. Orations that were unquestionably or, in some cases, arguably delivered to students make up about one half of the sixty pieces that have at least some text preserved in the standard edition of Himerius by Aristide Colonna;[2] and of the fifteen titles of completely lost orations given in Colonna's edition, eight (55–58, 67, 70,

---

[1] Some are labeled as having been delivered *ex tempore*: 16, 64, 66, 74, and see the critical apparatus of Colonna 1951 for what he believes to be a variant title of 61 preserved in Photius.

[2] Colonna 1951. I am only marginally interested here in *Or.* 9 and 44, because they celebrate only private events in the lives of individuals who happen to be students. *Or.* 9 is an epithalamium in honor of the marriage of Himerius' student Severus. *Or.* 44 celebrates the birthday of an ἑταῖρος—probably a student rather than merely a friend, for in this oration Himerius says that Xenophon "provided Cyrus [the Younger] with *an excellent arena in which to be schooled* [i.e., in the rebellion which Xenophon militarily supported]" (44.6), implicitly comparing himself and the addressee of the oration to Xenophon and Cyrus. Furthermore, in the context of a sophist's corpus, I think that it is legitimate to elevate the likelihood that ἑταῖρος has the sense "student."

71, 73) are unquestionably or arguably directed at students. I begin by reviewing these pieces, with the caveat, already hinted at, that some of the orations to students survive only in excerpts, sometimes very few excerpts; further, that some are lacunose because of the damage suffered by the sole manuscript, Parisinus bibl. nat. Suppl. gr. 352, that preserves the affected portions of the text; and that, when we have an apparently complete but short oration, we cannot normally know for sure whether the piece is, in fact, a complete but short *dialexis* or *lalia* or only a chunk from something that was originally longer.

I.

More than half of Himerius' orations to students at Athens were given on the occasion of the arrival or departure of Himerius himself or of his students.[3] First, consider orations associated with Himerius' own movements: we find him addressing his school once before departing for Corinth, the administrative seat of the province of Achaia (*Or.* 11); twice upon returning from Corinth (30, 70); once when he returned from "his homeland," i.e., Bithynian Prusias (63);[4] and once when he returned after an absence during which he had "contended [oratorically] in many great auditoria" (64). In one of the orations given upon returning to Athens (30), he tells his students that he missed them and is delighted to be back; but he adds, probably in a jocular tone, that his temporary absence will cause them to appreciate him more. When he returns from the tour in the course of which he spoke in "many great auditoria," he expresses delight at again seeing the "small auditorium" of his school, which, he says, "first welcomed the fruits of my eloquence" and where he had gained his reputation (64.3). The contrast between the small auditorium of his school and the great auditoria abroad leads to a lesson: great eloquence can be produced in a modest venue. Again there is a lesson for Himerius' students in his remarks upon returning "after a considerable lapse of time" (63.6) from Prusias. During that time he apparently did not orate. He is therefore rusty, he

---

[3] Section I is adapted from my translation of Himerius' orations (Penella 2007), which is also the source of the short quotations from Himerius in English.

[4] See *Suda* I 348 Adler.

says, and needs practice before speaking publicly: "[t]he piper does not dare to go on stage unless he first warms up on his instrument in private" (63.2).

Next, Himerius often addressed orations to a student or group of students arriving at or departing from his school.[5] The arriving students are sometimes referred to as νεήλυδες, "newly arrived," which I take as equivalent to "newly enrolled" or, in our terminology, "freshmen" (see the titles of *Orations* 13.6–8,[6] 14, 21, 26, 54, 55, 57, and the text of 54.3). The opening scholion of one oration (35) tells us that the students it welcomes came over to Himerius from the schools of other sophists, with whom they were apparently dissatisfied. Himerius saw these speeches of welcome as a continuation of the practice of Isocrates, who "always opened up the doors of his royal school to lovers of eloquence by means of an oration" (33 [7–9]).

Some recurring motifs can be seen in the remains of Himerius' welcoming orations. First, Himerius shows an interest in the fatherland of new students, praising or at least referring to it in his welcome.

---

[5] *Or.* 10, 13.6–8 (which I separate from 13.1–5 [see n6 below]), 14, 15, 17, 18, 21, 26, 27, 33, 35, 54, 55, 57, 58. I regard "the newly arrived followers of Piso" of 13.6–8 and the arriving Cyprians of 17 as groups of students. What is left of *Or.* 18 is not explicitly identified as a welcoming address, but excerpt 4 of it—"Rumor leads the young man [to me?] from there [Cappadocia?]"—suggests to me that that is what it is. I assume that in *Or.* 27 the young men from Prusias whom Himerius is addressing have just arrived either as newly enrolled or continuing students. *Or.* 54's title is "To Newly Arrived Students," but Himerius is actually addressing a mixed audience of new students and upperclassmen here. The lost *Or.* 58, to "the [student] who came [to Himerius' school] because of the oracle he received from Poseidon," is presumably a speech of welcome. *Or.* 59 and 60 welcome a group of Ionians identified as "guests" (ξένοι), not students. Yet at one point Himerius addresses them as "boys" (59.6). They may be youths whom Himerius was trying to attract to his school. At 61.4–5 and 69.8–9 some new students are greeted in passing.

[6] These three fragments survive in the *Excerpta Neapolitana* under the title "To the Newly Arrived Followers of Poseidon," with "Poseidon" emendable to "Piso" from the uncorrupted version of this title that appears in Photius, *Bibl.* cod. 165. Colonna 1951 joins them to 13.1–5, preserved in Photius, *Bibl.* cod. 243, under the title "From Another Protreptic Oration." Colonna's joining results from his desire to keep the order of the titles in Photius' Himerian bibliography (cod. 165) as well aligned as possible with the order of the excerpts in cod. 243. The joining *may* be right, but there is nothing in the content of 13.1–5 and 13.6–8 that argues that they should be joined, and I prefer to keep them separate.

"Every person, I think," Himerius said on one occasion (23.2), "is fond of what belongs to his own country. If an Egyptian should come here, he will find the Nile—that is, our conception of it—swelling in orations we deliver on Egypt"; and in a fragment of an oration cited in a Byzantine lexicon he remarks that "[t]he Muses entertain visiting guests on every occasion with eloquence that refers to their native country" (fr. 5). To a new Egyptian student he makes a point precisely by appealing to the Nile (*Or.* 14). New Cyprian students hear him praise Cyprus and its association with Aphrodite and are assured that "[h]er inhabitants [are] genuinely Greek in language" (17.4). A welcoming address to a young Cappadocian includes a story about the Cappadocian Melas River (18). *Oration* 60, addressed to Ionians who were probably prospective students,[7] praises Ionian accomplishments in Asia Minor and in Magna Graecia, including contributions to the development of the art of rhetoric. Next, Himerius notes ties between the students' homeland and Athens: he does this in addressing the prospective Ionian students (59, 60) and, on another occasion, a group of Asianic students that included Ionians (26), affirming their Attic ancestry and welcoming them to what was, in effect, their motherland. Finally, Himerius praises the students themselves. He appears implicitly if not explicitly to have told the newly enrolled Cyprians that they were in the camp of the heavenly, not the vulgar, Aphrodite (17.7–8) and to have made the Cappadocian feel that he was one of those youths who "look proud and carry their heads high because they were born right from Zeus' chest" (18.5).

In *Oration* 33, to a new student named Phoebus, Himerius remarks that Isocrates used welcoming speeches in his school to provide an introduction to his teachings. Himerius probably did this too. We certainly find general remarks about eloquence in what survives of the welcoming orations. *Oration* 13.6–8 notes that eloquence allows the rhetor to get control over the masses; 18 glorifies Apollo's arrow, which transported the Scythian Abaris all around the world, the arrow being understood to be eloquence; and 33 celebrates the traditions of Attic

---

[7] See n5 above.

eloquence. Himerius assures his new students that he will love them as well as teach them, that he will have a "cheerful bearing" and not use physical punishment (33 [27–28], 54.1–2). New students might be given general advice: the young Egyptian (14) is told that "Rome wasn't built in a day," that steady hard work leads incrementally to one's goal. Sometimes the advice needed to be tailored to special circumstances: the newly enrolled Severus was or just had been involved in a conflict, and in the welcoming *Oration* 21 Himerius seems to have urged him not to be obsessed by strife nor to resort to violence.

Two orations to students, 10 and 15, mark departures from Himerius' school and are titled "propemptics."[8] In *Oration* 10, which has the distinction of being largely in dialogue form, Himerius expresses sadness at the departure of the addressee (10.2, 16), praises him (10.15, 17, 19), and speaks of the love that characterizes the teacher-pupil relationship (10.9, 10, 15). He seems to suggest that the young man will one day have his own school (10.17). In the few remains of *Oration* 15 Himerius gives the departing student advice—about the need for a young man to establish his own reputation, about the relation of eloquence to virtue, about the cardinal virtues and the virtues that depend on them. He warns that a young man cannot lean on his father's reputation and that a father's renown can actually highlight the deficiencies of his children—which hints that the young man in question was the son of a prominent father.

Two orations to students, 61 and 69, mark the recommencement of studies after some break in them. *Oration* 61 was perhaps delivered at the beginning of the regular academic year, "the season for eloquence" (61.1). Himerius makes the point that celebrating the commencement of his students' studies by giving a display of his eloquence is appro-

---

[8] That 10 is addressed to a student is not in doubt (see 10.2). That 15 is addressed to a student is suggested by 15.1 and 15.4. When Himerius says in 10.20 that "I am not this fellow's [the addressee's] teacher, I swear by my love of you, O eloquence," he does not mean that literally; he is saying that, as a teacher, he is merely the instrument of eloquence personified.

priate, because it is precisely eloquence that they are hoping to acquire in his school. The opening scholion of *Oration* 69 informs us that it was delivered "after [Himerius'] wound healed, when studies were [re]commencing." The oration begins by asserting that "[i]t is time to open the lecture hall ..., since the Muses are giving eloquence its season." We may be at the regular beginning of the academic year or of a segment of it, which on this occasion followed closely on Himerius' recovery from a wound. Sections 3 and 4 of this oration can only mean that Himerius had been a victim of academic violence[9]—or, as he puts it, of "envy's fight against eloquence" (69.2). We know from Libanius (*Or.* 1.85) how dangerous the life of a fourth-century professor at Athens could be. One sophist there was assaulted and had his face rubbed in the dirt. Another was seized and taken to a well and would have been thrown in had he not agreed to leave the city. Besides commenting on his wound and his readiness to resume teaching, Himerius appropriately gives some general advice to his students as they ready themselves to resume their studies: apply yourselves to your studies, he tells them, and do not be distracted by amusements and pleasures.[10]

In their *in loco parentis* role, sophists must have often got involved in one way or another when their students became ill. Libanius mentions attending to sick students as a routine part of his activities (*Or.* 36.8). Himerius' Athenian rival Prohaeresius intervened on behalf of the health of Eunapius, his student-to-be, before even meeting him (*Vitae phil. et soph.* 10.2 [486]). In *Oration* 45 Himerius himself addressed his school on the occasion of a student's recovery from illness.[11] It is clear (45.3) that the person in question was Himerius' head student or student leader. His recovery will have demanded notice more pressingly

---

[9] Cf. the opening remarks of Wernsdorf 1790 on this oration; Walden 1909:313–314; Norman 1965:153; Völker 2003:352n2.

[10] For student laziness and distraction, see Lib. *Or.* 1.5, 3.6, 10–14, 34.10–12, 43.10, 62.6, 19; id. *Ep.* 175.4, 666.2; Walden 1909:319–324.

[11] He addresses his audience as φίλοι. For this term as, apparently, an equivalent of the more common vocative παῖδες, see *Or.* 27 [33].

than that of an ordinary student. Himerius celebrates that recovery, that escape from "the envy [of fortune]."

Sometimes student disorders elicited an oration. *Oration* 66 is addressed to students (φοιτητῶν) who, in some way, have been rebellious or unbridled (ἀφηνιάζειν). A story in this oration about Apollo's refraining from shooting arrows at misbehaving nymphs makes clear that Himerius, though he hopes his students will change their behavior, will not use physical punishment on them, a policy that he explicitly announces elsewhere (54.2).[12] The title of a completely lost oration on student disorders is "To the Followers of Quintianus, who had been Disorderly Auditors when [Himerius] was Speaking *Ex Tempore*" (67). It has been assumed that Quintianus was a rhetor;[13] he may actually have been one of Himerius' own students, the ringleader of a group of students who misbehaved in class.

The title of *Oration* 16 describes the occasion of this speech with the words ἐπὶ τῇ κατὰ τὴν διατριβὴν στάσει. The word στάσις is also used in excerpt 5 of the oration, and the word ἔρις ("strife") in excerpt 1. The title may be translated as "When Discord Arose within his School." It is not clear, though, whether this means discord among his own pupils or discord between his pupils and those of another sophist. In either case, Himerius believes that his oratory can quell that discord. In what we have of *Oration* 65 we do certainly seem to be dealing with a conflict between Himerius' students and those of another sophist. Himerius has apparently gathered his students and is lamenting the fact that some of them were wounded in this conflict and are therefore absent: the title is "To those Involved <in> a Conflict"—the Greek actually says "the conflict," τῇ συμπληγάδι—"and Absent from a Lecture." Himerius sympathizes with them. But the tone quickly changes: the injured students who are absent are retarding the performance of the class as

---

[12] On sophists' use of physical punishment, see Walden 1909:324–325; Marrou 1956:272–273; Festugière 1959:111–112; Booth 1973:107–114. Libanius eventually came to feel that it was counterproductive (*Or.* 58.1).

[13] By Colonna 1951 ad loc.

a whole; they must get over the disruptive incident and return to class as soon as possible.[14] Finally, as I have already mentioned, the fragmentary welcoming speech to the new student Severus (21) also addresses itself to some sort of conflict the young man was involved in. A version of the title of this speech preserved in Photius uses the same word, συμπληγάδι, that we find in the title of *Oration* 65 to describe Severus' plight. When Himerius reminds Severus that "Achilles ... did not forget his lyre even while battles were going on" (21.1) and remarks that Athena and Poseidon did not use violence in their strife over Athens (21.2), he is apparently urging Severus similarly not to neglect rhetoric because of the student conflict he had got involved in and to give up violence.

The last group of Himerian orations to be noted here are four pieces (13.1–5,[15] 19, 68, 74) on a variety of admonitory themes. Two of them (13.1–5 and 68) are referred to in their titles as "protreptic" orations; a third advertises its protreptic intentions by its use of the word προτρέπει in the text (74.1). Two of them, *Orations* 19 and 68, are unquestionably addressed to students: in both, Himerius calls his audience his "boys" (παῖδες), and in 68 he refers to them as having "tossed [their] books aside" (19.10; 68.8, 11). The theme of the fragmentary *Oration* 19 is that "fine things are rare things." We value highly what we do not see or experience regularly or what we are deprived of for stretches of time (cf. *Or.* 30 [20–34]). Conversely, Himerius argues, "familiarity breeds satiety" (19.8, 10). *Oration* 68 encourages variety, ποικιλία, in oratory (cf. *Or.* 35). Himerius notes the ubiquity of variety and maintains that innovation is one way by which it can be achieved: we should "refuse always to be satisfied with the ancient models and instead ... keep coming up with new works of art to fashion" (68.3). We can be fairly confident that *Oration* 74, arguing that "one must always be in [rhetorical] training,"

---

[14] According to Colonna 1951, the alternate title of this oration, a title that is preserved in Photius, is "A *Rebuke* of those who are Carelessly Following his Course of Instruction [i.e., by non-attendance]."

[15] See n6 above.

that practice makes perfect, was addressed to a student audience. Finally, the few remains of *Oration* 13.1–5 may also have been addressed to students. Himerius here urged that his listeners take advantage of opportunity, that they act "in season," "at the right time." He may have been telling them specifically to take advantage of their years of study and not to waste their time on trivial pursuits.

II.

The only extant orations that parallel these Himerian ones are found in the Libanian corpus.[16] We do not have as many Libanian orations to students as we do Himerian ones; but this is compensated for by the fact that those we do have all survive in full. Libanius addresses *Oration* 55 to a single student, Anaxentius of Gaza.[17] He urges the young man to resist pressure to break off his studies and return home. Anaxentius aspires to become a sophist. Libanius tells him that he will regret it if he does not continue to study under him.

The remaining Libanian orations I am surveying here are addressed to groups of students. In one of them (3) Libanius answers students who have complained that he has failed to deliver a customary speech for them. He explains that it is their poor behavior that has caused him to withhold the speech; if they improve, he will deliver it. On another occasion (*Or.* 58) Libanius berates some students who had mistreated a loyal pedagogue; even those not involved in the incident are chastised because they failed to prevent or condemn it. And students were among those whom Libanius criticized in *Oration* 23 for having fled from the city of Antioch (see 23.28).

If students were not the objects of "the oratory of reproof ..., a ... genre of which Libanius is by temperament and technique a past

---

[16] I marginalize Aelius Aristides' *Or.* 30 Keil, celebrating the birthday of his pupil Apellas, and his *Or.* 31 for his deceased pupil Eteoneus for the same reason that I marginalize Himerius' *Or.* 9 and 44: see n2 above. Furthermore, with regard to Aristides, *Or.* 31, I am concerned only with orations to the living.

[17] Most of this oration has been translated into French by Festugière 1959:434–441.

master,"[18] then they might have heard him reproving others. In *Oration* 34 he tells them about a pedagogue who has dared to criticize him, hoping that they will "hat[e] those who have given me offense" (34.29, transl. A. F. Norman). On another occasion (*Or.* 36) Libanius was being afflicted by sorcerers. He complains to his students that his friends and the city of Antioch have not given him the help he deserves. He tells them that they are more properly disposed towards him than his city friends are.

Finally, three Libanian pieces on a variety of topics. *Oration* 5 is a prose hymn to Artemis, in which the orator thanks the goddess for saving him and some students from a collapsing building. Libanius addresses his listeners first as ἄνδρες (5.1), then later as νέοι (5.21)—hence, apparently, a mixed audience of students and full adults. Libanius also had this same kind of mixed audience for *Oration* 6 (6.1 ὦ ἄνδρες, 6.6 ὦ νέοι), an address on the insatiable desires of human beings and the need to be thankful to fortune for what one has. In *Oration* 9, addressed exclusively to students, Libanius lauds the celebration of the New Year, when students get a break from teachers and pedagogues, but he also laments (9.18) the decline of pagan observances on that day.

To all of these Himerian and Libanian orations I can add an item from the *Suda*: it is recorded there (Γ 132 Adler) that the Palestinian sophist Genethlius of the late third century wrote a Προπεμπτικὸς πρὸς τοὺς ἑαυτοῦ ἑταίρους Δαδοῦχον καὶ Ἀσκληπιάδην. The word ἑταίρους here is likely to mean "students" rather than merely "friends."[19] I am unaware, though, of any further extant information on the kinds of oration I have been surveying—sophists' speeches to students on school matters, on *realia* of common interest to them and their students, or offering general academic or moral advice to their charges. We should not, however, automatically conclude that such orations were rare or peculiar. On the contrary, my own working assumption here will be that they were common and that it is only because of the accidents of transmission that we do not have more such texts or testimonia.

---

[18] Norman 2000:183. This volume includes translations of *Or.* 3, 34, 36, and 58.

[19] Heath 2004:79, glosses the word as "pupils or fellow-pupils."

It may be that those who made the editorial decisions that led to the survival or loss of ancient works—including the authors themselves—often felt that orations to students lacked the prestige and gravity that would have warranted their preservation. Yet in what follows I hope to convince my readers that such orations may be helpful for understanding the overall culture of the rhetorical schools.

III.

I turn now, as I promised at the beginning of this paper, to the *melete* or declamation.[20] Declamations were deliberative or judicial orations on imaginary topics. Their themes could be taken from myth or history, with greater or lesser fidelity to mythological tradition or historical fact; or a fictitious case could be constructed in which neither principals nor place nor time was specified, a case set in the generic land that D. A. Russell calls "Sophistopolis."[21] Declamations were delivered both inside and outside the schools; my interest here is restricted to school declamation. In the school, declamation was "the crown of the curriculum."[22] The central concern was the invention and marshaling of arguments; everything that the advanced student had already learned was to be deployed in concert in the crafting of these exercises. Despite the ubiquity of panegyric in the Roman Empire, deliberative and judicial oratory remained important for various functions that elite graduates of the schools would eventually perform. Persuasion, accusation, and defense were skills that had a practical value in adult society.[23] Sophists, of course, strove to be masters of declamation, to meet the expectations both of their pupils and of the extra-scholastic audiences that liked them to declaim for display and competitively. The Himerian corpus contains the remains of five *meletai* (*Or.* 1–5); the Libanian corpus includes 51, not all of them genuine.

---

[20] See Russell 1983; cf. Bonner 1949.
[21] Russell 1983:21–22.
[22] Russell 1983:12.
[23] Heath 2004: 277–298.

Ancient criticisms of the themes of declamation are well-known. These exercises were said to have little to do with the real world. In *Rhetorum praeceptor* 10, Lucian complains that sophists want their students "to dig up long-buried speeches as if they were something tremendously helpful" and to emulate Demosthenes and Aeschines "when no Philip is making raids and no Alexander issuing orders" (transl. A. M. Harmon). The court cases argued in declamations often seemed contrived, sensational, bizarre.[24] But Malcolm Heath contends— rightly, I think—that the ancient argument that declamation did not prepare students well for real-life advocacy is tendentious, that ancient criticism of declamation should not be given undue weight, and that "what is overwhelmingly most common in ancient discussions of declamation" is not complaints about it, but "advice on how to do it."[25]

The themes of declamation can be defended, or at least appreciated, on several grounds. First, what the student needed to learn was how to argue *tout court*. This is a transferable skill; it is irrelevant on what subject matter it is exercised. Getting up the facts of a particular real-life dispute, or case, or the laws involved is the easy part. It could be maintained that the fictional content of declamation implicitly teaches this very point, implying that argument, not the specific facts of the situation at hand, is what matters. "Faced with a [given] fiction, [the student] can fall back on pure argument,"[26] without the burden of having accurately and fully to get up facts that, in real life, are quickly retired once the dispute is over. And if declamatory premises were sometimes unrealistically contrived or complex, this would at least challenge *inventio* and encourage argumentative ingenuity.[27] Next, fictitious themes from mythology or history or attention-getting legal problems will have held students' attention better than, say, a curial debate on whether or not to extend Main Street or a courtroom dispute on some humdrum issue in inheritance law; and holding students' attention is a legitimate peda-

---

[24] See Sen. *Controv.* 3 *praef.* 12–14; 9 *praef.* 5; 10 *praef.* 12; Petron. *Sat.* 1–2; Quint. *Inst.* 2.10, 8.3.23, 10.5.14–21, 12.11.15–16; Tac. *Dial.* 35. But Quintilian is not completely averse to declamation.

[25] Heath 2004:302–304.

[26] Winterbottom 1982:65; cf. Heath 2004:301–302.

[27] Cf. Bonner 1949:83; Winterbottom 1982:65.

gogical goal.[28] Finally, we must remember that attachment to their past was a fundamental part of imperial Greek identity. The more that past could be put on display in a student's formative years, the better.[29] This exposure began in the progymnasmata[30] and culminated in declamations on mythological and historical themes. But even declamations in which time and place were not specified can have the feel of classical Athens;[31] and the city war-heroes, the tyrants, and the tyrannicides who often appear in them[32] seem to come more from the world of the classical Greeks than from that of the Greeks under Rome.[33]

If, then, the themes of declamation were distant from the real world, they arguably made good pedagogical sense nonetheless, providing training in skills that had a practical value. But the themes of the Himerian and Libanian orations to their students, with which I began, were *not* distant from the real world—at least not from the real world of the students to whom they were directed. We often hear our own students contrasting the academy with the "real world," which they imagine they will suddenly enter upon receipt of a diploma. But for students the academy *is* the real world. For Himerius' and Libanius'

---

[28] Cf. Bonner 1949:38–39; Sussman 1987:v; Quint. *Inst.* 2.10.5 *quid ergo? numquam haec supra fidem et poetica, ut vere dixerim, themata iuvenibus tractare permittamus, ut ... gaudeant materia ...?*

[29] Cf. Russell 1983:107–108; Heath 2004:253 ("the historical theme puts the student more closely *in contact with the cultural tradition* [than the historically non-specific theme]" [my emphasis]; and consider T. A. Schmitz's notion of the sophist "performing history" in declamations (Schmitz 1999:71–92).

[30] See Gibson 2004:103–129.

[31] Cf. Russell 1983:22: "[T]he imaginary city [Sophistopolis] ... is (like classical Athens) a democracy, where the rhetor—both politician and expert in oratory—is something of a hero"; Kennedy 1974:20: "Though the declamation [i.e., Lucian's *Tyrannicide*] is not historical and does not refer to any persons or places by name, the atmosphere is that of the Athenian democracy and thus not very different from the content of historical declamations." As for specific historical (and mythological) themes in ancient declamation, there is a useful list of them in Kohl 1915.

[32] When Philostratus first refers to declamation in his *Lives of the Sophists* 481, he thinks of themes involving "poor men and rich men, war-heroes, and tyrants."

[33] Russell 1983:32 rightly reminds us, though, that local tyrants were not unique to a particular period of history. On the other hand, in *Precepts of Statecraft* 805a-b, Plutarch does make the assertion that the overthrow of tyrants (*inter alia*) is no longer part of the urban political scene.

students, arriving at and departing from school, recommencing study, illness, disorders, their teachers' problems, and so on were the *realia* in their lives. So I want to suggest that there was an economy in their rhetorical experience by which the fictitious world of the declamations they both heard and composed was balanced and complemented by orations their teachers delivered to them on real-life issues of the school. These orations served to remind them of the practical functions of eloquence in the fully adult world. They could have learned that lesson, of course, by hearing real-life orations outside the school; but orations dealing with their own *realia* and addressed specifically to them would have made the point more memorably. If school declamations had too much Marathon and Demosthenes, too many "pirates standing in chains on the beach" and "tyrants pen in hand ordering sons to cut off their fathers' heads" (Petron. *Sat.* 1, transl. M. Heseltine), sophists' orations to their students on school *realia* would have been an ongoing reminder of the real-life purposes of oratory in the adult world in which those students would eventually play their roles: the sophist quelling student discord foreshadows the student-become-*curialis* addressing himself to citizen discord, the sophist defending himself before his students foreshadows the student-become-ex-official doing the same thing before the citizens of his city, the sophist welcoming new students foreshadows the student-become-sophist welcoming a Roman governor. We should not be too quick, then, to criticize the limitations of a particular school exercise or experience (in this case, declamation), because such limitations could be compensated for by other curricular or extra-curricular experiences.

IV.

So, then, students were brought back from the mythological or historical past or from the temporally abstracted world of Sophistopolis to the real, contemporary world as they moved from hearing and composing declamations to hearing their teachers orate to them on academic *realia*. But not so fast—at least not in the case of Himerius. For the very Himerian orations that address themselves to *realia* and underscore the practical uses of oratory are themselves filled with references to the past, to the classical encyclopedia and the classical canon. Photius remarked on this feature of Himerius' oratory, noting that "his writings are filled with examples from history and from all sorts of myth, either to prove something or make a comparison or to add pleasure and beauty to what is said" (*Bibl.* cod. 165.108b). I am especially interested in the making of comparisons (πρὸς ὁμοιότητα), that is, the comparing of the present situation with the past. Himerius does this repeatedly in his orations to students, sometimes making the comparison explicit, sometimes not; sometimes giving multiple *exempla*; sometimes briefly, sometimes developing an *exemplum* at some length; often with several points of comparison between the present situation and the mythological or historical *exemplum*. When Himerius' comparisons of past and present are numerous or thickly elaborated, one experiences something of the surreal: present and past time meld, as in a dream. The Himerian present is graced by comparison with the past: we may note here that, in commenting on how the sophist Prohaeresius brought Celeus, Triptolemus, and Demeter into an oration on the emperor Constans, Eunapius remarks that the present situation was thereby transformed and had an antique *gravitas* brought to it (*Vitae phil. et soph.* 10.7.8 [492]: μετέστησεν εἰς τὸν ἀρχαῖον ὄγκον τὰ γινόμενα). But the present also allows the past to be remembered, reiterated. Thus both present and past benefit from being juxtaposed.

Here are some examples from the Himerian orations to his students. In *Oration* 35 Himerius is Socrates, his new students who have abandoned other sophists are like the students who came to Socrates from other teachers. In the oration he delivered to his students after recovering from a wound, he is like Anacreon, Stesichorus, and Ibycus recovering from illness or accident (69.5). The newly arrived Severus of *Oration* 21 has just been involved in some sort of conflict. Himerius tells him a story about how "Achilles … did not forget his lyre even while battles were going on" and another story about Athena's and Poseidon's non-combative resolution of their strife over Athens. Himerius wants Severus to imitate Achilles' retreat from the fray and the deities' eschewal of violence. *Oration* 60 is addressed to Ionian visitors in Athens who are probably prospective students. It ends with a story about noble Ionians who once visited Pindar in Athens; Pindar could entertain them only with a short melody, but he promised that he would perform something longer on the next day. Pindar here is Himerius, the noble Ionian visitors of old are the young Ionians visiting Himerius' school, the short Pindaric melody is Himerius' short *dialexis*, and the promised longer Pindaric performance is the longer oratorical display that Himerius will give.

For Himerius there is no such thing as too many mythological or historical *exempla*. In the talk on the need for variety in one's orations (68), Himerius compares rhetorical variety with the varied artistry of Phidias, the variety of scenes on Achilles' shield, Apollo's various oracles and manifestations, Proteus' and Homer's multifacetedness, the diversity of living beings brought about (according to Protagoras) by Zeus' order through Prometheus and Epimetheus, and Amphion's varied activity as both lyre-player and wall-builder. In *Oration* 27 to students from Prusias, Himerius illustrates love of fatherland by invoking the examples of some nine deities, two Homeric figures, and five classical poets, as well as Lycurgus, Amphion, Socrates, Aesop, Plato, and Pythagoras—all in the space of a mere 30 lines! In praise of the small lecture hall of his Athenian school in *Oration* 64, some 50 lines in length, Himerius brings in Apollo's modest temple on Delos; small Ithaca, Pylos, and Aegina, preferred respectively by Odysseus, Nestor, and Aeacus to larger cities; the city of Croton, preferred by Democedes to the Persian Empire; the modest dwellings of Demosthenes, Socrates, Pindar, and Lycurgus, preferred by tourists to larger houses of historical interest; and the small workshops of Phidias and Praxiteles.

Examples of mythological or historical *exempla* developed at some length by Himerius are the sustained comparison with Isocrates in *Oration* 33, the story of Dionysus and the Telchines in *Oration* 45, a Homeric vignette in *Oration* 65, and the Aesopic story of Apollo and the nymphs in *Oration* 66. More examples of the use of the past in Himerius' orations to his students could be adduced, but these will suffice.

If we turn now to the Libanian orations to students reviewed above, what we find there is a much more restrained use of the past than in Himerius. To be sure, Libanius employs some mythological and historical *exempla*, some of them elaborated, some presented briefly, in his oration to Anaxentius (*Or.* 55.16–19, 21, 24, 35). His *Oration* 6, on insatiable desires, uses a few historical *exempla*; and *Oration* 5, the prose hymn to Artemis, necessarily contains mythological lore. But these instances apart, references to the classical encyclopedia and the classical canon in Libanius' orations to his students are few and made only in passing. The past is not used as richly (or obsessively) in Libanius as it is in Himerius. Now we could see in this a difference of style or of disposition, but I would also want to bring in the cultural dimension: since the Greek past was so important in the formation of imperial Greek identity, a cultural imperative, more tamed in Libanius, was encouraging what we might see as Himerius' excess. He is as much addicted to the past in real-life orations to full adults as he is in his real-life orations to students—reinforcing cultural identity, then, as well as forming it. One final point: when Himerius compares himself to Socrates, Pindar, and other illustrious figures, we should not be quick to accuse him of grandiosity. His audience is also sometimes flatteringly compared to figures of the past. In any case, these comparisons are not made primarily to flatter; rather the orator is using himself and his audience as occasions through which the past may be summoned up. Again, I suggest that we look to the cultural functionality of what is going on.

I began with a review of some specific Himerian and Libanian orations and have ended with some suggestions on how they might be better appreciated within their larger educational context. The key point is that students who experienced declamations set in the past or in a temporally abstracted world were reminded of the practical, real-life value of rhetoric by hearing orations on academic *realia*. That point should serve as a warning not to judge any single rhetorical experience in the schools in isolation from the students' total rhetorical experience. Then there is the matter of the importance of the past for the cultural formation of Greeks in the Roman Empire—so important that, however glaringly the past was present in much declamation, it could not be put away even when a sophist was orating on the most routine, quotidian business of the school.

FORDHAM UNIVERSITY

Bibliography

Bonner, S. F. 1949. *Roman Declamation in the Late Republic and Early Empire.* Liverpool.

Booth, A. D. 1973. "Punishment, Discipline and Riot in the Schools of Antiquity." *EMC* 17:107–114.

Colonna, A. 1951. *Himerii declamationes et orationes cum deperditarum fragmentis.* Rome.

Festugière, A. J. 1959. *Antioche païenne et chrétienne: Libanius, Chrysostome et les moines de Syrie.* Paris.

Gibson, C. A. 2004. "Learning Greek History in the Ancient Classroom: The Evidence of the Treatises on Progymnasmata." *CP* 99:103–129.

Heath, M. 2004. *Menander: A Rhetor in Context.* Oxford.

Kennedy, G. 1974, "The Sophists As Declaimers." In *Approaches to the Second Sophistic*, ed. G. W. Bowersock, 17–22. University Park, PA.

Kohl, R. 1915. *De scholasticarum declamationum argumentis ex historia petitis.* Paderborn.

Marrou, H. I. 1956. *A History of Education in Antiquity.* Transl. G. Lamb. Madison, WI.

Norman, A. F., ed. 2000. *Antioch as a Centre of Hellenic Culture as Observed by Libanius.* Liverpool.

Norman, A. F. 1965. *Libanius' Autobiography (Oration I).* London.

Penella, R. J., ed. 2007. *Man and the Word: The Orations of Himerius.* Berkeley, CA.

Russell, D. A. 1983. *Greek Declamation.* Cambridge.

Schmitz, T. A. 1999, "Performing History in the Second Sophistic." In *Geschichtsschriebung und politischer Wandel im 3. Jh. n. Chr.*, ed. M. Zimmermann, 71–92. Stuttgart.

Sussman, L. A. 1987. *The Major Declamations Ascribed to Quintilian: A Translation.* Frankfurt a. M.

Völker, H. 2003. *Himerios, Reden und Fragmente: Einführung, Übersetzung und Kommentar.* Wiesbaden.

Walden, J. W. H. 1909. *The Universities of Ancient Greece.* New York.

Wernsdorf, G. 1790. *Himerii sophistae quae reperiri potuerunt.* Göttingen.

Winterbottom, M. 1982, "Schoolroom and Courtroom." In *Rhetoric Revalued*, ed. B. Vickers, 59–70. Binghamton, NY.

7

ALMS AND THE AFTERLIFE
A MANICHAEAN VIEW OF AN EARLY CHRISTIAN PRACTICE

PETER BROWN

IT IS NOW THIRTY YEARS since I first met Glen. On that occasion, in 1976, I was present at a lecture which he delivered. And so, it is also thirty years since I first heard Glen praised. The speaker who introduced him on that occasion used a metaphor which has lingered in my mind as eminently appropriate. He spoke of Glen's books (at that time, his *Augustus and the Greek World* and the more recent *Greek Sophists in the Roman Empire*) as like those high-gravity stars which burn with incandescent, vastly condensed energy. This remark is now thirty years more true. Glen has filled the entire sky of late antiquity, from East to West, with vivid stars. His work spans the firmament of a late antique world far larger than we had once imagined. Not for him the conventional boundaries of the Greco-Roman Mediterranean. His is a Hellenism which reaches with ease into Edessa and down into the oases of central Arabia.[1] His martyrs (real and imagined) are not only those of Rome and Smyrna. They also include those of the pre-Islamic oasis city of Najran.[2] His synagogues are not only those of Palestine, but also those of the Yemen and the Hadramawt.[3] His Greek is not only that of Aelius Aristeides. It is the poignant, late, late Hellenism conjured up in the newly-discovered poems of Cavafy.[4] To look up into such a sky is to feel part of a bigger and more subtly interconnected world than we had previously dreamt of.

[1] Bowersock 1990.
[2] Bowersock 1995 and 2004.
[3] Bowersock 1993.
[4] Bowersock 1996.

But, in my personal experience, the joy of reading Glen has always been to share with him in the sharp joy of discovery. This sharp joy is what I owe most to him. It is not only that any article by Glen is, in itself, a find. Every one of them triggers the most delightful of all experiences—the discovery of something new, truly new, in a world with which we thought we were familiar: to identify a synagogue in the Hadramawt—where others had seen a camel-caravan; to spot a royal title similar to that of Constantine on a coin of Axum;[5] to bring alive for us a conventicle of *Euhemerioi*—of Happy Campers—in Asia Minor;[6] to draw attention to a mosaic of Romulus and Remus placed on the threshold of a sixth-century Christian hospital in Syria.[7]

As a discipline, we need this fresh, sharp zest for discovery—and, with it, we need to encourage the patient skills which make discovery possible: skills in languages (both classical and oriental), skills in reading in the works of many cultures, the hard, high skills of the epigrapher and the archaeologist. In all this, Glen is our model and, better than that, he is our breath of fresh air. As historians, we need to order and to explain. It is an altogether virtuous thing to wish to synthesize the past and to attempt to render it translucent to understanding. But if we are not careful, in modern conditions, synthesis can lapse into the opinionated recitation of master narratives, and interpretation can lapse into coy displays of methodological *Angst*. To turn to Glen is to know how to break out of this dull circle: through sharing in his joy in discovery we can find again the sweet, fresh water that lies so close to the surface, beneath the arid sands of our discipline.

Hence, it is an honor to be able to bring to Glen my thoughts on a recent discovery in the early history of Manichaeism, as it spread (both physically and as a gathering current of religious ideas) from the eastern borders of Glen's beloved Syria and the Province of Arabia, into the western world of Augustine and the early middle ages.

Only fifteen years ago, in 1990, a cache of Coptic letters was found in the corner of a room in a newly-excavated house at Ismant al-Kharab

---

[5] Bowersock to appear.

[6] Bowersock 1999.

[7] Bowersock 1998 and 2006.

(the ancient Kellis) in the Dakhleh Oasis of south-western Egypt. It was published by Iain Gardner and his colleagues seven years ago, in 1999. One such letter, *Papyri Kellis Coptici 32*, thanks and praises the pious lady Eirene, "she whose deeds resemble her name [Peace], our [spiritual] daughter." Eirene was

> The daughter of the holy church, the *catechumen* of the faith: the good tree whose fruit never withers, which is your love which emits radiance every day. She who has acquired for herself her riches and stored them away in the *treasuries that are in the heights, where moths shall not find a way nor shall thieves dig through to them to steal* (Matthew 6:19–20).

It then adds an explanation:

> which [treasuries] are the Sun and the Moon.

It was only this last, tell-tale reference to the Sun and the Moon as active agents in a cosmic drama of salvation, which identified the writer of the letter as a Manichee.[8]

The discovery of a cache of Manichaean letters and ritual texts in the houses of Kellis has further confirmed the growing consensus that, in the late third and fourth centuries, Manichaeism spread throughout the Roman empire as one form of Christianity among others. It was not, as its opponents claimed, an "exotic" and non-Christian religion, imported from distant Persia. In the words of the discoverers of the Manichaean texts of Kellis, the "Holy Church" of Mani fitted into the life of the little oasis town simply "as a superior and more effective kind of Christianity."[9]

But what sort of Christianity was it? The *Kellis Coptic Papyri* throw a vivid light on the manner in which the leaders of the Manichaean community, the Elect and the Teachers, expected to be supported by their rank and file. In the Manichaean community, the relation of Eirene and of other "*catechumens*" to the leaders of the movement was defined by a singularly clear-cut and high-pitched notion of religious

---

[8] *P Kell. Copt.* 32.1–13, ed. Gardner 1999:214–215.
[9] Gardner 1999:79.

giving. In return for purely spiritual services, deemed to be crucial for her salvation and for the salvation of those connected with her, as a "*catechumen*" or "hearer" of the faith Eirene (and men and women like her) would offer to these leaders total material support. The letters of the Elect are fulsome begging letters. Their editors were struck by "the unexpected juxtaposition of the practical and the uplifting."

> You being for us helpers and worthy patrons and firm and unbending pillars [of the Church]; while we ourselves rely upon you ... I was very grateful to you, ten million time! ... Therefore I beg you, my blessed daughters, that you will send me two of oil. For you know that we are in need.[10]

It is a very oily letter.

The Manichaean Elect of the Kellis documents recognizably stand at the end of three centuries of Christian history. The direct exchange between heaven and earth, by which "material" wealth was transmuted into "spiritual" benefit, had been implicit in the sayings of Jesus. The citation from *Matthew* 6:19–20: *Lay not up for yourselves treasures upon earth ... But lay up for yourselves treasures in Heaven*, was the only full citation from the Gospels in the Kellis Manichaean letters.

The notion of a "spiritual exchange" had been adumbrated, also, by Saint Paul. Writing on the collection of money "for the saints" in the community of Jerusalem, Paul had insisted, in *1Corinthians* 9:11, that *If we have sown unto you spiritual things, is it a great thing that we shall reap your carnal things?*[11] Thus, it is not at all surprising that the late fourth or fifth century Manichaean Latin text, discovered in a cave outside Theveste, should contain an exhaustive working through of Pauline and Gospel citations relevant to the "spiritual exchange" between leaders and their faithful—as the basis of the relationship between Elect and *catechumens/auditors* in the Holy Church of Mani. The sharp hierarchy of giving is made clear:

> That is why [Mani, following the words of Jesus] commands the rich ... who are known as 'disciples of the second order'

---

[10] *P Kell. Copt.* 31, ed. Gardner 1999:210–211.
[11] Georgi 1992.

to make friends with the Elect ... Each gives to the other through their abundant possessions, the Elect to the Hearers from their heavenly treasure [of prayers and teaching] and the Hearers to the Elect from their earthly wealth.[12]

The Manichaean Elect also fit easily into the wider background of the spiritual revolution of late antiquity in one crucial way. Not only was religion discussed more fervently and with more consequentiality in the third century AD than in previous centuries; some people came to be paid to talk religion on a full-time basis.[13]

Last but not least, the Manichaeans can now be seen as part of the wider background of an itinerant and frankly mendicant asceticism, which was common in the Christian Middle East. The recent excellent work of Philippe Escolan and Daniel Caner has revealed the existence of an entire "Third World" of "wandering, begging monks," of whose vigor and extent, throughout Syria and other Christian provinces (Egypt included), we had not previously dreamed.[14]

I would like to linger on one aspect only of the "spiritual exchange" which took place between the Manichaean Elect and *catechumens* such as Eirene, as this is discussed in the Manichaean *Kephalaia*. The *Kephalaia* were, originally, a mighty volume of over some 1000 pages. The manuscript dates from around 400 AD. Though they claim to record the questions and answers of Mani and his *catechumens*, they were almost certainly created after his death in 277. But maybe not too long after. What we may have here is a condensation of the practices of a radical Christian community, seen from the inside, in the late third or early fourth century.[15]

---

[12] *Codex Thevestinus*, ed. Be Duhn 1997 and Stein 2004. On Manichaeism in general, see Brown 1969, Lieu 1992, and Gardner and Lieu 1996.

[13] Schöllgen 1998.

[14] Escolan 1999 and Caner 2002.

[15] Funk 1997. The sections of the *Kephalaia* that came to Berlin have been known to us since 1940 and 1966, through the editions of Ibscher 1940 [*Kephalaia* 1–95] and Böhlig 1966 [*Kephalaia* 96–122]. Further Berlin *Kephalaia* have only been published recently: Funk 1999 [*Kephalaia* 122–150] and Funk 2000 [*Kephalaia* 150–173]. *Kephalaia* 1–122 have been translated by Gardner 1995. The Dublin *Kephalaia* are available in a fascsimile edition: Giversen 1986. They also contain significant material: Tardieu 1988.

I want to think aloud about the wider implications of the giving of alms (the *mntnae*), of the giving of an oblation (*prosphora*), the celebration of a "love feast" (the *agape*) and the "making of memory" (*prpmeue*) on the occasion of the "going of the soul out of the body" of an Elect or of a *Catechumen*.[16] This ritual is, of course, only a small part of an immense complex of ritual processes, which has now been brought alive for us by the masterly study of Jason Be Duhn.[17] But it is worthwhile lingering over this particular ritual for the light that it throws on contemporary Christian practice.

Let me cite from parts of *Kephalaion* 115. First, the title:

> The *Catechumen* asks the Apostle: will Rest (*matnes*) come about for Someone who has come out of the Body, if the Saints [the Elect] pray over/for him and make an alms-offering (*nser oumntae*) for him?

The question is, basically, do such prayers work and, above all, does such an offering of alms (*mntnae*) work?

> So now I beseech you, my Master, that you may instruct me about this matter/lesson (*pisedje*): whether it is true? For it is [a practice] very great and honored among the people.[18]

To which the Master replies, in effect, "Make My Day." Of course, such practices work; and he will tell you exactly why—and that they do so on a cosmic scale. In this, Mani is very much an intellectual of the third century. He shared the driving force of that age, which, in the elegant words of Aline Rousselle, was a drive towards "l'explicitation du croire"—a drive towards making traditional practice and belief transparent to understanding.[19] Altogether, Mani's attitude to religous rituals, in the *Kephalaia*, is like that of the Irishman when confronted with a complex working piece of machinery, running smoothly: "Tell

---

[16] Richter 1997:61–67.

[17] Be Duhn 2000.

[18] *Kephalaion* 115, ed. Böhlig 1966:270–280, translated in Gardner 1995:276. See also *Kephalaion* 144, ed. Funk 1999:346–348.

[19] Rousselle 1999:433–438.

me, now," says he, "does it work ... *in theory?*" For Mani, as we know, everything works "in theory." He knows the workings of the *cosmos* from its very beginnings. So he can explain why the rituals of his church are effective in terms of a grandiose cosmic drama.

But what about the working machine itself? For the *Catechumen* takes the machine for granted. Alms-offerings, oblations, and "the making of remembrance" are, for him, "very great and honored amongst people." His concern is less *how* they work, but *do* they work? For he very much wants them to work. It is on this point that Mani's cosmic explanation reassures him. Now he can be certain that:

> alms on his behalf and a remembrance on his behalf [of the one who has died], for his brother, for his father, or his mother or his son, or else his daughter or his relative who shall come out from the body ...[If] he has made alms ... He did not lack his hope.

Yes, says Mani:

> What you are doing is a great good ... you redeem it [the passing soul] from thousands of afflictions.[20]

The tendency of the *Kephalaia* is to offer grandiose and convincing explanations of rituals which are already well known to the *Catechumens*. And these rituals are not exclusively Manichaean rituals. Many are pre-existing rituals of the Christian communities which have been, as it were, "Manichaeized." They have had a Manichaean "spin" put upon them. What Mani offers is the assurance (based on his own revealed knowledge of the true workings of the *cosmos*) that, in his church, at last, they are guaranteed to work—"in theory" and, therefore, in practice. The rituals themselves and the expectations which the rituals were expected to meet are already there. There were already part of the spiritual landscape of the Christian communities of the Middle East.

To see a Christian ritual in a Manichaean text is like glimpsing a building beside a railroad, caught, for a moment, in the reflection of the

---

[20] *Kephalaion* 115, ed. Böhlig 1966:277 and 280, translated in Gardner 1995:282 and 283–284.

windows of a passing train. The Manichaean *Kephalaia* were documents very much driven by Mani's magnificent and idiosyncratic obsession with the secrets of the universe. But they also offer us, for a moment, a glimpse of the solidly established, day-to-day practice of the Christian neighbors of the Manichees in the early fourth century.

It is on the issue of alms offered for the departed that I wish to concentrate. Let me begin at the end of the story. If we move ahead a full century from the *Kephalaia* to the works of one of Mani's most startling (if temporary) converts, Augustine of Hippo, one contrast is striking.

Questioned about the afterlife, Mani tells all. He reassures his hearers that, in His Holy Church, rituals for the dead worked. Thus, in *Kephalaion* 87, *On Alms*, he makes plain that the *catechumens* of "every sect" (by which he means all previous Christianity—and, perhaps, also Jews and Zoroastrians) give alms in the name of God. But only in the Holy Church of Mani do these alms "work:"

> it is this holy church itself that is the place of rest [the *mmantan*: the end-point, the 'place of cessation'] for all those that shall rest therein; and it becomes a doorway and a conveyance to the land of rest.[21]

Mani even has a clear view of the history of the Christian Church, which he makes plain in *Kephalaion* 144. Mani asserts that the practice of giving alms for the dead was a tradition handed down to the Apostles by Jesus. But in Christianity, the *agape* meals rapidly became corrupt. They came to include drunkenness and the eating of impure foods. They lost their effect until they were "reformed" by Mani. Due to the reforms of Mani, rituals which had become corrupted in other Christian communities were now both rendered intelligible and were guaranteed to work. They protected the souls of the dead. And they did so particularly at the dread moment of the soul's departure from the body for another world. [22]

---

[21] *Kephalaion* 87: *On Alms*, ed. Ibscher 1940:216–218, trans. Gardner 1995:224–226.
[22] *Kephalaion* 144, ed. Funk 1999:346.13.

It is important to point out that, in these answers, we are plainly dealing with a man of the third century, and not a man of the western Middle Ages. What concerned Mani and his hearers was not a medieval notion of Purgatory. That notion involved imagining some middle time and place, carved out of the immensity of a timeless other world. What mattered, for Mani's contemporaries, was a far older and darker theme: the terror which faced the soul as it entered the other world at the moment of death.[23] On this issue, Mani spoke clearly and reassuringly. Alms given to his Holy Church in the persons of the Elect protected the laity from peril at the moment of its passing into another world in a manner in which alms and *agape* meals given to the poor in "mainline" churches did not.

The letters and even the account books of Kellis are scattered with references to the *agape* offered for the souls of the dead. It was a matter of sadness, among the Manichees of Kellis, that one old lady should have died without the consolation of such rites:

> We are remembering her very much and I am distressed that she died when we were not with her and that she died without finding the Brotherhood gathered around her.[24]

Already we can see in *Kephalaion* 158 and from other sources, the Holy Church of Mani had acquired considerable property in the form of "alms"—buildings, liturgical vessels, even oblate slaves and, one suspects, children given to the Elect as servants and as copyists of the Manichaean Holy Scriptures.[25] The wealth of the Manichaean church did not only consist in alms: it came through alms. And these were, to a great extent, alms given for a death ritual whose effectiveness, for the souls of the believers, had been guaranteed by Mani himself.

When, in 421, Augustine came to write his *Enchiridion* (the *Ready-to-Hand Book of Christian Doctrine*), he also wrote (like the author of the *Kephalaia*) for a lay enquirer. He dealt with exactly the same questions as those posed to Mani by his *catechumens*. Yet his answer—deeply

---

[23] Brown 1999.

[24] *P Kell. Copt.* 21.51–56, ed. Gardner 1999:188–189.

[25] *Kephalaion* 158, ed. Funk 2000:395–397; cf. August. *Contra Faustum* 13.6.

pondered after almost forty years of meditation and of pastoral work—
is the opposite of Mani's. It was, basically, "God only knows and He is
not telling." Oblations for the souls of the dead are, indeed, a tradition
handed down from the Apostles. But, when we ask how they work in
particular, and for what particular categories of persons, we are met by
the immense silence of God.[26]

The answers may be different; but it is the convergence of concerns
between Mani and Augustine which interests me. The questions which
Augustine has been asked are exactly the same as had been posed to
Mani.

Above all, Mani had been asked to fill in a lacuna in his own system.
His hearers had pressed him hard on this issue. This is made plain
in *Kephalaion* 92. Mani had drawn an entire picture of the universe.
But why, in this cosmic map, had he found no place for the average
believer?

> Why did he not depict the Middle Way of the *catechumens* ...
> Why did he not show how the *catechumen* [rather than the
> saintly Elect] goes out of the body and how he is brought
> before the Judge?[27]

Augustine was pressed by exactly the same questions. They were
not merely questions of pious practice. They had been kept open in
mainline Christian circles by a tension within the Christian Scriptures
themselves. How was it possible to reconcile the overwhelming sense of
immediate salvation, conveyed in the *Gospel of John* (as in *John* 5:24: *Truly,
he who hears my word ... he does not come into judgement, but has passed from
death to life*) and the archaic dismissiveness of *Psalm* 1:5: *Therefore, the
wicked shall not stand in the judgement*, with a Universal Judgement of
good and bad alike, at the end of time, as presented in *Matthew* 25:32?[28]

Faced by this tension, Augustine took refuge in a trenchant formula.
He offered what can be called a Van Ness Diagram of the Other World.
In this diagram, it was only the area of overlap which involved ritual

---

[26] August. *Enchiridion* 29.110.
[27] *Kephalaion* 92, ed. Ibscher 1940:235.2–11, transl. Gardner 1995:241–242.
[28] Durst 1987.

action by believers. The prayers and oblations of the faithful were not relevant to the *valde boni*: for they could be assumed to have reached heaven with no difficulty. Nor were they relevant to the *valde mali*: for they could be assumed to be either *in* Hell or destined *for* Hell. The "friction point" of early Christian eschatology, and of Early Christian pastoral care, was the fate of the *non valdes*—the *non valde mali*, the *non valde boni*: the "not altogether bad" and "not altogether good."

The lapidary phrases of the *Enchiridion*—which laid out this three-fold division of the faithful in relation to their hope for help in the other world through rituals performed in this world by the faithful—achieved an almost gnomic authority in early medieval Latin discussions of the effect of prayers and oblations for the souls of the dead. Like well-worn stones, they slide smoothly into place, again and again, in all subsequent medieval treatments of this topic.[29]

But, for Augustine himself, we can sense, behind the rock-like opacity of his answers, the building of a dam, intended to hold back (rather than to satisfy) the mute pressure of the *non valdes* of the Christian communities. These people wanted considerably more circumstantial and, if possible, more reassuring answers than he was prepared to give them.

From this I would conclude one thing. First and obvious: Manichaean literature in Christian regions can still offer us surprisingly valuable insights into what other Christians thought and felt—and often, given the time of its compilation, in periods earlier and less well documented than the deceptively articulate Golden Age of the Fathers of the Church.

Second, and not so obvious: the history of Christian notions of the afterlife is the history of great silences. As has been shown in a brilliant new study by Éric Rebillard, *Religion et Sépulture*, what is significant about much of early Christian burial practice and beliefs about the afterlife is how *silent* the clergy tended to be on these issues. Burial and the rituals of death were a *terrain vague*, an unclaimed territory, dominated by lay practice and by lay belief, on which the clergy of the

---

[29] Carozzi 1994.

Christian churches, in east and west alike, were surprisingly reluctant to put up new buildings. There was not, at this time, a brisk and authoritative taking over, by the clergy, of the shadowy world of the dead.[30]

As Éric Rebillard has made plain, late antiquity is a world, still, without large Christian cemeteries. It is a world, also, without extensive and circumstantial lucubration by Christian writers on the fate of the dead and on the exact effect of rituals which had long been performed, by Christians, on behalf of the dead. Yet, behind this silence, one senses an oceanic pressure of lay demand for explanation. To this demand for explanation and reassurance, the existing Patristic sources gave singularly tongue-tied answers.[31]

Here the Manichaean evidence is crucial. The discussions of oblations and almsgiving for the dead in the Manichaean *Kephalaia* are a momentary break in the silence of our sources. They reveal the urgency of the expectations which had already built up around such rituals within the Christian communities of the late third and early fourth centuries. Furthermore, in the euphoric circumstantiality of his Teach-Ins for *catechumens*, in the *Kephalaia*, Mani and his disciples showed how the expectations raised by these rituals might be resolved.

Indeed, as we know from the history of Christian piety in the early middle ages, this was how they were resolved. It was agreed that the Mass worked, and many authors (most notably Gregory the Great in Book Four of his *Dialogues*) came forward to tell the anxious and the uninformed exactly how it did, and with what effect for the souls of their loved ones.[32] In this sense, Mani, along with Augustine, deserves a place as one of the Founders of Medieval Christendom.

PRINCETON UNIVERSITY

Bibliography

Be Duhn, J. and G. Harrison. 1997. "The Tebessa Codex: A Manichaean Treatise on Biblical Exegesis and Church Order." In *Emerging from*

---

[30] Rebillard 2003.
[31] Rebillard 2005.
[32] Brown 1999:296–302.

Darkness, ed. P. Mirecki and J. Be Duhn, 33–87. Leiden.

Be Duhn, J. 2000. *The Manichaean Body in Ritual and Discipline*. Baltimore, MD.

Böhlig, A. 1966. Kephalaia. *Zweite Hälfte: Lieferung 11/12*. Stuttgart.

Bowersock, G. W. 1990. *Hellenism in Late Antiquity*. Ann Arbor, MI and Cambridge.

———. 1993. "The New Greek Inscription from South Yemen." In *To Hellénikon: Studies in Honor of Speros Vryonis, Jr. 1: Hellenic Antiquity and Byzantium*, ed. J. S. Langdon, S. W. Reinert, J. S. Allen and C. P. Ioannides, 3–8. New Rochelle, NY.

———. 1995. *Martyrdom and Rome*. Cambridge.

———. 1996. "The New Cavafy: Unfinished Poems 1918–1932." *The American Scholar* 65:243–257.

———. 1998. "The Rich Harvest of Near Eastern Mosaics." *JRA* 11:693–699.

———. 1999. "Les *Euémerioi* et les confréries joyeuses." *CRAI* 1999:1241–1256.

———. 2004. "The *Hadramawt* between Persia and Byzantium." In *Convegno internazionale: La Persia e Bisanzio*, 263–273. Rome.

———. 2006. *Mosaics as History: The Near East from Late Antiquity to Islam*. Cambridge, MA.

———. Forthcoming. "Helena's Bridle and the Chariot of Ethiopia." In *Antiquity in Antiquity*, ed. G. Gardner and K. Osterloh. Tübingen.

Brown, P. 1969. "The Diffusion of Manichaeism in the Roman Empire." *JRS* 59:92–103.

———. 1999. "*Gloriosus Obitus*. The End of the Ancient Other World." In *The Limits of Ancient Christianity: Essays in Late Antique Thought and Culture in Honor of R. A. Markus*, ed. W. E. Klingshirn and M. Vessey, 289–314. Ann Arbor, MI.

Caner, D. 2002. *Wandering, Begging Monks: Spiritual Authority and the Promotion of Monasticism*. Berkeley, CA.

Carozzi, C. 1994. *Le voyage de l'âme dans l'au-delà: D'après la littérature latine (Ve–XIIIe siècle)*. Rome.

Durst, M. 1987. "*In medios iudicium est*: Zu einem Aspekt der Vorstellung vom Weltgericht bei Hilarius von Poitiers und in der lateinischen Patristik." *JbAC* 30:29–57.

Escolan, P. 1999. *Monachisme et Église: Le monachisme syrien du ive au viie siècle. Un ministère charismatique.* Paris.

Funk, W.-P. 1997. "The Reconstruction of the Manichaean *Kephalaia.*" In *Emerging from Darkness,* ed. P. Mirecki and J. Be Duhn, 143–159. Leiden.

———. 1999. *Kephalaia.* Part 2: *Lieferung 13/14.* Stuttgart.

———. 2000. *Kephalaia.* Part 2: *Lieferung 15/16.* Stuttgart.

Gardner, I. 1995. *The Kephalaia of the Teacher.* Leiden.

——— and S. N. C. Lieu. 1996. "From Narmouthis (Medinat Madi) to Kellis (Ismant al-Kharab)." *JRS* 86:146–169.

———, A. Alcock and W.-P. Funk, eds. 1999. *Coptic Documentary Texts from Kellis.* Oxford.

Georgi, S. 1992. *Remembering the Poor: The History of the Pauline Collection for Jerusalem.* Nashville, TN.

Giversen, S. 1986. *The Manichaean Coptic Papyri in the Chester Beatty Library 1:* Kephalaia. Geneva.

Ibscher, H. 1940. *Kephalaia.* Part 1: *Lieferung 1/10.* Stuttgart.

Lieu, S. N. C. 1992. *Manichaeism in the Roman Empire and Medieval China.* 2nd ed. Tübingen.

Rebillard, É. 2003. *Religion et Sépulture: L'Église, les vivants et les morts.* Paris.

———. 2005. "*Nec deserere memorias suorum*: Augustine and the Family-based Commemoration of the Dead." *AugStud* 36:99–111.

Richter, S. G. 1997. *Die Aufstiegspsalmen des Herakleides: Untersuchungen zum Seelenaufstieg und zur Seelenmesse bei den Manichäern.* Wiesbaden.

Rousselle, A. and J.-M. Carrié. 1999. *L'empire romain en mutation des Sévères à Constantin 192–337.* Paris.

Schöllgen, C. 1998. *Die Anfänge der Professionalisierung des Klerus und der kirchliche Amt in der Syrischen Didaskalie.* Münster.

Stein, M. 2004. *Manichaica Latina 3:1.* Codex Thevestinus. Paderborn.

Tardieu, M. 1988. "La diffusion du Bouddhisme dans l'empire kouchan, l'Iran et la Chine d'après un *Kephalaion* manichéen inédit." *Studia Iranica* 17:153–180.

8

DE PÉTRA À JÉRUSALEM ... ET RETOUR!

MAURICE SARTRE

COMMENT, pour honorer un savant qui est aussi un tel globe-trotter, ai-je pu avoir l'idée de vous convier à parcourir avec moi si peu de chemin? Car, si les péripéties de l'histoire récente nous ont pendant longtemps interdit d'aller directement d'une ville à l'autre et ont contribué à nous les faire considérer trop facilement comme deux mondes étrangers l'un à l'autre, la géographie reste la plus forte et il faut se résoudre aux évidences: de Pétra à Jérusalem, il n'y a qu'un saut de puce à l'échelle de la Méditerranée.

Mais il y a d'autres barrières, d'autres frontières que celles que dressent les États! La spécialisation de plus en plus grande des savants, imposée en quelque sorte par l'avalanche des publications, dresse entre les champs d'études des obstacles presque infranchissables. Peut-être le phénomène est-il plus marqué dans certains pays que dans d'autres, et peut-être suis-je abusivement influencé par l'expérience française où, traditionnellement, on se déclare professeur d'Histoire "grecque" ou d'Histoire "romaine," rarement d'Histoire "ancienne." Et l'histoire grecque s'arrête prudemment à Actium, quand l'histoire romaine semble oublier de prendre en compte les provinces de langue grecque. Glen Bowersock est l'un de ces rares—et donc précieux—savants qui ont su embrasser d'un même regard l'Orient et l'Occident, et, en Méditerranée orientale, Grecs et Araméens, Romains et Perses, Juifs et Arabes. Puisque c'est l'Arabie qui nous a fait nous rencontrer—il y a trente ans exactement—on comprendra que j'aie voulu, pour cet hommage, revenir sur un sujet qui nous tient à cœur à tous deux, en l'enrichissant de ce que, durant cette longue période, j'ai appris ou mieux compris grâce, notamment, aux travaux de Glen Bowersock.

I.

Arabes et Juifs! Ce simple énoncé semble nous plonger dans l'histoire la plus contemporaine, mais la période dont je voudrais vous entretenir se situe il y a plus de deux millénaires, plus exactement, entre le IIe siècle avant J.-C. et, disons, le IIIe ou le IVe siècle après J.-C. Et abandonnons sur le champ l'idée d'un affrontement tel que celui qui déchire ces terres aujourd'hui. Certes, des guerres entre les uns et les autres, il y en eu, et plus d'une, mais ce n'est pas cela qui me retiendra, pour l'essentiel.

Si l'on se place vers le milieu du IIe siècle, la situation géopolitique du Levant Sud paraît relativement claire. À l'est du Jourdain, mais aussi dans le Néguev, un État s'est construit peu à peu, le royaume nabatéen.[1] Ses origines ne sont pas très claires, mais il ne fait guère de doute que l'organisation étatique est relativement précoce. On reviendra plus loin sur quelques détails, mais précisons d'emblée que cet État est, sinon peuplé, du moins dominé par des Arabes. On a essayé de remettre en cause récemment cette identification entre Nabatéens et Arabes, comme d'ailleurs, de déplacer dans le Néguev l'assaut des forces d'Antigone le Borgne en 312 contre leur capitale, Pétra,[2] mais la démonstration n'a rien de convaincant. Toute la tradition antique identifie les Nabatéens comme des Arabes, du moins selon la définition ethnographique qu'en donnent les Anciens, à savoir des nomades. Nomadisme limité pour beaucoup, mais dont il reste probablement une tradition de pastoralisme chamelier et l'aptitude à conduire des caravanes commerciales sur de longues distances. Leur installation ancienne dans le Sud de la Transjordanie, au contact des populations araméennes—ou du moins de langue araméenne—les a sans doute conduits à adopter nombre de traits culturels des populations sédentaires de Syrie, dont la langue araméenne. Mais l'onomastique et les cultes plaident en faveur de leur origine arabe.

---

[1] On me permettra de renvoyer à Sartre 2003:411–424, où l'on trouvera l'essentiel de la bibliographie utile; version résumée dans Sartre 2005:16–23.

[2] Restö 2003:366–367 (sur Arabes et Nabatéens) et 285–290 (sur la localisation dans le Néguev de la Pétra attaquée en 312).

Sur l'autre rive du Jourdain—mais aussi en partie à l'est du fleuve, dans ce que l'on nomme la Pérée—un État juif s'est également créé, plus récemment.[3] Au milieu du IIe siècle, il est en pleine phase de constitution, après la violente révolte des Maccabées. L'installation de Jonathan à Jérusalem, son accession au grand pontificat en 152, l'évacuation des troupes séleucides de l'Akra en 142, la proclamation de Simon comme grand prêtre, ethnarque et stratège par la Grande Knesset à l'automne 140 sont autant d'étapes essentielles dans l'édification de l'État hasmonéen. État à la superficie d'abord limitée aux environs de Jérusalem, mais qui s'étend rapidement à une grande partie de la Palestine grâce à l'énergie des grands prêtres et à la faiblesse de rois séleucides englués dans les querelles dynastiques.

Entre ces deux peuples, entre ces deux États, entre ces deux cultures, quels points communs? La spécificité indéniable des Juifs en matière religieuse ne dresse-t-elle pas un obstacle insurmontable à toute comparaison? La littérature savante n'a-t-elle pas fait preuve de sagesse en séparant soigneusement les Juifs de leur environnement?

Je ne le pense évidemment pas, car adhérer à ces positions *a priori* serait s'enfermer dans des schémas mal fondés, que l'archéologie et l'histoire démentent. Tout montre au contraire des convergences constantes, dont certaines proviennent peut-être d'une compétition avérée entre les deux États.

Je ne veux pas insister sur la compétition territoriale qui les oppose, bien qu'elle serve de toile de fond à leur coexistence durant plus d'un siècle, jusqu'à ce que Rome leur interdise des combats qui nuisent à la sécurité de la région. Mais gardons présent à l'esprit que Juifs et Arabes entrent en conflit à plusieurs reprises, sur deux fronts privilégiés: d'une part le Néguev et le Nord du Sinaï, où les Nabatéens tentent d'accéder à la mer et à un bon port, Gaza; d'autre part la Transjordanie, du pays de Moab jusqu'au Golan, seule possibilité pour les Nabatéens de dominer des zones agricoles où œuvrent des populations sédentaires. Il est d'autres enjeux, mais on peut se limiter ici à ceux-ci. Il serait cependant abusif de placer l'ensemble de leurs relations sous le signe de la rivalité

---

[3] Sartre 2003:383–397; Sartre 2005:12–16.

et de la concurrence. Des relations amicales sont attestées à plusieurs
reprises: le grand prêtre Jason trouve refuge d'abord chez Arétas le
Nabatéen en 169 (*2Macc.* 5.8), c'est aux Nabatéens que Jonathan veut
confier ses bagages lorsqu'il est en difficulté (*1Macc.* 9.35–36). Et lors
des menaces qui justifient l'intervention des troupes maccabéennes
dans le Hauran en 163, les Nabatéens de la région se montrent amicaux
(*1Macc.* 5.25).

Un arrière-plan d'ardente concurrence se développe néanmoins
à partir du milieu du IIe siècle, lorsque les deux États cherchent à
s'étendre. Il me semble expliquer, au moins en partie, certaines évolu-
tions parallèles, même si celles-ci se produisent avec un certain décalage dans le temps. Mais la concurrence n'explique pas tout et l'on peut
trouver bien des ressemblances dans la manière dont Juifs et Arabes
réagirent face à la domination politique des Grecs d'abord, des Romains
ensuite, et, plus largement face à la culture grecque que les uns et les
autres véhiculaient, sans que le contexte de rivalité soit un facteur
explicatif.

Bien que les deux États soient nés à des moments différents de
l'histoire hellénistique, ils surgissent l'un et l'autre d'une confron-
tation avec un royaume hellénistique. On ne sait rien des Nabatéens
avant le coup de main lancé par Antigone le Borgne sur Pétra en 312,
et je me garderais donc de considérer que la résistance offerte aux
troupes gréco-macédoniennes à cette occasion constitue l'acte fonda-
teur de l'État. Mais si les Nabatéens n'avaient pas encore mesuré l'am-
pleur des changements intervenus en 332 en Syrie, ils en prirent alors
la pleine mesure. On ne peut douter qu'à partir de ce moment l'État
nabatéen dut tenir compte de la présence de puissants royaumes à
l'ouest et au nord de son territoire. Toute progression territoriale ne
pouvait se faire qu'au détriment des Lagides, puis, à partir de 200–198,
des Séleucides.

La naissance de l'État hasmonéen, plus tardive, fut aussi plus
douloureuse puisqu'il fallut une longue guerre de libération. Après
l'évacuation de l'Akra en 142, les Juifs ne furent pas à l'abri d'un retour
offensif des troupes séleucides comme on le vit bien en 131 avec la
campagne victorieuse d'Antiochos VII contre Jean Hyrcan, puis celle,

malheureuse, d'Antiochos XII en 87.[4] Néanmoins, là aussi, la création
d'un État territorial qui dépassât le seul pays occupé par les Juifs se fit
très rapidement, en un demi-siècle, au détriment du royaume séleu-
cide, plus rarement au détriment des voisins nabatéens.

Confrontés l'un et l'autre à des royaumes hellénistiques beaucoup
plus puissants, les deux États adoptèrent peu à peu les structures de
ces royaumes, et parfois presque en même temps. Ainsi, on a longtemps hésité sur la date d'apparition d'un monnayage à Pétra comme
à Jérusalem. Il apparaît maintenant comme à peu près assuré que les
premières séries monétaires nabatéennes remontent aux années 129–
128, au temps d'Arétas II,[5] suivies d'assez près par les premières émis-
sions hasmonéennes vers 110.[6] Je ne crois pas que ce phénomène soit
anecdotique car il s'inscrit dans un processus plus ample qui comporte
la mise en place des structures d'un État hellénistique et l'adoption de
certains aspects de la culture grecque. Sans chercher à être exhaustif, il
faut en rappeler quelques éléments afin d'appuyer l'analyse du phénomène chez les deux peuples voisins.

La prise du titre royal symbolise mieux que tout cette adhésion aux
modes ou modèles helléniques. On a longtemps hésité sur la date d'apparition de ce titre chez les Nabatéens, faute de documents fiables, et
une découverte récente ne me paraît pas modifier complètement la
situation. En effet, l'une des épigrammes du Papyrus de Milan récemment édité, très mutilée, mentionne sur deux lignes successives un
"Nabatéen," "roi des cavaliers combattants."[7] Même si l'on laisse de
côté la possibilité de restituer "Malichos" comme nom du Nabatéen en
question, il demeure la mention très probable d'un roi des Nabatéens

---

[4] Antiochos XII vise en réalité les Nabatéens, mais il a entrepris de contourner la
mer Morte par le Sud et donc de traverser l'essentiel du royaume d'Alexandre Jannée. La
défaite cuisante de celui-ci près de Joppé n'eut pas de suites en raison de la défaite et de
la mort d'Antiochos XII face aux Nabatéens: Flavius Josèphe, *AJ* 13.390–391.

[5] Meshorer 1975 optait pour le règne d'Obodas II, mais la série avec Athéna casquée
au droit et Niké au revers avait déjà été attribuée aux Nabatéens par Robinson 1936:290–
291, et Kushnir-Stein et Gitler 1992–1993:13–20, ont montré que ces séries remontaient
aussi haut que les années 129–128. Meshorer s'était rallié à cette position.

[6] Cf. Sartre 2003:391 et n70 avec la bibliographie antérieure.

[7] Texte édité par Austin et Bastianini 2002:n° 10. Sur cet aspect du dossier, cf. Graf
2006.

entre les années 280 et le milieu du IIIᵉ siècle av. J.-C. Cette découverte donne du poids à une hypothèse de J.-T. Milik[8] qui datait résolument du IIIᵉ siècle une inscription nabatéenne d'Elousa portant mention d'un Arétas, roi des Nabatéens.[9] Or, en 169, *2Macc.* 5.8 traite encore un Arétas de "tyran des Arabes," ce qui paraît contredire l'épigramme de Posidippos comme l'inscription d'Elousa. Sans que l'on puisse aboutir à une certitude, il me semble que l'on ne doive pas trop se fonder sur des appellations transmises par les sources littéraires. L'auteur de *2Macc.*, Juif hellénisé à l'évidence, peut bien réserver le titre de τύραννος à un chef "barbare" sans se soucier de son titre réel. On pourrait évidemment en dire autant de Posidippos de Pella qui, à l'inverse, aurait pu attribuer au chef des Nabatéens le titre qui convient pour un chef suprême; mais, si Milik a raison pour la date, l'inscription d'Elousa, qui est un document issu des Nabatéens eux-mêmes, confirmerait la justesse du terme. Il est donc fort possible, sinon probable, que le titre royal apparaisse en Nabatène dès le IIIᵉ siècle.

Chez les Juifs, Aristobule, selon Flavius Josèphe, aurait été le premier à porter le titre de *basileus*, vers 104–103 au plus tôt.[10] A Jérusalem et à Pétra, l'emprunt aux monarchies hellénistiques ne fait pas de doute. Certes, il existe chez les Juifs une tradition royale davidique, mais rien dans la monarchie hasmonéenne (et encore moins hérodienne) ne rattache celle-ci à ce lointain ancêtre,[11] et Josèphe précise bien qu'Aristobule fut le premier hasmonéen "à placer le diadème sur sa tête." Ainsi, aucun effort n'est fait pour que le roi apparaisse comme roi juif: sur les monnaies d'Alexandre Jannée, le revers porte le nom hébreu de Jannée et son titre de grand-prêtre, alors que le droit (*a priori* plus visible) porte la mention *Basileōs Alexandrou*, comme un banal souverain hellénistique. Certes, on se garde bien de graver l'effigie du souverain, ce qui aurait été un sacrilège, mais la légende grecque suffit à mesurer la volonté hellénisante du souverain. Chez les Nabatéens, la tradition aniconique des dieux ne s'applique pas aux rois, et le portrait

---

[8] Cité par Starcky 1966:col904.
[9] Inscription publiée d'abord par Cowley 1914–1915:145–147.
[10] *AJ* 13.301.
[11] Mendels 1997:55–79.

des souverains apparaît, avec une légende uniquement araméenne, à partir d'Obodas II, soit avec un certain décalage par rapport à l'apparition de la monnaie: crainte de l'image ? Probablement pas puisque les premières séries nabatéennes affichent Athéna et Nikè dans les années 120, à l'imitation des monnaies d'Alexandre.

La vie de cour elle-même paraît marquée d'influences ou de pratiques helléniques. Chez les Nabatéens des titres auliques imitent ceux des cours hellénistiques. Strabon qualifie Syllaios de "frère du roi," et les reines portent habituellement le titre de "sœur" du roi.[12] Je ne connais rien de tel à la cour hasmonéenne, mais l'influence grandissante des femmes (ce qui justifie qu'Aristobule fasse emprisonner sa mère), les intrigues sanglantes, le recours à l'assassinat politique (Simon assassiné par son gendre Ptolémée), et, plus pacifiquement, la pratique des banquets où nombre d'anecdotes rapportées par Josèphe ou par d'autres trouvent place, tout me paraît assimiler la cour de Jérusalem à celles d'Alexandrie et d'Antioche.

De même, la construction de tombeaux monumentaux appartient à la volonté de manifester la toute puissance royale. Certes, il est regrettable que nous n'ayons pas trace des tombeaux royaux lagides, séleucides ou attalides, mais la description du tombeau de famille des Hasmonéens à Modiin, telle que le décrit l'auteur de *1Macc.* 13.25–30, établit l'inspiration hellénistique de leur aspect monumental: "Simon fit bâtir au-dessus du tombeau de son père et de ses frères et le suréleva pour qu'on le vît, avec de la pierre polie, par derrière et par devant; puis il dressa sept pyramides, les unes en face des autres, pour son père, pour sa mère et pour ses quatre frères; il leur fit une garniture en les entourant de grande colonnes; il fit sur les colonnes des panoplies pour assurer à ceux-là un renom éternel, et, à côté des panoplies, des navires sculptés de façon à être vus de tous ceux qui navigueraient en mer." La volonté d'ostentation est manifeste et appartient clairement au système de valeur des monarchies hellénistiques. Les pyramides rappellent certains des tombeaux un peu plus tardifs de la vallée du Cédron, ainsi que certains tombeaux de Pétra comportant pyramides

---

[12] Je ne crois pas du tout que cela implique de réels liens du sang, dans une tradition tribale, comme l'indique Teixidor 1995:114; naturellement cela ne les exclut pas.

ou obélisques. Le rapprochement avec Pétra (et Hégra) paraît d'autant plus justifié que les tombeaux de la capitale nabatéenne relèvent aussi de la volonté d'ostentation des rois et des riches habitants de la ville. On aimerait pouvoir comparer de la même manière les palais hasmonéens et hérodiens avec leurs homologues hellénistiques, mais on sait combien sont rares les exemples de palais hellénistiques. Néanmoins, celui de Pétra—abusivement dénommé "Great Temple" par ses découvreurs—témoigne du même goût pour le décor et les aménagements hellénisants que celui de Jéricho par exemple.[13]

D'autres traits hellénisants sont repérables dans l'un et l'autre royaume, et plus encore chez les Hérodiens. On mentionnera pour mémoire la constitution d'un domaine foncier royal, attesté chez les Hasmonéens dès le règne de Jonathan avec le domaine d'Ekron qu'il distribue en *klēroi* à ses soldats. L'armée porte aussi la marque de ces hellénisations: système des clérouques, emploi de mercenaires étrangers dès les Hasmonéens, ce que les Hérodiens développèrent. Des textes peu connus, voire inédits, de Syrie du Sud montrent que les Hérodiens embauchèrent des mercenaires non seulement en Babylonie et en Idumée, mais aussi des Grecs, installés par eux à Danaba. Ils n'hésitèrent pas à emprunter le vocabulaire grec ou romain pour désigner leurs propres créations: un Hérodien fonda même une colonie, dotée d'une ère propre, sur la bordure du Trachôn, à Shaara.[14] On a cru parfois que des officiers romains avaient été détachés auprès de l'armée hérodienne; je ne crois pas que ce soit le cas et il s'agit seulement de mercenaires de haut rang apportant avec eux les méthodes et le vocabulaire de l'armée romaine.[15]

Les Nabatéens ne furent pas en reste, eux qui empruntèrent des termes comme éparque,[16] chiliarque,[17] stratopédarque ou *centurion*,

---

[13] Joukowsky 1998, avec les doutes émis très tôt sur la nature de l'édifice par Bowersock 2000:60; cf. déjà Zayadine 1987:139.

[14] Inscription inédite mentionnant l'an 23 de la colonie, dans le cadre d'une dédicace clairement d'époque hérodienne.

[15] C'est le cas de L. Obulnius, officier d'Agrippa Ier ou II, ou de Modius Aequus au service d'Agrippa II.

[16] *CIS* 2.214 = H 32.

[17] *CIS* 2.201 = H 29.

transcrits en araméen, ce qui dénote un emprunt direct, et non une simple traduction conventionnelle lorsque l'on passe d'une langue à l'autre. De même les Nabatéens empruntèrent-ils des termes pour l'administration civile comme *stratège* ou *epitropos*.[18] Or, je ne considère pas ces emprunts comme un simple vernis pour faire "moderne," une manière de donner un nom grec à des institutions traditionnelles: il y a sans doute adoption des modes nouveaux d'organisation militaire et administrative.

Je ne cherche évidemment pas à montrer que les deux royaumes voisins se transformèrent en royaumes hellénistiques comme les autres, et je n'ignore pas combien ils restèrent profondément originaux par d'autres aspects. Il n'est pas la peine d'insister, chez les Juifs, sur le maintien des règles de la *Torah*. Et la description du fonctionnement de la société nabatéenne et de l'entourage royal par Strabon et par Diodore[19] montre tout ce qui sépare l'État nabatéen d'un royaume hellénisé.

II.

Ce n'est pas seulement l'État qui s'hellénise, mais la société tout entière, à Pétra comme à Jérusalem. L'hellénisme gagne en profondeur les diverses couches de la société: on est loin d'une simple hellénisation des structures étatiques. Et le premier paradoxe est sans doute de trouver l'hellénisme à l'œuvre avec autant de vigueur, en Judée, chez ceux qui le rejettent que chez ceux qui l'acceptent avec ferveur. On mesure ici combien nous manque un Jason de Cyrène ou un Flavius Josèphe nabatéens, qui auraient décrit les réactions de la société nabatéenne aux innovations. Nous observons les changements, nous en mesurons éventuellement les incidences culturelles, mais nous ne pouvons deviner les oppositions éventuelles qu'il fallut vaincre.

---

[18] *CIS* 2.234, 235, 238, 270 (JSa N 43): '*srtg*'. Cf. Teixidor 1995:111–121, 115–116; on y trouvera commodément rassemblées les attestations de mots et d'institutions grecques.

[19] Peut-être faut-il réévaluer ces témoignages à la lumière des procédés rhétoriques de l'ethnographie antique. Il serait intéressant de connaître les sources de Diodore; en tout cas, on trouve chez Diodore des éléments qui rappellent la description des Rékabites chez *Jérémie* 35.6–7.

Il est frappant d'observer que sur le plan culturel les changements sont pour l'essentiel les mêmes de chaque côté du wadi Arabah et du Jourdain. Ainsi, l'onomastique des Judéens a accueilli très tôt des noms grecs. Chacun connaît les noms de Jason et de Ménélas, mais on pourrait en ajouter bien d'autres, comme Eupolémos, Dosithéos, etc.[20] L'usage se répand dans les milieux juifs cultivés dès la fin du IIIe siècle, sans que l'on puisse en déduire un relâchement des observances chez ceux qui les portent: il y a autant de Juifs opposés à Jason qui portent un nom grec[21] que de partisans de Jason et de Ménélas. La mise en route d'un corpus systématique de la Palestine permettra de faire un inventaire plus précis, mais on voit bien que les noms grecs sont présents en quantité dans l'onomastique des Juifs de Judée. C'est frappant dans les milieux hellénisés, ceux qui font écrire en grec, mais on l'observe aussi bien dans des milieux plutôt traditionnels, où les noms sémitiques abondent. Il suffit de relever les noms de la nécropole de Beth Shearim pour en être convaincu, même s'il est vrai qu'une partie des Juifs enterrés là provient de la diaspora.[22] L'acculturation de ceux-ci a pu favoriser cette évolution, mais ce n'est pas certain si l'on compare avec la situation attestée plus à l'Est.

On ne peut parler d'une diaspora "arabe," même si elle existe (à Délos, à Rhodes, en Italie), compte tenu de sa faible importance numérique, et il est donc exclu que l'emprunt de noms grecs par les Nabatéens subisse l'influence d'une diaspora. Or, l'habitude de prendre un nom grec se répand dans la société nabatéenne bien avant la disparition

---

[20] Cf. les analyses assez générales de Hengel 1980; plus détaillé, Hengel 1974; sur l'onomastique grecque des Juifs, Hengel 1974:61–65.

[21] Ainsi les ambassadeurs de Judas à Rome, Jason fils d'Éléazar, et Eupolémos (*1Macc.* 8.17). Plus tard les ambassadeurs de Jonathan à Rome sont Numénios fils d'Antiochos et Antipater fils de Jason (*1Macc.* 12.16); les mêmes sont aussi envoyés à Sparte (*1Macc.* 14.22) et Numénios seul à Rome (*1Macc.* 14.24; cf. 15.15, où l'on précise qu'il est avec d'autres, non nommés) par Simon. Il faudrait encore mentionner les officiers juifs opérant en Transjordanie, Dosithéos, et Sōsipatros (*2Macc.* 12.19 et 24), le traducteur juif du livre d'*Esther* en grec à Jérusalem (Lysimaque fils de Ptolémée, ainsi que ceux qui l'ont apporté à Alexandrie, Dosithéos, et son fils Ptolémée: *Esther* Suppl. 10.3.11). Cf. aussi la liste des LXX dans la *Lettre d'Aristée*.

[22] Les noms relevés à Beth Shearim sont très variés, et parfois inattendus, comme une Dionysia; mais la plupart sont neutres sur le plan religieux.

du royaume nabatéen. J.-T. Milik avait naguère relevé les noms grecs attestés dans les inscriptions nabatéennes au temps de l'indépendance; et Abraham Negev a complété l'enquête.[23] Le total est assez impressionnant compte tenu du faible nombre de textes, ce qui me semble être la preuve d'une relative banalisation du phénomène chez les élites. Les noms choisis sont extrêmement variés, y compris des noms assez rares comme Glaucos ou Damasippos, et il faut aussi prendre en compte les noms d'origine indigène pour lesquels on adapte une terminaison à la grecque (Μαλχίων). Tous se trouvent en transcription araméenne, non en grec, ce qui me paraît très révélateur d'une volonté hellénisante. Il peut y avoir quelques étrangers, mais je doute fort que des Grecs de passage ou des Romains fassent graver des inscriptions en nabatéen!

On doit mettre ce goût pour les noms propres grecs en parallèle avec l'adoption d'une architecture funéraire fortement marquée par le goût alexandrin, par l'introduction aussi d'un décor de la maison emprunté à l'art gréco-romain. Les stucs, les peintures de style pompéien relevés à Pétra, y compris maintenant dans le pseudo "Grand Temple" qui a de bonnes chances d'être le palais royal, contribuent de la même manière à créer un cadre "grec" pour la vie de ces notables. Les maisons rupestres du wadi Siyyagh[24] comme les belles maisons construites de ez-Zantour[25] en portent témoignage. L'hellénisme a pénétré tôt à Pétra si l'on suit les spécialistes de la peinture, qui estime que les peintures de style gréco-romain appartiennent au plus tard à la fin du IIᵉ siècle av. J.-C.

La même diffusion des goûts grecs existe en Judée. Les tombes de la vallée du Cédron,[26] la tombe de Jason et son épigramme, le décor

---

[23] Negev 1991.

[24] Cf. Zayadine 1987:131–142; Nehmé et Villeneuve 1999:62–71; Zayadine 1986:248 et ill. 49. D'autres traces de murs peints avaient été relevées dans les thermes situés au sud de l'arc monumental: Zayadine 1986:217, ill. 5.

[25] Kolb 2000:42–43.

[26] Cf. présentation d'ensemble dans Fedak 1990:140–148. Sur le tombeau de Zachariah, cube à couronnement pyramidal, Avigad 1954:79–90; Stutchbury 1961:101–113; tombe de Jason, du début du Iᵉʳ siècle av. J.-C., mêlant ordre dorique et ordre corinthien: Rahmani 1967:61–100; Avigad 1967:101–111; Benoît 1967:112–113. Cf. aussi Avigad 1975:17–20. Noter encore le tombeau des Bene Hezir, d'ordre dorique, et celui d'Absalom, avec sa couverture en forme de calice de lotus.

des maisons hellénistiques de la Cité de David, dont les plus anciennes
remontent de la même façon à la fin du IIe siècle,[27] tout invite au
rapprochement. Josèphe mentionne aussi les belles maisons des grands
propriétaires juifs de Chabulôn, en Galilée occidentale, "construites
dans le même style que celle de Tyr, de Sidon et de Bérytos."[28] Le décor
général s'apparente à celui du royaume voisin[29] et la même volonté de
paraître moderne a saisi les notables juifs et arabes, en même temps.
Même si les Juifs pieux refusent certains aspects de cette modernité—
comme les images—c'est peut-être un aspect secondaire par rapport
à l'ambiance culturelle d'ensemble. Et le mouvement ne cessa de se
développer après la ruine de Jérusalem, notamment dans ce refuge du
judaïsme que fut la Galilée, comme en témoignent les découvertes de
Sepphoris.

Quittant Pétra par la ville basse, le Siq et la route vers wadi Mousa, et
arrivant à Jérusalem par la vallée du Cédron, le voyageur ne changeait
pas radicalement de monde culturel. Le décor urbain et péri-urbain
devait lui paraître familier. Car je ne crois pas que l'on puisse douter
que la même ambiance culturelle ne règne à Jérusalem et à Pétra. La
spécialisation des historiens a contribué à isoler les Juifs de leur milieu,
comme cela s'est produit aussi pour l'Égypte dont on voudrait faire un
isolat culturel. Certes, des traits spécifiques puissants existent, en Judée
comme en Égypte, mais pas au point d' exclure ces communautés du
monde dans lequel elles vivent. Comme Sylvie Honigman,[30] je considère que la littérature grecque produite par des Juifs aux IIe av. J.-C.-
IIe s. apr. J.-C. appartient pleinement à la culture grecque du temps et
qu'il est illusoire de créer une catégorie "littérature juive d'expression
grecque."

[27] Avigad 1972:198 notamment. Cf. des illustrations dans Avigad 1975 (il s'agit des
fouilles des années 1968–1974), et dans Geva 1994 (notamment pl. VI). Cf. aussi Avigad
1989, qui présente le musée installé sur les fouilles et fournit plans des maisons et riches
illustrations; les maisons appartiennent aux Ier s. av.- Ier s. ap. J.-C., toutes détruites en 70.

[28] *BJ* 2.504.

[29] Cf. Rozenberg 1996:121–138, qui n'exclut pas la présence d'artistes italiens; Fittschen
1996:139–161.

[30] Honigman 2003.

Il en va de la littérature comme des autres arts. Quiconque parcourt Pétra aujourd'hui découvre une ville "grecque," je veux dire une ville imprégnée de l'urbanisme gréco-romain de son temps. Certes, Pétra n'est ni Rome, ni Athènes, ni Alexandrie—je ferai silence sur Antioche que nous connaissons si mal—mais le cadre urbain d'ensemble n'est pas si fondamentalement différent. Ce n'est en aucun cas un art gréco-arabe, même si des motifs étrangers à l'art gréco-romain ornent nombre de tombeaux ou de maisons. Comme les géologues parlent de faciès, j'aurais tendance à considérer que Pétra offre aux visiteurs le faciès nabatéen de l'art gréco-romain de son temps. Il ne reste malheureusement rien ou à peu près rien de la littérature des auteurs grecs d'origine arabe de cette époque, et la plupart ne sont plus que des noms. Mais le peu que l'on sait d'eux révèle des auteurs grecs sans attache particulière avec l'Arabie.

Généthlios de Pétra se distingue comme spécialiste de Démosthène, et son rival et compatriote Callinicos ne s'occupe guère plus d'affaires syriennes que bien d'autres auteurs grecs. Certes, il a bien composé en dix livres un ouvrage intitulé Περὶ τῶν κατ' Ἀλεξάνδρειαν ἱστοριῶν, dont il subsiste un extrait sur les guerres entre Antiochos IV et Ptolémée VI Philométor, mais il n'a aucune saveur "arabe" particulière. En réalité, ces rhéteurs ou sophistes "arabes" ne sont pas plus "arabes" que leurs confrères de Phénicie ne sont phéniciens: ils appartiennent pleinement à la littérature grecque de leur temps. Fergus Millar a rappelé naguère[31] comment des auteurs originaires de Phénicie étaient totalement étrangers à leur terre d'origine, comme Porphyre de Tyr qui, lorsqu'il cite à deux reprises la Syrie, s'appuie sur le témoignage de deux auteurs grecs d'Asie Mineure. Peut-être faudrait-il faire une exception pour des auteurs comme Glaucos ou, surtout, Ouranios, dont Glen Bowersock a montré la fiabilité et l'excellente connaissance de l'Arabie;[32] le second, à l'évidence, connaît le sens exact des mots arabes ou araméens. Mais les pauvres fragments qui subsistent ne permettent sûrement pas de le cataloguer comme un auteur gréco-arabe!

---

[31] Millar 1997:241–262.
[32] Bowersock 1997:174–185.

Rien ne me paraît plus semblable, du moins en apparence, que la Galilée des IIe et IIIe siècles: un décor urbain gréco-romain tel qu'il apparaît à Sepphoris, avec des mosaïques, et un décor des maisons qui ne déparerait pas les belles maisons de n'importe quelle autre ville grecque de la même époque. Même les synagogues n'échappent pas à la mise au goût du jour si l'on en croit une anecdote rapportée par *BT Shabbat* 72b où un Juif, croyant entrer dans une synagogue, se retrouve dans un temple païen. La confusion serait-elle possible si les mêmes éléments décoratifs n'ornaient pas l'un et l'autre? Dans la ville, et dans toute la région, des rabbins à l'évidence connaissent souvent le grec, même s'ils ne l'utilisent ni pour enseigner, ni pour écrire. On a depuis longtemps mis en évidence l'influence déterminante de l'hellénisme sur le développement de la pensée juive depuis l'époque hellénistique. Je ne fais pas ici allusion à Philon et autres auteurs juifs de la littérature grecque que j'évoquais plus haut. Je veux parler de ceux qui paraissent les plus étrangers à cette littérature et que l'on ne saurait considérer comme des auteurs "grecs," je veux dire les maîtres du Talmud.

Les élites intellectuelles juives avaient adapté à leurs propres besoins les procédés rhétoriques de l'hellénisme dès l'époque hellénistique. Le phénomène s'observe dès le livre de l'*Ecclesiaste* (*Qohélet*) car en dépit des contorsions des exégètes, je reste persuadé que le modèle de ce livre de sagesse réside davantage dans les maximes stoïciennes de l'époque que dans des modèles mésopotamiens improbables remontant à plus d'un millénaire. Quelle que soit la force de la tradition des livres de sagesse, la saveur hellénisante de *Qohélet* me paraît incontestable. On admettra qu'il est difficile de ne pas considérer un peu plus tard les livres de *Judith* et d'*Esther*, dans la version finale qui nous est parvenue, celle du IIe siècle, comme des romans hellénistiques dosant avec soin les ingrédients de ce type de littérature, suspense, sexe et sang, la piété en plus!

Trop d'études savantes ont porté sur ces sujets pour que je développe davantage ce point. Mais il est plus intéressant de souligner que les rabbis des premiers siècles n'hésitent pas davantage à emprunter à l'hellénisme. On a montré naguère combien les images empruntés aux concours grecs sont présentes dans la littérature talmudique,[33] comme

---

[33] Chambers 1980, essentiel.

chez Paul de Tarse. On a établi à juste titre un parallèle entre la maïeu-
tique socratique et certains dialogues des rabbis avec leurs élèves, et
plus généralement entre les dialogues platoniciens et l'enseignement de
ces maîtres. On peut discuter de la forme, mais les influences quant au
fond sont d'une autre importance et les exemples sont multiples.[34] On
connaît le célèbre dialogue rapporté dans le traité *Avodah Zarah* entre
un rabbi Gamaliel (II ou III) et un philosophe grec (sans doute imagi-
naire) nommé Proclos au sujet de l'image d'Aphrodite dans les thermes.

> Proclos ben Philosophos posa cette question à Rabban
> Gamaliel à Akko, alors qu'ils se baignaient dans les thermes
> d'Aphrodite: "Il est écrit dans votre *Torah* 'tu ne mettras
> la main sur rien de ce qui est voué à l'interdit' (*herem*)
> (*Deutéronome* 13.18); pourquoi alors te baignes-tu dans les
> thermes d'Aphrodite?" Il répondit: "on ne peut pas répondre
> [aux questions relatives à la *Torah*] dans des thermes." Quand
> ils furent sortis, Rabban Gamaliel dit: "Je ne suis pas entré
> sur son territoire, elle est entrée sur le mien. Tu ne dis pas
> 'les thermes sont construits comme un ornement pour
> Aphrodite,' mais 'Aphrodite est placée comme un orne-
> ment des thermes.' De plus, même si on te donnait beaucoup
> d'argent, tu n'entrerais pas dans ton temple nu, juste après
> avoir éjaculé, et en urinant devant la déesse. Or, ici même,
> elle se tient au-dessus de l'égoût et chacun urine devant elle.
> Il est écrit 'leurs dieux, dans les situations où ils sont traités
> comme des dieux, sont interdits, quand ils ne le sont pas, ils
> sont autorisés.' (*Mischna Avodah Zarah* 3:4)

Dans ce texte fondamental, on voit en réalité r. Gamaliel séparer
le sacré et le non-sacré, en inventant la catégorie neutre du décor. On
mesure le chemin parcouru depuis l'époque des Maccabées, lorsque
l'auteur de *2Maccabées* s'étouffait d'indignation devant la présence des
Juifs dans la palestre ou l'envoi d'une délégation aux *Hérakleia* de Tyr où,
pourtant, ils se gardaient bien de sacrifier aux dieux. Pour r. Gamaliel,

---

[34] Cf. notamment la belle démonstration de Satlow 1998:135–144, sur les arguments
nouveaux des rabbins dans leur condamnation de l'homosexualité.

se baigner nu aux thermes, au milieu des païens (on est dans une cité grecque, Ptolémaïs) et en présence d'une statue d'Aphrodite ne constitue pas une gêne, si ce n'est pour parler de questions religieuses.

On ne peut s'étonner dans ces conditions de trouver des mythes grecs représentés dans des milieux juifs. Le sarcophage de Méléagre trouvé à Beth Shearim,[35] daté du IIIᵉ siècle, ne devait plus choquer personne. Et l'on sait comment l'interdiction de représenter les êtres vivants fut abandonnée à Doura comme à Sepphoris.[36]

Il n'est pas abusif, je crois, de parler d'une hellénisation en profondeur de la société juive dans les premiers siècles de notre ère. En dépit des refus, des révoltes, l'imprégnation se fait en profondeur car, quoi qu'en disent les rabbis, la séduction de l'hellénisme joue à plein sur de larges pans de la société juive. Le cadre multiculturel, multi-religieux, et polyethnique dans lequel vivent désormais les Juifs de Palestine leur impose de réfléchir à leur propre identité et à ce qui en constitue l'essence. Et ils le font avec les armes que leur fournit la rhétorique grecque aussi bien qu'avec les ressources de l'exégèse juive du commentaire des Écritures. En inventant la catégorie neutre du décor, les rabbins abandonnent la vision traditionnelle où tout est religieux. Puisque les Juifs ne sont pas plus insensibles aux charmes du modernisme que les autres peuples de la région, il fallait d'urgence faire sortir de l'interdit ce qui pouvait l'être, faire la part entre l'accessoire et l'essentiel. En d'autres termes, la concurrence de l'hellénisme obligeait le judaïsme à accomplir une mutation intellectuelle et sociale fondamentale.

Car des Juifs ne craignent plus de souligner leur appartenance au monde grec. Une jeune juive, dont on a retrouvé les archives sur les bords de la mer Morte, Salomé Komaisé, fait inscrire dans son contrat de mariage "l'engagement de bonne foi dudit Yeshu'a (son époux) de la nourrir et la vêtir elle et ses enfants à venir en accord avec les *habitudes grecques* et les *manières grecques* au péril de tous ses biens." Même si, à l'évidence, il s'agit pour elle de souligner une certaine qualité de vie, j'ai envie de dire "un certain *standing*," et si l'hellénisme dont elle se prévaut apparaît d'abord comme un critère de différenciation

---

[35] Koch 1975:n° 200.
[36] Cf. en particulier Levine et Weiss 2000.

sociale, on imagine quel chemin parcouru depuis l'époque où l'auteur de *2Maccabées* dénonçait la création d'un gymnase à Jérusalem. Sous la pression de l'hellénisme et avec l'aide de ses outils intellectuels, le judaïsme a bien effectué une véritable révolution. En quelque sorte, il a "digéré" l'hellénisme ou, si l'on préfère, surmonter la crise moderniste.

III.

Salomé Komaïsè nous ramène sur les bords de la mer Morte. Revenons donc à Pétra. Aucun des interdits qui obligent les rabbis à tant d'efforts pour suivre les penchants de leurs ouailles ne pèse, apparemment, sur la société nabatéenne. Apparemment dis-je, car nous manquons de preuves, et quelques indices restent difficilement exploitables. Naturellement, si des Nabatéens pieux se sont indigné de voir Doushara, al-Uzza, ou Allat représentés sous forme de dieux grecs, nous n'en avons pas de traces. Quoique ... le maintien de stèles "aux yeux," ou plus simplement la sculpture de bétyles dans le défilé du Siq jusqu'aux IIe–IIIe siècles de notre ère montre un réel attachement aux traditions, au moins de la part de certains fidèles, et une certaine conception des dieux. Mais nous ignorons si les mêmes qui honorent les dieux en faisant graver leur bétyle dans certaines circonstances n'offrent pas, en d'autres occasions, une statuette parfaitement anthropomorphe. Nous ne pouvons donc faire la part entre attachement aux traditions et refus des innovations. Un seul indice me paraît aujourd'hui dénoter un refus d'une habitude grecque: l'absence de concours grecs dans la ville. Louis Robert l'avait souligné jadis et y voyait une claire limite de l'hellénisation, à Pétra comme à Palmyre. On pourrait y ajouter la Judée. Encore faudrait-il connaître les raisons de cette absence chez les Nabatéens et chez les Palmyréniens. S'agit-il, comme le laissait entendre Louis Robert, d'un refus de la nudité athlétique? Peut-être, mais il y avait des thermes à Pétra, comme en Judée ... Auraient-ils été utilisés par les seuls Romains de passage ou résidents? Faut-il au contraire mettre l'absence de concours sur le compte d'un manque de moyens? Je ne crois pas l'argument tenable car rien n'indique un appauvrissement de la ville avant le grand tremblement de terre de 363. La raison invoquée par Louis Robert reste peut-être la plus vraisemblable, et le parallèle avec Palmyre la renforce. Mais c'est le parallèle entre Nabatène et Judée qui importe ici, ce que Louis Robert n'avait pas souligné.

Ainsi Pétra s'est modernisée, hellénisée, mêlant sans doute comme Jérusalem et, plus tard, les villes juives de Galilée, traditions indigènes et emprunts à l'hellénisme. Pétra, mais d'une façon plus large, toute l'Arabie romaine, de Hégra à Pétra. Il reste sans aucun doute beaucoup à découvrir encore à Hégra où seuls les tombeaux du Ier siècle ont réellement été étudiés. Or, une découverte récente, une inscription latine, prouve que l'agglomération indigène a été transformée en cité par les Romains.[37] De quoi cela s'accompagna-t-il? Le repérage de l'agglomération, effectué récemment par prospection archéométrique, permettra peut-être d'en savoir plus si une fouille a lieu. On connaît beaucoup mieux les transformations de Bostra et des villages du Hauran où les monuments gréco-romains pénètrent jusque dans les campagnes: théâtres, thermes, temples, mais aussi nécropoles. Mais les villes juives de Galilée n'ont pas échappé à cette adaptation. Et, de ce point de vue, la diffusion du christianisme en Arabie n'apporta pas de modification particulière, les sociétés d'Arabie suivirent le mouvement "moderne" du moment, sans qu'on y devine de particulières réticences.

Au total, les deux peuples voisins, porteurs de deux cultures différentes, suivent une même évolution, celle de la modernité ambiante. L'un sans état d'âme, l'autre dans une dialectique permanente du refus et du maintien de son identité. Or, au bout du compte, on peut s'interroger sur le résultat dans la très longue durée. Que reste-t-il de l'hellénisme des Arabes Nabatéens? Que reste-t-il de l'héritage grec dans le Judaïsme?

Même si cela ne fut pas ressenti comme tel dès le début, l'invasion musulmane de 634–636 constitua un réel bouleversement pour toute la région. Bouleversement politique, certes, mais plus profondément religieux. Tout ne s'effondra pas d'un seul coup, on le sait bien, et la construction et l'embellissement d'églises se poursuivirent jusqu'au milieu du VIIIe siècle. Mais j'ai toujours été frappé par l'effondrement rapide de l'hellénisme en Syrie et Arabie où même la minorité chrétienne ne maintint guère le flambeau d'un hellénisme vivant. On sait que l'effon-

[37] Al-Talhi et al-Daire 2005:205–217.

drement fut plus rapide encore et plus radical en Afrique du Nord et que les historiens s'interrogent toujours sur les raisons profondes de ce bouleversement dans une province qui passait pour la plus romanisée de toutes. Sans aucun doute, l'Islam imposait une rupture nette comme seul peut l'exiger un monothéisme. Le christianisme, bien que né du judaïsme, avait été presque dès ses débuts lié indissolublement à la culture gréco-romaine puisque c'était celle de ses fidèles les plus nombreux. Il avait fallu trier dans l'héritage, en rejeter l'inacceptable, adapter sans cesse, faire en somme ce que les rabbis avaient si bien fait au bénéfice du judaïsme entre le temps des Maccabées et le IVe siècle. Le parallèle n'est pas innocent et Guy Stroumsa a montré brillamment comment les pratiques juives expliquaient largement la réussite de la mutation de la société polythéiste gréco-romaine à une société chrétienne radicalement différente sans qu'elle ait eu à rompre avec la culture qui était la sienne.[38]

Dans l'Empire romain, Arabes et Juifs avaient eu, chacun à leur manière, à réagir. On a vu combien Pétra témoigne d'une hellénisation forte des élites, au point que la ville pouvait s'enorgueillir d'avoir donner naissance à des rhéteurs grecs de renom, comme Callinicos ou Généthlios. Rien, dans la Pétra chrétienne ne distingue la ville d'une autre communauté chrétienne du Proche-Orient hellénisé. Or, non seulement on assiste à une conversion massive, mais surtout il ne reste rien de la culture antérieure, même si l'on a bien montré que des artistes byzantins ont travaillé pour les nouveaux maîtres de la Syrie. On peut naturellement invoquer des solidarités ethniques, mais jouaient-elles vraiment? Quelle conscience pouvaient avoir les habitants de Pétra d'une parenté avec ceux de Médine? On ne le saura sans doute jamais, mais force est de constater que l'hellénisme fut rapidement balayé sans laisser de traces, comme si tout cela n'avait été qu'un décor superficiel, une culture empruntée plutôt qu'assimilée. La survie de l'hellénisme que l'on observe pendant un temps ne pèse rien face à la nouvelle culture dominante.

À l'inverse, les Juifs—on ne peut dire Jérusalem, devenue depuis 135 une ville païenne puis chrétienne—avaient réagi d'abord avec violence,

---

[38] Stroumsa 2005.

du moins pour le plus grand nombre. Or, dans la lutte contre l'hellénisme, le judaïsme se forgea des armes nouvelles, adopta, consciem-
ment ou non, certains concepts de l'adversaire. Nabatéens de Pétra et
Juifs paraissent sensibles aux charmes du modernisme, et y succom-
bent volontiers. Mais, chez la plupart des Juifs, cela passe par une
rigoureuse analyse de ce qui est licite et de ce qui ne l'est pas. Certes,
quelques uns, comme Hérode, ne s'embarrassent guère de scrupules de
ce genre—d'où les scandales qu'il suscite—mais tandis que le plus grand
nombre succombe, les rabbins sont à l'œuvre pour faire entrer les
nouveautés dans la *Torah*. Tout se passe comme si, d'un côté, à Pétra, les
Nabatéens adoptaient les nouveautés grecques sans se préoccuper de
ce que cela peut modifier quant aux bases intellectuelles sur lesquelles
repose leur civilisation. De l'autre, les rabbins se sont sans doute rendus
compte assez vite de l'importance de l'hellénisation de la société juive
et des risques que cela faisait courir aux racines mêmes du judaïsme.
Ils surent alors adapter les fondements intellectuels de leur religion
au modernisme, faire leur ce qu'ils ne pouvaient éviter. Et à terme, le
judaïsme conserva cet apport fondamental. À l'inverse, les Nabatéens,
comme pratiquement toute la Syrie chrétienne, ne conservèrent rien
d'une tradition grecque qui, pour l'essentiel n'était guère assimilée, et
qui, plus encore, paraissait fondamentalement liée au christianisme.
Face à un monothéisme conquérant, les Juifs sauvèrent leur héritage
grec en restant fidèle à leur foi, les Nabatéens ou leurs descendants
abandonnèrent dans le même temps leur foi chrétienne et leur culture
grecque. Entre Pétra et Jérusalem, devenues des symboles plus que des
réalités, le fossé paraissait désormais immense, infranchissable.

Université François-Rabelais (Tours)
Institut Universitaire de France

Abréviations

H = Healey, J. F. 1993. *The Nabataean Tomb Inscriptions of Mada'in Salih.*
Oxford.
JSa = Jaussen, A. et R. Savignac. 1997 [à l'origine édité 1909–1914].
Mission archéologique en Arabie. Le Caire.

Bibliographie

Austin, C. et G. Bastianini. 2002. *Posidippi Pellaei quae supersunt omnia.* Milan.

Avigad, N. 1954. *Ancient Monuments in the Kidron Valley.* Jérusalem.

———. 1972. "Excavations in the Jewish Quarter of the Old City of Jerusalem. 1971." *IEJ* 22:193–200.

———. 1975. *Jerusalem Revealed: Archaeology in the Holy City 1968-1974.* Jérusalem.

———. 1989. *The Herodian Quarter in Jerusalem.* Jerusalem.

Bowersock, G. W. 1997. "Jacoby's Fragments and Two Greek Historians of Pre-Islamic Arabia." In *Collecting Fragments/Fragmente sammeln,* éd. G. W. Most, 174–185. Göttingen.

———. 2000. "La surprise du bouleutérion." *Le Monde de la Bible* 127:60.

Cowley, A. E. 1914-1915. "Inscriptions from Southern Palestine: Greek, Nabatean, Arabic. II. Semitic." *Palestine Exploration Fund Annual* 3:145–147.

Chambers, R. R. 1980. *Greek Athletics and the Jews, 65 BC–AD 70.* Diss. University of Miami.

Fedak, J. 1990. *Monumental Tombs of the Hellenistic Age: A Study of Selected Tombs from the Pre-Classical to the Early Imperial Period.* Toronto.

Fittschen, K. 1996. "Wall Decorations in Herod's Kingdom: their Relationship with Wall Decorations in Greece and Italy." In *Judaea and the Greco-Roman World in the Time of Herod in the Light of Archaeological Evidence,* éd. K. Fittschen et G. Foerster, 139–161. Göttingen.

Geva, H. éd. 1994. *Ancient Jerusalem Revealed.* Jerusalem.

Graf, D. F. 2006. "The Nabateans in the Early Hellenistic Period: The Testimony of Posidippus of Pella." *Topoi* 14:47–68.

Hengel, M. 1974. *Judaism and Hellenism.* London.

———. 1980. *Jews, Greeks and Barbarians: Aspects of the Hellenization of Judaism in the Pre-Christian Period.* London.

Honigman, S. 2003. *The Septuagint and Homeric Scholarship in Alexandria: A Study in the Narrative of the* Letter of Aristeas. London.

Joukowsky, M. 1998. *Petra: The Great Temple.* Vol. I: *Brown University Excavations 1993-1997.* Providence, RI.

Koch, G. 1975. *Die mythologischen Sarkophage* VI: *Meleager*. Berlin.

Kolb, B. 2000. "Les maisons patriciennes d'az-Zantûr." *Le Monde de la Bible* 127:42–43.

Kushnir-Stein, A. et H. Gitler. 1992–1993. "Numismatic Evidence from Tel Beer-Sheva and the Beginning of the Nabatean Coinage." *Israel Numismatic Journal* 12:13–20.

Levine, L. I. et Z. Weiss, éd. 2000. *From Dura to Sepphoris: Studies in Jewish Art and Society in Late Antiquity*. Portsmouth, RI.

Lindner, M. 1986. *Petra: Neue Ausgrabungen und Entdeckungen*. Munich and Bad Windsheim.

Mendels, D. 1997. "Jewish Kingship in the Hasmonaean Period." In id., *The Rise and Fall of Jewish Nationalism*, 55–79. Grand Rapids, MI.

Meshorer, Y. 1975. *Nabataean Coins*. Jerusalem.

Millar, F. 1997. "Porphyry: Ethnicity, Language, and Alien Wisdom." In *Philosophia Togata II*, éd. J. Barnes et M. Griffin, 241–262. Oxford.

Negev, A. 1991. *Personal Names in the Nabatean Realm*. Jerusalem.

Nehmé, L. et F. Villeneuve. 1999. *Pétra*. Paris.

Rahmani, L. Y., N. Avigad et P. Benoît. 1967. "Jason's Tomb. Aramaic Inscriptions of the Tomb of Jason. L'inscription grecque du tombeau de Jason." *IEJ* 17:61–114.

Restö, J. 2003. *The Arabs in Antiquity: Their History from the Assyrians to the Umayyads*. London and New York.

Robinson, E. S. G. 1936. "Coins from Petra etc." *NC*, 5th series, 16:290–291.

Rozenberg, S. 1996. "The Wall Paintings of the Herodian Palace at Jericho." In *Judaea and the Greco-Roman World in the Time of Herod in the Light of Archaeological Evidence*, éd. K. Fittschen et G. Foerster, 121–138. Göttingen.

Sartre, M. 2003. *D'Alexandre à Zénobie. Histoire du Levant antique (IVe siècle av. J.-C.-IIIe siècle ap. J.-C.)*. 2e éd. Paris.

———. 2005. *The Middle East under Rome*. Cambridge, MA.

Satlow, M. L. 1998. "Rhetoric and Assumptions: Romans and Rabbis on Sex." In *Jews in a Graeco-Roman World*, éd. M. Goodman, 135–144. Oxford.

Starcky, J. 1966. "Petra et la Nabatène." In *Dictionnaire de la Bible*. Suppl.

VII, éd. L. Pirot, A. Robert, H. Cazelles and A. Feuillet, coll. 886–1017.

Stroumsa, G. 2005. *La fin du sacrifice.* Paris.

Stutchbury, H. E. 1961. "Excavations in the Kidron Valley." *PEQ* 93:101–113.

Talhi, Dh. Al- et M. al-Daire, 2005. "Roman Presence in the Desert: A New Inscription from Hegra." *Chiron* 35:205–217.

Teixidor, J. 1995. "Le campement, ville des Nabatéens." *Semitica* 43–44:111–121.

Zayadine, F. 1986. "Ein Turmgrab in Bab es-Siq." In *Petra: Neue Ausgrabungen und Entdeckungen,* éd. M. Lindner, 217–221. Munich and Bad Windsheim.

———. 1987. "Decorative Stucco at Petra and other Hellenistic Sites." *Studies in the History and Archaeology of Jordan* 3:131–142.

INDEX OF SOURCES

INDEX OF SUBJECTS

This book was composed by Ivy Livingston
(Department of the Classics, Harvard University)
and manufactured by Sheridan Books, Ann Arbor, MI.

The cover was designed by Joni Godlove (big*bang creative).

The typeface is Gentium, designed by Victor Gaultney
and distributed by SIL International.